Silicon Samurai

Also by Tom Forester

The Microelectronics Revolution (ed.) (1980)
The Information Technology Revolution (ed.) (1985)
High-Tech Society (1987)
The Materials Revolution (ed.) (1988)
Computers in the Human Context (ed.) (1989)
Computer Ethics (1990)

Silicon Samurai

How Japan Conquered the World's IT Industry

Tom Forester

First published 1993

Blackwell Publishers
238 Main Street, Suite 501
Cambridge, Massachusetts 02142
USA

108 Cowley Road
Oxford OX4 1JF
UK

Library of Congress Cataloging-in-Publication Data
Forester, Tom.
Silicon Samurai : how Japan conquered the world's IT industry / Tom Forester.
p. cm.
Includes bibliographical references and index.
ISBN 1–55786–292–3
1. Computer industry—Japan. 2. Computer industry. 3. Semiconductor industry—Japan. 4. Semiconductor industry. 5. Information technology—Japan. 6. Electronic industries—Japan. 7. Electronic industries. I. Title.
HD9696.C63J3153 1993 92–44815
338.4'7004'0952—dc20 CIP

ISBN 1–557–86292 3

British Library Cataloguing in Publication Data

A CIP catalogue record for this book is available from the British Library.

Typeset in 11½ on 13½ pt Garamond at The Spartan Press Ltd,
Lymington, Hants

Printed in Great Britain by Hartnolls Ltd, Bodmin, Cornwall

This book is printed on acid-free paper

"We might dress in jeans, but we are still samurai, wearing swords."

TV anchor Hiroshi Kume, *Fortune,* May 6, 1991

Contents

Preface

Japan is about to overtake the US to become No. 1 in information technology, the key strategic technology of our times. This book tells the story of how the Japanese did it – and it reveals the techniques Japanese companies have used to systematically displace the once dominant American and European manufacturers from sector after sector of this critical industry.

Already, six out of the top ten microchip companies in the world are Japanese; five out of the top ten electronics companies are Japanese and the three fastest growing computer companies in the world are Japanese. The vast majority of VCRs, laptop computers, photocopiers and faxes we buy today have been manufactured in Japan. They join the transistor, the color TV, the microwave oven, the microprocessor chip, optical fiber, video games, industrial robots and LCD screens on the long list of twentieth-century inventions which were born in the USA, but are now made in Japan.

Starting four decades ago with transistor radios and televisions, the Japanese had by the 1970s come to dominate audio, video and most other areas of consumer electronics. In the 1980s, Japanese companies targeted and swiftly captured leadership of the vitally important semiconductor industry. Since then, the Japanese have steadily moved up the so-called technology "food chain," quietly building market share in laptop computers, workstations, mainframe computers, supercomputers and software. Along the way, they have gained a stranglehold over key areas of advanced manufacturing technology such as automated machine tools, robots and flexible manufacturing systems; they have come to reign supreme in major items of modern office equipment such as faxes and photocopiers; and they have become No. 1 in the huge global telecommunications equipment market.

In each sector, the Japanese have pursued the same basic game-plan of importing and improving upon Western technology obtained through a variety of ways – some legitimate, some illegitimate; building up productive capacity and gaining production experience in a protected domestic market in which consumers pay inflated prices and from which foreigners are largely excluded; launching coordinated attacks on overseas markets – especially the US – by slashing prices in order to "buy" market share and by absorbing losses for as long as it takes to force foreign competitors out of business; and finally, having relentlessly pursued market share at the expense of profits, Japanese companies have then raised prices in order to reap super-profits on key components – for which they are now monopoly suppliers. They also move upscale to more profitable, sophisticated products. The profits are then reinvested – rather than distributed to stockholders – in order to maintain Japanese domination of a captured sector. This pattern of conquest has been played out time and time again.

If America and Europe continue on their present course and basically pursue business-as-usual policies, then by far the greater part of the IT industry will slip inexorably into the hands of the Japanese. Moreover, the entire high-tech sector – including growth areas such as biotechnology, new materials, pharmaceuticals and medical equipment – is at risk from Japanese domination unless America and Europe make drastic changes to their industry, trade, and technology policies, as well as their industrial structure and indeed their whole approach to business and wealth-creation. Unless the West learns the lessons of Japan's high-tech business strategy and changes course, there is a grave danger that America and Europe could become little more than industrial museums – and Japan's economic triumph will be complete.

Tom Forester

1
Japan: Land of the Rising Computer

Technology: The New Wealth of Nations – Japan Becomes No. 1 in Information Technology – Japan's Push into America and Europe

When America's legendary Apple Corp. launched a new range of notebook computers in late 1991, reviewers marveled at the ingenuity of these neat little machines. It therefore came as something of a shock to learn that the basic Powerbook 100 model was entirely made, not in the USA by Apple, but in Japan by the Japanese consumer electronics giant Sony – a company not normally associated with computers. What's more, when Apple announced its Newton pentop computer in 1993, it turned out that the Newton was also to be made in Japan – by the consumer electronics firm Sharp.

Apple – the very symbol of American entrepreneurship – had apparently turned to Sony and Sharp for assistance because it did not have enough engineers, the capital or the expertise in miniaturized manufacturing to swiftly put the Powerbook 100 or the Newton into production. Sony had leapt at the chance to learn more about the personal computer business and gave the Powerbook project top priority, delivering the finished version from a half-page specification in less than thirteen months. Sharp was simply waiting for the call from Apple, knowing that it had a virtual stranglehold on LCD (liquid crystal display) technology.

There could hardly have been a better illustration of the current economic and technology trends in the IT (information technology) industry – and the way they seem to be working in Japan's favor. Japanese companies have unrivaled manufacturing facilities and the vast sums of capital needed to set up new high-tech production lines. More significantly, the cases of the Powerbook and the Newton demonstrated all too clearly how the US computer industry has been "hollowed out" by the Japanese, who now have command over the supply of key computer components like memory chips, LCD screens and floppy disk drives. As Japanese-American author Sheridan Tatsuno obligingly points out, in the Oriental game of Go, "one doesn't attack one's rival head-on but conquers by surrounding him."[1]

Technology: The New Wealth of Nations

Most economists and historians now agree that the possession of technological know-how largely determines the wealth of nations. According to Robert U. Ayres of Carnegie-Mellon University, "wealth" was once thought to reside in objects such as gold, silver, pearls, diamonds, and rubies. Later, in the nineteenth century, leading economists came to see wealth in terms of Labor and Capital – for example, Karl Marx promulgated his "Labor Theory of Value," which proved influential in some parts of the world. But, says Ayres, the central tradition of neoclassical economics – from Adam Smith to Ricardo and Keynes – was that wealth was some sort of fixed stock of resources. More recently, he says, wealth has been thought to reside in oil ("black gold") or the possession of "critical" materials.[2]

Earlier this century, the German thinker Joseph Schumpeter was one of the first to reject this static view of wealth and to focus on the process of economic growth and wealth-creation. He argued that wealth is not a zero-sum game – it is not simply something that can be captured through wars or redistributed between classes. Rather, wealth could be created – especially through the intelligent application of new technology. Many other economists like Verdoorn, Denison, Arrow, and Solow built on his key insight that technological innovation is essential for economic growth and they developed new theories to help us understand the process of technological change.

Ayres himself argues that wealth is primarily knowledge or stored-up information and that most wealth today originates in technological innovation: "Labor and capital play a role, but while wealth has material aspects, it is essentially a form of 'condensed' useful information or knowledge. Its ultimate origin is the human mind. In other words, wealth is not a gift of nature, nor is it derived from 'labor' in traditional Marxian terms. Nor is it a simple consequence of the law of compound interest as applied to money in the bank. Money is a convenient measure of relative wealth, at least for some purposes, but money by itself does not create new wealth."[3]

Today, he says that the contribution of raw material products and of natural resources to national wealth is small ("a few percent of GNP") and growing smaller. This is primarily because technology is becoming a substitute for natural resources. The physical process of refining, and adding value to raw materials can be seen as a process of adding useful *information* to materials, as can the process of manufacturing products. Wealth therefore is mainly derived from technological innovation, which in turn is dependent upon knowledge and information, not on the possession of raw materials.

US economist George Gilder, author of *Microcosm: The Quantum Revolution in Economics and Technology* (1989), points out that raw material inputs – chiefly silicon derived from beach sand – constitute only about 2 percent of the cost of microchips, the exemplary technology of our era. The microchip, says Gilder, epitomizes the worldwide shift in the value of goods from materials to ideas. "Combining millions of components on a single chip, operating in billionths of seconds, these devices transcend most of the previous constraints of matter. The most valuable substance . . . is the idea for the design."

For centuries, writes Gilder, nations grew rich by winning control over territory and treasure, slaves and armies. "Today, the ascendant nations and corporations are masters, not of land and material resources, but of ideas and technologies. Japan and other barren Asian islands have become the world's fastest-growing economies. Electronics is the world's fastest-growing major industry. Computer software, a pure product of mind, is the chief source of added value in world commerce. The global network of telecommunications carries more valuable goods than all the world's supertankers. Today, wealth comes not to the rulers of slave labor but to the liberators of human creativity, not to the conquerors of land but to the emancipators of mind."[4]

The devaluation of matter in the world economy, says Gilder, originates in the fundamental re-evaluation of matter in quantum physics. This has overthrown the comfortable belief that the world consists of solid material objects. Likewise, he says, it is interesting to note that the electron, the basic entity of electronics and communications, is not a material form. "The new industrial revolution is a revolution of mind over matter," writes Gilder. "The use of steel, coal, oil, and other materials is plummeting as a share of the value added in the economy . . . A few pounds of optical glass fiber, made of the same elements of sand . . . will soon carry as much information as a ton of copper. A satellite now displaces many tons of copper wire . . . Chip producers build volume not chiefly by processing more silicon but by placing more circuits on a given area, which is almost entirely a function of accumulated knowledge and experience."[5]

Probably the most comprehensive account of how national wealth and international competitiveness are underpinned by innovation – and in particular technological innovation – is provided by Harvard University's Michael E. Porter in his treatise, *The Competitive Advantage of Nations*. Porter argues that possession of natural resources is a poor predictor of national wealth. "National prosperity is created, not inherited," he writes. "It does not grow out of a country's national endowments, its labor pool, its interest rates, or its currency's value, as classical economics insists." Rather, he says that national success is determined by a nation's ability to innovate and to upgrade its industries. "Companies gain advantage against the world's best competitors because of pressure and challenge. They benefit from having strong domestic rivals, aggressive home-based suppliers, and demanding local customers . . . Ultimately, nations succeed in particular industries because their home environment is the most forward-looking, dynamic and challenging."[6]

Thus Porter proposes a "diamond" configuration which explains a nation's level of competitive advantage. Inside the diamond are "factor conditions," such as natural and human resources, including skill levels and wage rates; "demand conditions," such as size of domestic market and the sophistication of consumers; "company strategy, structure and rivalry," such as number of companies in an industry and the intensity of competition; and "related and supporting industries," especially the existence of technological clusters. Such clusters, he says, can rapidly accelerate the pace of innovation and thus dramatically boost competitive advantage. Once upon a time, the most important electronics cluster in the world was Silicon Valley, California. Now the most significant IT clusters, he says, are located in Japan.

The "fundamental lesson," Porter writes, "is that the quiet life is an enemy of competitive advantage. Industries thrive when they are forced to overcome high labor costs or a lack of natural resources, when their customers won't accept inferior or outmoded products, when their local competitors are many and murderous, and when government offers no protection from fair competition and sets tough technical and regulatory standards." In the 1950s and 1960s, he says, this description best fitted the USA. But in recent decades, the nation possessing the greatest competitive advantage is Japan: "Japan has been the premier postwar success story . . . The extent and speed of Japan's evolution is unparalleled in modern competitive history."[7]

Japan Becomes No. 1 in Information Technology

Japan's astonishing economic success in the postwar era has been based not on the acquisition of territory, but on the acquisition and application of modern technology. By far the most important technology in recent decades has been information technology.

Information technology is a core or fundamental technology which pervades nearly all products and production processes. It is an enabling tool, whose control functions enhance the abilities of other tools. Without information technology, very few complex modern products could be made or be made to work. Industry and commerce as we know it today would cease to function. The basic building blocks of IT systems are semiconductors or microchips. They are the core components of electronic controls and the staple diet of computers – indeed, the Japanese actually refer to microchips as the "rice" of industry. Any nation that wishes to remain on the cutting edge of IT must also be on the cutting edge of microchips. But that is not all: as Anton Peisl of Germany's Siemens recently put it, "The nation or continent that aspires to be internationally independent and competitive in the information technology sector must command the entire electronic 'food chain' from semiconductors to end products."[8]

Thus IT is not only a fundamental technology in a technical sense. IT is also a potent competitive weapon. Companies and countries which first master the techniques for producing IT items – i.e. those fastest down the "learning curve" – will gain the largest market share and will stand to reap increasing returns to scale. Those who master the intelligent *use* of IT will gain competitive advantage from being more efficient in their operations and more effective at serving their customers and in developing new products. Conversely, a nation which falls behind in the production and application of IT will lose competitive advantage in all its other products. If it becomes dependent on another nation for the supply of key components or state-of-the-art technology – as the US is becoming increasingly dependent on Japan for supplies of such things as memory chips and LCD screens, then that nation could be doomed to become an also-ran in the global commercial race. At best, it will have to spend billions of dollars on getting back into the race.

From the military point of view, IT is a vital strategic resource. No country can aspire to geopolitical leadership in the world if it is not on the cutting edge of information technology. No country can be truly free if it is dependent on potential enemies for vital components. These days, it is impossible to fly a fighter plane or launch a missile without the help of microchips – but if you no longer make them, you're clearly at a disadvantage. As long ago as 1987, the US Defense Science Board warned that the American military was becoming dependent upon Japan for supplies of microchips and it is said that when US troops went to war in the Gulf in early 1991, they did so largely on Japanese-made chips. In 1989, a US Department of Defense report revealed that Japan was leading the US in five out of twenty technologies which the Pentagon considered vital to military power. Three of these – semiconductors, robotics, and photonics – were varieties of information technology.

Japan has already grabbed the lion's share of the world IT

market, which has grown from $200 billion in 1987 to nearly $800 billion in 1993. While Japanese companies do not yet have the market lead in computers and software per se, they now dominate in consumer electronics, office equipment and manufacturing equipment, they have a healthy lead in telecommunications (telecoms) equipment and they are about equal in semiconductors. Six out of the top ten semiconductor firms in the world are Japanese. Five out of the top ten electronics companies in the world are Japanese. Three out of the top ten telecoms equipment companies and three out of the top ten "computers and office equipment" firms in the world are also Japanese.[9] While the United States has been busy fighting wars, invading countries, holding peace talks and generally acting as the world's policeman, Japan has quietly gone about the business of consolidating its hold on the world's IT industry.

Japan's rise and America's decline is well illustrated by the dramatic turnaround in America's trade performance over the past two decades. From the turn of the century right up until 1972, the US ran a positive trade balance. Then the US plunged into deficit and the deficit blew out to $150 billion by the mid-1980s. The US–Japan trade imbalance in electronics alone reached a staggering $18 billion by 1985 and $22.3 billion by 1990 (when the next largest US–Japan deficit, in cars and trucks, stood at $20.5 billion). In every IT and high-tech sector, US exports were down and imports were up, so that by 1990, for instance, foreigners had nearly 20 percent of the entire American IT market. In every high-tech sector, Japan was steadily gaining market share. By 1991, America's trade profile with Japan was beginning to make the US look like a Third World country: five of the top ten US exports to Japan were cigarettes, corn, timber, aluminum, and soybeans; all ten of the top ten Japanese exports to the US were high-tech – and eight of these were categories of information technology.[10]

US leadership in information technology has been fading fast. Two decades ago, America held a comfortable technological lead in most areas of IT and shared the lead with Europe in the rest. But today, no matter what indicator is used – production figures, company performance, R&D expenditure, records of innovation or expert opinion – it is apparent that the US is slipping behind in key areas like computers and telecoms and is falling badly behind in areas like consumer electronics and manufacturing equipment. The picture is sometimes patchy: for example, while the US is still ahead in microprocessor design, computer networks and software, Japan is ahead in chip-making equipment, fiber optics, displays, and printers. However, the general pattern is clear: Japan is up and the US is down.[11] In the US, successive reports in recent years from such bodies as the National Science Board and the Council on Competitiveness have warned in the strongest possible terms that the US is losing its high-tech lead and is in danger of becoming a second-rate "also-ran." What's more, recent opinion polls suggest that the American public now believes that the loss of high-tech leadership is inevitable.

Europe's decline in IT has been equally spectacular in the past decade. Back in 1979, Europe had an electronics deficit of $1.5 billion, but during the 1980s this blew out to reach a staggering $35 billion in 1991. Today, both US and European firms in the European market are under siege from the Japanese in semiconductors, consumer electronics, cellular phones, computers, and office equipment. While European "national champions" like Siemens, Olivetti, Bull, Philips, and Thomson-SGS struggle to maintain market share and to keep pace with innovation, successive cross-national mergers and government-funded research consortia like ESPRIT and JESSI have failed to stem the decline. As recently as 1988, a European IT revival looked possible, but by early 1991 EC President Jacques Delors had to call leading industry players to a "crisis" summit in Burgundy. European companies like ICL, Bull, and Olivetti were being hollowed out or taken over by the Japanese, while Philips was in such dire straits that it was forced to pull out of semiconductors altogether. Meanwhile, "liberal" and *dirigiste* bureaucrats in Brussels argued about how best to "save" what was left of the European IT industry. Some said that a measure of protectionism was Europe's only hope.

The astonishing success of the Japanese in IT – and the relative failure of America and Europe – can be explained in terms of industrial policy, trade policy, technology transfer policies, industrial and financial structure, attention to manufacturing, and the nature and values of the respective societies.

Thus Japan's industrial policy of close government–industry collaboration and the active "targeting" of markets and technologies by MITI (the Ministry of International Trade and Industry) has contrasted markedly with the US policy of having no industrial policy and Europe's general lack of dynamism and direction. In trade policy, Japan's blatant use of domestic protectionism and the subsidizing of exports have clearly proved more successful than America's rigid adherence to free-market ideology and its misguided belief in level playing fields. Meanwhile, Europe has suffered from national rivalries and the fact that it did not become a truly common market until 1993.

In technology policy and especially policies for R&D, while America and Europe have been guilty of doing too much "R" and not enough "D," the Japanese in contrast have been absolutely brilliant at commercializing R&D. Their techniques for systematically transferring Western technology back to Japan for further creative refinement – whether through "partnerships," direct acquisitions, industrial espionage, or the blatant theft of intellectual property – have enabled Japan to rapidly "catch up" with the West and then to embark on "take-lead" strategies. Meanwhile, the US research effort has suffered from fragmentation and military domination and in Europe the history of information technology research has been one of lost opportunities, EC wrangles, and botched "big" projects.

Japan's industrial structure is dominated by the *keiretsu*, or families of companies which trade with each other, work together, plan for the long term, have deep pockets, and have access to patient capital. In contrast, American business suffers from chronic entrepreneurialism, short-term thinking, and the tyranny of stockholders over management. European industry has been badly divided by nationalism and suffers from bureaucratic management, social barriers between management, technical staffs and production personnel, and a belief that big is still beautiful. While Japan has played close attention to manufacturing excellence and quality control, in America and Europe manufacturing has been neglected and suffers from low status.

In addition, the values of Japanese society are very different from those prevailing in both America and Europe. The Japanese *do* work longer hours, they save more, they spend less, and individually they appear to have fairly modest aspirations. Japan is a very homogeneous society which emphasizes cooperation rather than conflict and collectivism over individualism. On the other hand,

American society is very heterogeneous and is characterized by individualism, cut-throat competition, and self-aggrandizement. Americans save very little and spend lots. European society is more collectivist, but it has a weaker work ethic and is slow to change.

For many years, Japanese companies have ruthlessly and relentlessly acquired foreign IT secrets using a variety of tried-and-tested "technology transfer" techniques, such as offering "partnerships" or "joint ventures" to Western companies in possession of technology secrets; the direct acquisition of US and European companies, especially promising high-tech start-ups; the licensing of technology from cash-starved Western companies; the deployment of thousands of graduate students and researchers into US and European universities and research facilities, as well as the endowment of chairs and research institutes in leading Western universities in order to gain access to the West's best minds; and the outright theft of technology secrets through break-ins, bribery and corruption, as occurred in the well-documented cases in the Silicon Valley semiconductor industry.

Probably the most controversial of the Japanese "catch-up" techniques has been the blatant disregard of Western intellectual property rights and in particular the systematic breaking of Western patent laws. The kind view of Japanese behavior in this regard is that the Japanese operate by different rules and that whereas the goal of Western law is to protect the rights of the innovator or entrepreneur, the Japanese prefer to see technological know-how shared around for the benefit of all. The less charitable view is that the Japanese are simply cheats and thieves who steal other people's ideas because they are not creative enough.

There are many instances of Japanese companies breaking US patents (for example, Minolta was ordered to pay Honeywell $96 million damages in 1992 for infringement of its patent on autofocus cameras[12]); of Japanese firms rushing to take out patents in Japan on devices they have seen or acquired in the West (such as Kawasaki patenting Clay Jacobson's original design for the jet-ski and Mitsubishi copying the fusion lamp[13]); of Japanese firms simply stealing US technology (video game maker Sega was ordered to pay US inventor Jan Coyle $43 million compensation in 1992[14]); and of Japan refusing to grant US companies patents until after long delays which have allowed Japanese manufacturers to catch up (as was the case with Corning Glass's optical fiber, described in chapter 7). Some argue that Japan has been totally unethical with regard to patents, while others say that this is merely smart business practice.

Japan's Push into America and Europe

Japan's conquest of IT has occurred in the context of growing concern in America and Europe over Japan's international business strategy and heightened fears about the rise of Japanese economic power.

In America, the continuing impact of Japan's trade, industry, and technology policies on the US–Japan trade balance meant that the US still had a huge trade deficit with Japan of $41 billion in 1991 and a provisional deficit of $43 billion in 1992 (although it had been as high as $52 billion in 1987). Many US–Japan "partnerships" or "joint ventures" launched in the 1980s have now fallen apart amid mutual recrimination and the role of Japanese manufacturing plants in the US – the so-called "transplants" – has come under increasingly critical scrutiny. A number of highly publicized Japanese purchases of US companies like Columbia Pictures and CBS Records, and of landmark properties like the Rockefeller Center in New York, has further inflamed US public opinion. On top of this, there have been revelations about the extent of Japan's influence-buying in the US, especially the amount spent by the Japanese on political lobbying in Washington.

American disapproval of Japan reached a new high in 1992 after Japan's perceived lack of support in the Gulf War and President Bush's abortive trip to Tokyo with US industry leaders. Opinion polls indicated that a clear majority of Americans saw Japan as America's least trustworthy ally and as a country which did not play fair in trade and should be discouraged from investing in the US. Some commentators expressed the view that America had helped Japan back onto its feet after World War II, but now Japan appeared to be seeking revenge for its wartime humiliation. Matters were not helped when Yoshio Sakurauchi, the Speaker of the Lower House of the Japanese Diet, described American workers as lazy and illiterate, and the boss of the Japanese video game firm

Nintendo tried to buy a Seattle baseball team. Anti-Japanese fervor even led the Los Angeles transport department to cancel a contract with Sumitomo for the supply of a light-rail transit system.

On the trade front, the early 1990s show has been like a re-run of an old movie: the script is essentially the same as that laid down by Clyde V. Prestowitz in his seminal study, *Trading Places: How We Allowed Japan to Take the Lead* (1988). Prestowitz was the first to bring together various threads of the story of US–Japan trade relations in the postwar era and to outline the basics of the Japanese game-plan. In the early 1990s, the same pattern he identified of protectionism at home and predatory pricing abroad, combined with hidden subsidies, collusion, patent infringement, etc., has become more apparent. The script calls for frustrated American exporters to lobby the US government over unfair Japanese trading practices, US trade negotiators or even presidents then visit Japan to demand that the Japanese open up their domestic market, the Japanese agree to mend their ways, the Americans promise to try harder, nothing appreciable happens, and the process is repeated over again a couple of years later. Meanwhile, the US trade figures show no sign of improvement, Japan's trade surplus just grows and grows (to a record $97 billion, for example, in 1991), Japan plans its next push into foreign markets with a new wave of products, and the Japanese get richer while Americans get poorer.

In addition, there has been growing resentment over certain aspects of Japanese industrial policy, such as the behavior of the *keiretsu*, or large families of companies which tend to do business among themselves. Both the financial *keiretsu* structured around banks and the production *keiretsu* based on a single industry have come under fire, first, for effectively creating barriers to the sale of foreign goods in Japan and second, for exporting their business practices abroad to, for example, the US auto and autoparts industries. A major study of the *keiretsu* system by Robert Lawrence of the Brookings Institution and the frustration experienced by US investor T. Boone Pickens with the Koito company in Japan seemed to confirm the fears of those who believe that the *keiretsu* cannot be beaten. Some have even called for the creation of American *keiretsu* to counter the threat.

The appearance of Japanese *keiretsu* in the US has caused alarm – especially in the auto industry. When Japanese companies began seeking joint ventures with American autoparts suppliers in the 1970s and actually setting up plants (or "transplants") in the US in the 1980s, many US firms thought they would be participating in a bonanza. But divergent management styles, wrangles over quality and a distinct lack of profitability for the American "partners" has meant that many of these joint ventures have fallen apart. At the same time, the transplants themselves have become the target of US critics who have challenged their claims to use a high percentage of US parts. In fact, many are little more than "screwdriver" operations which assemble cars made from parts imported from Japan. In 1991, the US Customs took a close look at the leading transplant company, Honda, and revealed systematic exaggeration of the US content of its cars. Some now argue that far from narrowing the US auto trade gap with Japan, as was intended – the transplants have actually exacerbated it.

Fingers have also been pointed at Japan's growing political clout in the US – and in particular the $4.5 billion or so that Japanese interests are alleged to have spent between 1980 and 1990 on winning friends and influencing people. This has included corporate philanthropy, research contracts for universities, sponsorship of sports, and direct public relations. But by far the most sinister, in many people's minds, is the $400 million or so a year the Japanese are now said to be spending on Washington lobbyists and grass-roots political propaganda. In his book, *Agents of Influence* (1990), Pat Choate says that the Japanese retain more than 1,000 Washington lobbyists, lawyers, and advisers, and outspend both the Republican and Democratic parties combined and the five largest US business organizations combined. Two great achievements of Japan's Washington lobbyists, says Choate, were to prevent the imposition of dumping penalties on Japanese color TVs sold in the US and the re-classification of Japanese light trucks as cars, which allegedly saved Japanese companies $500 million a year.[15]

Choate lists six Japanese "excuses" which, he says, Japan's lobbyists and public-relations hirelings repeat endlessly. These are that Japanese firms create jobs for Americans (a myth, says Choate); that Japan's critics are either "Japan-bashers" or racists;

that America's problems are all homegrown; that nationalism is outdated and that we are all really part of a "borderless" world; that Japan is very different from other nations – indeed, unique – and therefore requires special treatment, especially to maintain its "special relationship" with the US; and that Japan itself is changing and will become "more like us" (i.e. the US) given time. Choate is scathing about all these arguments – and in particular the suggestion that Japan is "different": on separate occasions, he recalls, Japanese trade negotiators have claimed that the Japanese have different blood, different dirt, different snow, different sewage, different intestines, and different earthquakes – as ploys to keep out foreign products.

The evident success of the Japanese lobbying effort is made possible, says Choate, by the greed and venality of Washington public servants who regularly "defect" to the "enemy." Scores of federal employees have left to become lobbyists for the Japanese, including three recent US Trade Representatives – America's top trade negotiators. Choate says there is a dire need for improved ethics in Washington, a greater sense of national duty among public servants, and new rules to stop those holding top federal posts from ever becoming registered foreign agents or paid lobbyists.

The familiar argument (or "excuse") that Japan is changing and will become more like the West in time – sometimes called the "convergence" thesis – has come under serious challenge in recent years from so-called "revisionist" writers like Clyde V. Prestowitz, James Fallows, Karel van Wolferen, and William J. Holstein.[16] They have "revised" the traditional view – which has been the official orthodoxy in US government circles for most of the postwar era – that the US–Japan trade problem will somehow fade away as Japanese society opens up. But the revisionists argue that there is very little sign of the Japanese changing: most Japanese are still working and saving as hard as ever, most are dedicated to the greater glory of their *keiretsu* company, and most have a strong patriotic allegiance to Japan. It is simply wishful thinking to believe that their relentless pursuit of economic success will somehow evaporate. As TV anchor Hiroshi Kume put it: "We just don't think like you. We might dress in jeans, but we are still samurai, wearing swords. For us, Japan equals the Earth."[17]

The revisionists therefore argue that in this sense the Japanese *are* different from Americans and Europeans. In Japan, economics dominates public policy. Production is emphasized more than consumption. Imports are kept out ("unfair" says the West) and exports subsidized because this is in the long-term interest of Japan Inc. Nothing must stand in the way of continuing economic growth at home and expansion abroad. Every institution, rule and regulation in Japanese society is geared up to protect and promote Japan Inc. The welfare of individuals in Japan, its corporations and its government are seen as one and the same. In short, say the revisionists, the Japanese are playing by an entirely different set of rules – rules which do not look like being changed in the short term. And according to the authors of one recent book, *The Coming War with Japan*, if Japan and America continue on their present path, then the current economic problems will get much worse and political and military conflict will inevitably follow.[18]

In Europe, growing concern about the Japanese – and in particular fears that the Japanese would be the ones to benefit most from the creation of a truly Common Market in 1993 – was reflected in a series of statements attributed to the short-lived French premier, Edith Cresson in 1991. Madame Cresson was quoted as saying that the Japanese were "ants" bent on "a strategy of world conquest" who sat up nights thinking of "new ways to screw the West." Although they did not use the same colorful language of Madame Cresson, many other European politicians and bureaucrats argued that whereas the US had been Japan's target in the 1980s, Europe looked like becoming its target in the 1990s (the Japanese did not deny this). By 1991, Europe was already running a huge $27 billion deficit with Japan (compared with $41 billion in the US). In 1993, Europe became the world's biggest market for many consumer goods and the premier three-way battleground between US, European, and Japanese producers.

The Japanese push into Europe may have occurred later than that into the US, but many of the techniques have been the same. Japanese companies have approached technology-rich and/or cash-starved European firms with a view to launching "joint ventures" or "strategic alliances." Where such overtures have been rejected, the Japanese have resorted to direct acquisitions or have built new plants, with the result that total Japanese inward investment in

Europe rocketed from a few hundred million dollars in 1980 to $54 billion in 1991. There are now so many Japanese companies in the UK that it is estimated that 16 percent of British workers will have Japanese bosses by the year 2000. The activities of Japanese manufacturers have provoked endless EC arguments over "local content" rules and have led to quotas being introduced on Japanese products, especially autos. For example, the Japanese are restricted to 1.23 million units or 15 percent of the European car market until 1999. As in America, the Japanese are also actively involved in propaganda and influence-buying, and they have been particularly astute at exploiting local, regional, and national rivalries. In France, this provokes regular bouts of *Nipponphobie* – or "fear of Japan."

Notes

1 Sheridan Tatsuno, *Created in Japan: From Imitators to World Class Innovators* (Harper & Row, New York, 1990), p. 158.
2 Robert U. Ayres, "Technology: The wealth of nations," *Technological Forecasting and Social Change*, 33 (1988), pp. 189–201.
3 Robert U. Ayres, "Technology," pp. 189 and 199.
4 George Gilder, *Microcosm: The Quantum Revolution in Economics and Technology* (Simon & Schuster, New York, 1989), pp. 17–18.
5 George Gilder, "The world's next source of wealth," *Fortune*, August 28, 1989, pp. 78–82.
6 Michael E. Porter, *The Competitive Advantage of Nations* (Free Press, New York, 1990). Quote from *Harvard Business Review*, March–April 1990, pp. 73–4.
7 Michael E. Porter, "Why nations triumph," *Fortune*, March 12, 1990, p. 55; and Michael E. Porter, *The Competitive Advantage of Nations*, pp. 569–70.
8 Peisl quoted in *Harvard Business Review*, September–October 1990, p. 180.
9 *Fortune*, July 30, 1990 and July 29, 1991.
10 Reports in *Business Week*, February 5, 1990; and *Fortune*, May 6, 1991 and December 30, 1991.
11 Reports in *Fortune*, June 17, 1991 and March 9, 1992; *Business Week*, June 25, 1990.
12 Reports on the Minolta case, *New Scientist*, March 14, 1992 and *Business Week*, February 24, 1992.
13 Reports on the fusion lamp, *Harvard Business Review*, September–October 1990, pp. 58–67; and on the jet-ski, *Business Week*, August 19, 1991.

14 Report on the Sega–Coyle case, AFP in *The Australian*, May 19, 1992.

15 Pat Choate, *Agents of Influence: How Japan's Lobbyists in the United States Manipulate America's Political and Economic System* (Knopf, New York, 1990); see also Pat Choate, "Political advantage: Japan's campaign for America," *Harvard Business Review*, September–October 1990, pp. 87–103.

16 Clyde V. Prestowitz, *Trading Places: How We Allowed Japan to Take the Lead* (Basic Books, New York, 1988); James Fallows, *More Like Us* (Houghton Mifflin, New York, 1990); Karel van Wolferen, *The Enigma of Japanese Power* (Knopf, New York, 1989); William J. Holstein, *The Japanese Power Game: What It Means for America* (Charles Scribner's & Sons, New York, 1990).

17 Kume quoted in *Fortune*, May 6, 1991, p. 27.

18 George Friedman and Meredith Le-Bard, *The Coming War with Japan* (St Martin's Press, New York, 1991).

2
Consumer Electronics: The Soft Underbelly of IT

First Blood: Transistor Radios and Televisions – VCRs and Videodiscs: A Great American Disaster – Video Games: How Nintendo Zapped Atari – To CD or not to CD, DAT is the Question – HDTV: The Mother of All Video Battles? – Staying Ahead: Multimedia, Screens and Things

Japan's conquest of the IT industry stems directly from its earlier conquest of consumer electronics. Consumer electronics has been described as the "soft underbelly" of IT and there seems little doubt that Japanese companies realized very early on that the West was vulnerable to attack in this sector. Success with transistor radios and record turntables gave the Japanese a foot in the door in the 1950s. They followed this up by capturing the major market share in a succession of what the Japanese call "boom items" – namely, black and white TVs and stereo hi-fis in the 1960s; color TVs, cassette decks and video games in the 1970s; and VCRs, CD players, Walkmans, and camcorders in the 1980s. In fact, by the early 1990s the Japanese completely dominated the world audio and video markets – and America's trade deficit with Japan in consumer electronics stood at more than $10 billion.

With their success in consumer electronics, the Japanese have simply turned on its head the traditional American and European view that technological innovations "trickle down" from scientific or military research to the commercial or consumer market. Rather, the Japanese have shown that innovations in consumer electronics, such as flat-panel displays and HDTV, can "trickle up" to the office automation and even military markets. Cross-pollination between the home and office sectors, for instance, has forged new products such as home copiers and home fax machines, while laptop computers and video systems developed for the mass market are now in regular use on the battlefield. As William Spencer, chief executive officer of Sematech, the US semiconductor consortium, recently commented, "Today's technology is not being driven by the Strategic Defense Initiative. It's being driven by Sony camcorders."[1]

The consumer electronics saga is instructive in many other ways. It illustrates, for example, the importance of traditional Japanese strengths in miniaturization and in the manufacturing process. It demonstrates the importance of capturing the market for key components – in this instance, items such as memory chips, turntables, tape decks, small TV tubes, LCD screens, and CDs. It also reveals significant processes at work – processes such as the "hollowing out" of US and European industry through excessive reliance on imported components, the re-labeling of complete products bought in from foreign competitors and the establishment of manufacturing bases in "cheap-labor" countries – all of which lead to a loss of skills and manufacturing capabilities.

Perhaps most interesting of all, the consumer electronics story illustrates the pattern of Japanese conquest: first, Japanese companies imported and creatively refined key technologies obtained through licensing deals with Western companies; second, they built up production and experience in a well-protected domestic market in which consumers were heavily "taxed" in the form of higher prices; third, they attacked overseas markets (particularly the lucrative US market) by cutting prices and absorbing losses until competitors – denied access to the Japanese market – were forced out of business; and finally, they raised prices for overseas consumers on key components and more sophisticated products in order to reap super-profits which could be reinvested to maintain and reinforce Japanese domination of the industry.[2] In the overall IT story, we will see this game-plan played out time and time again.

But that is not to say that American and European firms have not been at fault. Far from it: in a damning indictment of US companies published in 1990, *The Consumer Electronics Industry and the Future of American Manufacturing*, the Washington-based Economic Policy Institute concluded: "In one branch of electronics after another, US firms have failed to achieve commercial advantage from technical innovation, while the Japanese and the newly-industrializing countries of Asia have caught up with and in many instances have surpassed their US rivals. This pattern is repeated in cases where the technology is stable – toasters, radios and irons – and where the technology is changing rapidly – TVs, video recorders, semiconductors and computers."[3] For the West, the consumer electronics story is indeed a sad and sorry tale.

First Blood: Transistor Radios and Televisions

Back in 1955 – when the rock 'n' roll revolution was getting underway and America was the greatest country in the world – an unknown Japanese company by the name of Sony introduced the US public to something called a "transistor radio." Although the tiny TR-55 model made Elvis Presley sound decidedly tinny, American teenagers and housewives loved it. Prior to the introduction of the portable tranny, people had to gather around kitchen table-top radios or living-room consoles in order to hear their favorite hits. Now popular music could be taken to the bedroom or even outside – to the park or to the beach. The transistor radio boom had begun.

Sony sold half a million TR-55 radios in the first year. A subsequent pocket-sized model, finished in the fifties colors of pink and white, and pale turquoise and white, sold by the million worldwide. Here was a boom item and a mass market if ever there was. Few people back in 1955 – except perhaps Sony's ambitious chairman, Akio Morita – could have ever imagined that 35 years later Sony would be not only a household name in TVs, camcorders, CD players, and portable Walkman tape recorders, but the company would be so huge that it would have annual revenues of $27 billion and would have gobbled up, among others, America's CBS records and Columbia Pictures.

Japanese electronics companies, guided by MITI, had correctly identified two important trends, one social and one technical. First, the audio technology-based social revolution, propelled by postwar economic growth and the rising generation of "teenagers" would create massive demand for portable music in the form of radios and record players. With 45 rpm and 33 rpm vinyl records making their debut, the pop music industry was set for take-off – indeed, it was to reach dizzy heights in the pop-culture dominated "Swinging Sixties." The audio industry alone was to become worth $30 billion a year by the mid-1980s, but even in the 1950s the Japanese only saw audio hardware as a beachhead, a wedge into world markets from which an attack could be launched on the entire consumer electronics sector.

Second, the Japanese further recognized the key strategic importance of transistorized solid-state technology. While the established US companies like General Electric, Motorola, RCA, and Zenith, and the European giants like Philips, Grundig, Telefunken, and Thorn, blundered badly by dismissing the transistor radio as a fad and a passing gimmick, Japanese companies saw that transistor technology was the wave of the future in both electronics and computing. Those with most experience in transistors, those who were furthest up the learning curve and those possessing the greatest economies of scale in manufacturing and distribution, they reasoned, would be in a position to triumph later in what became known as information technology.

Accordingly, Japanese electronics production leapt five-fold between 1957 and 1962, by which time transistor radios accounted for 20 percent of all electronics production. Some 80 percent of Japanese-made transistor radios were exported, one half of them to the USA. Even more significantly, in 1955 MITI formed a Computer Research Committee, specifically charged with promoting transistor research. Two further computer projects were launched by Japanese corporations in 1956–8 which would lay the foundations of Japan's commercial transistor-based computer industry. Most governments in the West were oblivious to these developments in a funny country on the other side of the world.[4]

From the beachhead established in transistor radios, the Japanese electronics companies moved on to attack their next major target: the multi-million dollar TV industry. According to Clyde V. Prestowitz, of all the Japanese advances into the US market, the conquest of the television industry was the most significant.[5]

Prestowitz, a Japan specialist and a leading US trade negotiator for many years, describes how the US television manufacturers Motorola, RCA, General Electric, and Zenith held a comfortable technological and market lead over foreign products in the postwar years. But in the early 1950s, RCA and General Electric made the fatal mistake of licensing monochrome (black and white) television technology to Japanese producers. Although this generated short-term earnings for the US companies – there was very little else they could do because the Japanese market was effectively closed to them – it helped close the technological gap between US and Japanese producers and, even more significantly, locked American companies into the position of producing exclusively for the US domestic market. US producers would thus never be able to achieve the economies of scale and learning-curve advantages open to the Japanese.

Within a few years, the trickle of Japanese monochrome sets reaching the US market became a flood. By 1972, no less than 62 percent of black and white TVs sold in the US were imports (although this figure included those from overseas subsidiaries of American companies). As US producers lost money as they lost market share, they were attracted by generous Japanese offers to supply low-cost, low end of the range models which could be re-labeled and sold as their own products.

For example, in his book, *The Chip War* (1989), Fred Warshofsky describes how Sony approached RCA with an offer to supply black-and-white TVs for a price cheaper than RCA could make them. RCA agreed, put RCA labels on them and on-sold them to Sears. Later, the Japanese approached Sears and offered to supply them direct. Sears took them and put their own Kenmore label on them, thus cutting out RCA. Then Sony turned to RCA, accused it of breaking an agreement to take large numbers of sets, and refused to supply RCA any longer.[6] In such ways, the Japanese were able to capture key distribution channels and rapidly increase their market share. By the end of 1976, imports accounted for no less than 98 percent of the US monochrome market.

Meanwhile, in 1962, RCA had licensed its color television technology to Japan, and despite the fact that Motorola had announced the world's first solid-state color television set in 1966, it was the Japanese firm Hitachi which was first to market with a commercial model in 1969. As Prestowitz puts it, the monochrome story was about to be repeated "in living color." Between 1970 and 1976, the Japanese share of the US TV market leapt from 17 percent to 45 percent. The number of US manufacturers of TV sets, which stood at 27 in 1960, shrank in the face of the Japanese onslaught. By 1980, just three were left – General Electric, RCA, and Zenith.[7]

The Hitachi color television introduced in 1969 was a solid-state model, which utilized semiconductor devices rather than old-fashioned vacuum tubes. In 1970, approximately 90 percent of Japanese sets were solid-state, yet RCA and Zenith did not offer solid-state models until 1973 – by which time it was too late. Apart from being the wave of the future, solid-state televisions had two key advantages over traditional TVs – they were more reliable and they were more compact.

Japanese sets quickly gained a deserved reputation for quality and reliability – indeed, Ian Mackintosh, in *Sunrise Europe* (1986), cites this as the "major reason" for their success.[8] American and European consumers started to demonstrate a marked preference for TVs made in Japan, so the Japanese were able to command premium prices for their models, thus swelling their profits even further. European and American producers launched crash-programs to go solid-state and match the Japanese on quality, but they missed the boat.

In addition, Japanese solid-state TVs were typically smaller than American and European models – and this proved popular with consumers. Apart from replacing tubes with semiconductors, Japanese producers had also increased the deflection angle in the main picture tube, which further reduced the size of the TV box, thus making tabletop and portable TVs possible. By concentrating on large stand-alone or wood-cabinet console models, Western companies had once again misread their own markets.

The three remaining American TV makers became two in 1986, when General Electric merged with RCA. In 1987, the GE–RCA television business was sold off to the French conglomerate, Thomson. That left Zenith as the sole remaining US producer of TVs – but even that didn't last, because in 1991 Zenith (which had lost $52 million in the previous financial year) merged its TV business with Lucky-Goldstar of South Korea and moved its remaining US production line to Mexico. Meanwhile, in the European market, despite early attempts to stem the Japanese TV tide by controlling the patents to the PAL (West Germany) and SECAM (France) systems and later some tough trade negotiations, the major Japanese makers emerged triumphant.

Many explanations have been put forward to account for the American and European television debacles. Some – such as Japanese strengths in technology and quality, and Western marketing blunders – have already been mentioned. However, Prestowitz argues that three key factors led to the demise of the US television industry.

First, the wide open US distribution system, in which merchandizers and consumers show very little loyalty to domestic manufacturers. For the consumer to be king is not a bad thing, but consumers do not always act in the broader national interest. Second, he says that Japanese producers colluded in controlling prices and distribution of TVs in the US. When American producers complained of dumping, the Japanese changed the prices on official invoices and US Customs documents, while granting covert kickbacks to US distributors using Hong Kong and Swiss bank accounts. Third, US government policies, which favored free trade and opposed protectionism, played right into the hands of the Japanese. A lack of resources to investigate dumping, customs fraud, and antitrust allegations did not help. And US tax laws offered every encouragement to American companies wishing to move their manufacturing operations abroad – thus adding a further twist to the hollowing-out spiral.[9]

VCRs and Videodiscs: A Great American Disaster

Compared with the bloody battle for the TV market, Japan's triumph in the next phase of the video revolution was a walkover. Only Europe's Philips put up a fight in VCRs, while America's RCA blundered badly with the videodisc – so badly, in fact, that it wrecked this once great US company.

Back in the late 1950s, a number of consumer electronics companies around the world began working on systems which would allow people to record video images and play them back on a TV set. But as Ian Mackintosh points out, the main technical problem was the much larger frequency bandwidth required to record video as opposed to audio signals. The first solution to the problem was offered by the US company Ampex, which used two-inch wide magnetic tape and a high-speed rotating drum containing four recording heads. The Ampex VTR (video tape recorder) worked, but it was very bulky, very costly, and consumed vast quantities of expensive tape. It was quite out of reach of the ordinary consumer and was only really suitable for use by broadcasting companies.[10]

A major breakthrough came in the early 1960s when the Japanese firm Toshiba developed the helical-scan system, a meticulous engineering refinement of the Ampex machine which used half-inch tape following a helical path around a small, rapidly spinning drum. The Japanese had succeeded in making a VTR so compact and so simple that it could sit on a tabletop and be used by almost anyone. Even so, it was an expensive machine and was aimed mainly at the educational and commercial markets. But the Japanese had signaled that they were further refining the VTR concept – principally by reducing recording-head costs and placing the tape inside a cartridge or cassette – in readiness for a major assault on the consumer electronics market.

That attack came in the mid-1970s. Although the European company Philips actually introduced the first commercial video cassette recorder (VCR) in 1971, the Philips model was still too expensive for most consumers and it only offered a 1-hour maximum recording time – nowhere near long enough to record, for example, a standard feature film. Meanwhile Sony and JVC of Japan were working on cheaper, longer playing cassette systems called Betamax and VHS, convinced that a mass market could be found for the VCR. In 1975, Sony introduced its VCR, followed by JVC in 1977. From worldwide annual sales of just 400,000 in 1976, sales of VCRs rocketed to 24 million units a year by 1984, eventually peaking out at about 36 million units sold in 1986 (34 million of them were made in Japan – creating around 250,000 direct jobs in that one industry alone).

This meant that the VCR rated as one of – if not *the* – most successful consumer products in history. Spurred by the royal wedding of Prince Charles and Lady Diana in 1981, Britons rushed out to buy VCRs in enormous numbers, giving VCRs a household penetration rate of 19 percent in the UK by the end of 1982, compared with just 6 percent in the US. But Americans soon caught up, buying 4 million VCRs in 1983 and a staggering 12 million in 1985. By 1988, VCRs had achieved a US household penetration rate of 65 percent, while 18 percent of US households owned more than one.[11] Today, VCR household penetration is more like 85 percent and US sales of VCRs are still running at around 1 million a year.

Sheridan Tatsuno, author of *Created in Japan: From Imitators to World Class Innovators* (1990), says that the VTR is a classic example of Japan's genius for creative refinement – which is not to be confused with imitation or copying. Although the American company Ampex pioneered VTRs for professional use, it was the Japanese who improved the product technically *and* found a mass market for it. While the technical refinements were important – and a good illustration of the Japanese propensity for *kaizen*, or constant improvement – the crucial breakthrough was achieved by selling the concept of "time-shifting" to ordinary consumers.[12] The ability to record TV programs for later viewing accounted for the VCR's mass appeal and explains why millions of people rushed out to buy one in the early 1980s. One US survey found that 77 percent of VCR buyers rated time-shifting as very important, compared with only 27 percent giving a similar rating to playing rented cassettes. Many users preferred taping shows for later viewing because it enabled them to zap the advertisements – much to the chagrin of Madison Avenue.

Another factor was standardization. When JVC/Matsushita brilliantly outmaneuvered Sony by offering VHS licenses to other companies, they realized only too well that in a business like consumer electronics – which is technically complex, which has huge economies of scale, and where the consumer is required to match components to machines – standardization is paramount. Once consumers felt secure with VHS, they embraced it with vigor. As a result, Sony with its unsuccessful Beta format suffered one of its few defeats in the consumer electronics market.

VCRs will be a hard act to follow. When VCRs were a boom item in the early and mid-1980s, they accounted for one half of the entire output of the Japanese consumer electronics industry – just as color TVs did in the 1970s and monochrome TVs did in the 1960s. Japanese companies earned an average $10 billion a year from VCR sales through the 1980s. Unlike CDs, DAT decks, HDTVs, and camcorders, the VCR was neither a replacement for nor an improvement of an existing device, but a brand-new product. Some say that there will be nothing to match the importance of the home VCR. Even so, sales of camcorders were ticking over nicely at about 1.5 million a year in the late 1980s. Smaller, cheaper, more robust, and more user-friendly versions are boosting sales further in the 1990s, but they are still a long way off the 36 million VCRs sold in 1986.

An account of Japan's victory in VCRs would not be complete without reference to the videodisc – the megaflop of the video revolution and a chapter in the consumer electronics story which one US company, RCA, would rather forget. For it was RCA which put all its eggs in one basket in the 1970s when it spent huge sums of money developing its Selecta Vision system, the video equivalent of a long-playing (LP) record. With Sony and JVC already pushing sales of VCRs to record levels, RCA launched its videodisc players into the 1981 US Christmas market. It sold a disappointing 105,000 by year's end and sales stayed in the doldrums throughout 1982–3. In early 1984, RCA stunned the world by announcing that its Selecta Vision system was being ditched altogether after racking up trading losses of $280 million in addition to a staggering $300 million in development costs. A grand total of 550,000 videodisc players had been sold, while VCRs were selling at the rate of 24 million a year.

Videodisc players failed primarily because they were unable to record TV programs and could only show pre-recorded material, of which there was a shortage. But there were other problems: for instance, the cost of VCRs fell from $1,300 on introduction in 1976 to $900 in 1981 – while the less useful videodisc player still cost $500. The relative cheapness of the disc player made it less attractive to dealers, who received higher margins from the Japanese VCR producers. Delays in getting the player to market also gave VCRs an early and unbeatable lead.

In her book, *RCA and the Videodisc* (1986), Margaret Graham describes the stresses and strains within RCA as it came to terms with the enormity of its gamble. Although all the arguments against the videodisc and in favor of the VCR were scrutinized by the company, it appears that it had such a financial and psychological investment in the videodisc concept that it found it impossible to backtrack. The company came to believe its own myth that the videodisc player would appeal more to the ordinary person. Yet the idea had originally come from scientists in RCA's research department – not the people most likely to be in tune with the American consumer. In fact, Graham concludes that top management must keep a much closer check on what their research departments are up to if they want to avoid the kind of mistakes made by the unfortunate RCA.[13]

Video Games: How Nintendo Zapped Atari

The familiar story line of an early US or European lead being eroded by Japanese creative refinement of an existing product was repeated in the case of video games.

In the beginning there was Pong, the simple black and white "tennis" game introduced in 1972. Its inventor, Nolan Bushnell, founded Atari in the same year. Business was brisk, although young consumers soon became bored with Pong-type games. Bushnell sold Atari to Warner Communications in 1976 for $28 million. But in 1977 Atari introduced its new-generation Video Computer System, which enabled users to switch cartridges, just like a cassette recorder. After a two-year delay, sales of Atari machines suddenly took off like a rocket in 1979–80 and when Bally came out with the "Space Invaders" game, the market went crazy. Sales of games like "Missile Command" and "Asteroids" ran into millions, video games arcades sprouted everywhere and there were national competitions to see who could keep a 25-cent game going longest. Although doctors identified horrendous new injuries like "Space Invaders wrist" and educationists intoned that figures like Atari's "Pac-Man" were turning young people into morons, video games became the most sensational craze of all time. US sales hit a staggering $3 billion in 1982, making it one of the fastest growing industries ever.

But the video games bubble burst as quickly as it had developed. Despite a rush of new products coming onto the market like Mattel's Intellivision, Coleco's Coleco Vision, Activision and "Dragon's Lair" from Cinematronics, US sales hit the wall – slumping to less than $1 billion in 1984 and a mere $100 million in 1985. Shares in video game companies plummeted on Wall Street and the companies quit the market as quickly as they had entered. Cartridge makers laid off workers and video games arcades closed their doors. Before it went bust, Atari even had to bury truckloads of unsold game cartridges in a New Mexico landfill. It was "Game Over" for video games – they had been well and truly zapped.[14]

The big turnaround came in the Christmas market of 1987, when a hitherto unknown Japanese playing-card manufacturer by the name of Nintendo produced a video game system which became that season's smash hit. The Japanese had learned two lessons from the great video games bust: kids wanted better sound and graphics and more challenging, sophisticated games. While the quality of Atari displays had left users with sore eyes, Nintendo's system had clearer definition, more vivid colors and more realistic animation. And instead of saturating the market with lookalike games which quickly bored people, Nintendo's boss Hiroshi Yamauchi insisted that only a select number of engrossing Nintendo games be made available at any one time – and even they would be retired and replaced regularly before they outwore their welcome in the family home. Even so, games like the oddly named Super Mario Bros, Mike Tyson's Punch Out and The Legend of Zelda sold in their millions. Nintendo's US revenues rose to $800 million in 1987 – out of a total US video game market of $1.1 million.[15]

American companies were completely caught off guard by Nintendo's sudden and stunning success. Most believed that video games would once more prove to be a passing fad which would surely end in another bust. But they were wrong: Nintendo machines were making their way into more and more American homes. By 1990, no less than 24 million units had been sold in the US, annual revenues had reached $2 billion and Super Mario Bros had clocked up sales of 40 million worldwide. While US start-ups were focused on producing software for computer games, they seemed not to notice that personal computers could still cost $1,000, compared with a mere $85 for a Nintendo console. As for video game software, they had left it too late: Nintendo and its mostly Japanese suppliers had 90 percent of the video game market. Nintendo's revenues accounted for an astonishing 21 percent of all US toy sales in 1990.

In 1991 Nintendo displaced Toyota as Japan's most successful and most profitable company (1991 profits: a cool $1 billion). In Kyoto, Yamauchi and colleagues were figuring out ways to keep the profits flowing. While the name Nintendo actually means "leave it to Heaven" in Japanese, the company was apparently leaving absolutely nothing to chance. Apart from leaning on suppliers and distributors to maintain their near-monopoly position, Nintendo's strategists were working on games using CD-ROMs, games for grown-ups, educational applications, and the extension of Nintendo clubs, tournaments, and advisory services. With one poll of US schoolchildren showing that Mario was more popular than Mickey Mouse, there were even suggestions that Nintendo of Japan could become the next Disney.[16]

But Nintendo slipped up badly when it delayed until late 1991 the US introduction of its second generation, 16-bit machine or "super" Nintendo. This enabled Japanese rival Sega to jump in with its 16-bit Megadrive/Genesis system featuring, among other things, Sonic the hedgehog. Sega's new system was not only cheaper – it was compatible with the earlier 8-bit system, meaning that old games did not have to be junked. Many Sega games also featured better graphics and more action. By early 1993, Nintendo and Sega were running neck-and-neck in world markets.[17]

To CD or not to CD, DAT is the Question

Just as Japanese companies have come to dominate in home video, so they have triumphed in home audio – although they have not had it all their own way and they have had some expensive false starts, such as DAT (digital audio tape).

The colossal audio boom of the 1960s continued right through the 1980s. Between 1983 and 1989, the world audio market grew in value from $12 billion to $22 billion. In 1990, it was worth $24 billion. In 1989, a massive 1.5 billion audio cassettes were sold worldwide, along with 600 million CDs (compact discs) and 450 million vinyl records. CDs had clearly won the war with LPs (long-playing records), which were fast going out of production.

Introduced by Philips and Sony as recently as 1982, CDs and CD players rapidly became one of the great success stories of consumer electronics. Sales of CD players in the US zoomed from just 35,000 in 1983 to 240,000 in 1984 and 700,000 in 1985. In 1990, a staggering 6.5 million units were sold. CDs are basically small versions of the ill-fated videodisc – except that they have sound rather than pictures recorded in the form of digital code engraved as tiny identations on the disc. As the disc spins, a laser beam "reads" the code, which contains millions of digits and runs for 3.3 miles on each side of the disc. The code is translated back into signals for the amplifier. Since nothing touches the disc, there's no hiss, crackle, or pop you get with records – and no wow or flutter you get with tapes. What's more, CDs are good for thousands of plays – they never wear out.

Although the European company Philips is credited with inventing the CD, it is the Japanese who have explored digital audio technology more thoroughly. Already, we have seen the development of video CDs (for use in video jukeboxes, for example), CD-Is (or interactive CDs), with which sound and/or pictures can be randomly accessed, and CD-Es (or erasable CDs), which can be wiped and re-recorded. An American company, Optical Data of Beaverton, Oregon, announced that it had developed a CD-E in 1988, but it was a Japanese company, Taiyo, which first began selling recordable (although not erasable) blank CDs in November, 1988. Through their use of technology "trees" and "road maps," Japanese companies like Sharp are systematically exploring future directions and possible new applications of digital audio technology.[18] These techniques have proved useful in the past for identifying trends, indicating links between technologies, mobilizing financial and research support – and generally enabling the Japanese to stay one jump ahead of the competition.

However, the Japanese are not infallible. In the case of DAT, Japanese companies blundered badly by completely misjudging the market for this technology and badly underestimating the strength of opposition to DAT from American and European record companies, recording artists, and songwriters. Introduced by Sony in Japan and Europe in 1987, DAT recorders offered CD quality on pre-recorded audio cassettes. They also raised the prospect of easy copying of CDs with no deterioration in quality. So confident were the Japanese that DAT would replace conventional cassettes – and maybe even become the successor to CDs – that they hurriedly geared up for mass production. Matsushita's JVC predicted that DAT recorder sales would reach 1.1 million a year by 1990 and account for 40 percent of its audio sales, while Sony's Aiwa actually forecast annual sales of 6 million units by 1990![19]

But DAT immediately ran into a storm of criticism from the American recording companies, European CD producers such as Philips, and powerful bodies like the IFPI (International Federation of Phonogram and Videogram Producers). The "threat" from DAT and the "danger" of DAT began making headlines around the world, as opponents claimed that pirate taping would massively reduce royalty income in the music industry. It would be the end of civilization as we know it and it was all a Japanese plot. Through IFPI, the recording companies demanded compensation for likely lost sales, called for all DAT recorders to be fitted with anti-copy circuitry, and at the same time refused to make available DAT versions of popular albums. Sales of DAT recorders remained in the doldrums: in 1987–8, at most only about 30,000 units were sold worldwide.

In June, 1989, hopes were raised when Japanese, European, and American negotiators meeting in Athens reached agreement on a new technical standard, known as the Serial Copy Management System (SCMS). This decreed that every DAT recorder would contain a microchip that encoded a signal on the tape when a first copy was made. The code would then prevent subsequent copies being made. This single-copy or "Solocopy" policy seemed to offer a solution to the potential piracy problem – until the music industry realized that there was nothing to stop people from making several copies of a CD on to as many different tapes as they liked.

One year later, in June, 1990, American songwriters launched political and legal actions to stop the sale of DAT recorders in the US market, where they had already been effectively barred for three years. However, in July 1991, a settlement to the long-running dispute was finally reached, with the manufacturers agreeing to pay 2 percent royalties on the machines and 3 percent royalties on blank tapes. The royalties would be split between the record companies, recording stars, songwriters, and music publishers.

But sales of DAT machines were already stalled worldwide – for different reasons. No more than about 100,000 were sold in 1990, compared with 190 million record and cassette players of various kinds. The DAT market had turned out to be no more than a niche market. DAT machines were expensive, they could not play conventional cassettes and very few titles were available in DAT format. Most consumers were only just converting their record collections from vinyl to CD: another major change in so short a time was needed like a hole in the head. DAT was likened by one retailer to a dessert brought to the table when the guests were unable to eat another thing. Only the dedicated audiophile was likely to taste the new dish. However, it's possible that DAT could just be a slow starter and may yet take off.

A couple of serious rivals to DAT finally appeared in late 1992 in the shape of the erasable-recordable compact Mini Disc (the MD) and the conventionally shaped and sized Digital Compact Cassette (the DCC). Announced by Sony in 1991, the Mini Disc is half the size of a normal CD and is aimed at the portable or "joggable" market. This is because it is immune to jolts like a cassette player – but the sound quality is that of a CD. Based upon magneto-optical technology, MDs can also be used to re-record music – a key characteristic of DAT. However, Sony's launch of the Mini Disc was overshadowed by fears that the DCC would be the real market winner.

The Digital Compact Cassette (DCC), announced by the Dutch firm Philips in 1991 and co-developed with Matsushita, is technically simpler than the MD and offers digital sound quality in the same shape and size as a conventional music cassette. This means that conventional cassettes can be played on DCC machines (so-called "backwards compatibility"), so consumers will not have to junk all their old tapes or discs, as they have to do if they switch over to DAT or MD. Recognizing that we might be seeing a re-run of the bloody Betamax versus VHS battle, Sony and the Philips/Matsushita team have both agreed to license their technology to each other, so nobody will be a big loser in any MD–DCC conflict. However, it remains to be seen whether DCCs become another boom item like the CD.

HDTV: The Mother of All Video Battles?

Of all the consumer electronics policy issues of the last few years, more time and effort by governments and more column inches in the media have been devoted to high-definition television (HDTV) than just about anything else. This is because HDTV has been widely seen as the next big video battle, the one which will decide who will control not only an important sector of consumer electronics but a number of other crucial IT markets in the next century. Yet all the hullabaloo over HDTV has occurred without anybody knowing for sure whether or not digital broadcasting is technically feasible or whether HDTV will be a success with consumers.

HDTV offers wide, crisp, movie-quality pictures and CD sound instead of the indifferent sound and pictures of a conventional TV set. It achieves this "you are there" quality chiefly by using around 1,125 lines or 1,250 lines, instead of the 525 lines used in conventional TVs in the US and the 625 lines used in Europe.

Japan targeted HDTV way back in 1968. The Japanese Broadcasting Corporation (NHK) subsequently spent many years and many Yen researching HDTV and developing its "Hi-vision" or MUSE (multiple sub-Nyquist sample encoding) standard under the guidance of MITI. Both MITI and MPT (Ministry of Posts and Telecommunications) saw in HDTV a way of creating a lucrative new consumer electronics market and giving Japanese companies a further edge over foreign competitors. They forecast a huge HDTV market developing toward the turn of the century and envisioned applications not only in broadcasting but in libraries, hospitals, schools, and universities.

NHK made strenuous efforts throughout the 1980s to get MUSE adopted as the new standard in Europe and North America. In 1988, NHK became the first organization in the world to broadcast HDTV pictures when it used HDTV cameras to cover the Seoul Olympics. In 1990, NHK began regular HDTV test broadcasts in Japan and in 1991 began broadcasting eight hours of HDTV programs per day. But at $30,000 a set, there were few takers and by early 1992 only a few hundred "Hi-Vision" sets had been sold.

The Japanese met strong resistance to MUSE in Europe and America. European governments meeting in 1986 strongly opposed the adoption of MUSE and subsequently leading European companies got together under the umbrella of EUREKA 95 to develop HD-MAC, a 1,250-line analog system allegedly more suited to European TV sets. HD-MAC built on a new EC-sponsored standard for conventional TV called MAC, which was supposed in time to replace the incompatible PAL and SECAM systems. But low-power satellite broadcasters like Luxembourg's Astra and Britain's Sky television were left free to use PAL and other European broadcasters remained opposed to MAC. The wrangles continued and in November 1992 the EC finally threw in the towel on MAC – and with it went European hopes for the HD-MAC system. Holland's Philips and France's Thomson are believed to have spent $2 billion on HD-MAC research.

In the United States, competing standards proliferated in the late 1980s, partly because the US electronics industry was made up of warring factions and partly because confusion seemed a useful tactic to help slow down the Japanese advance. At this time, the HDTV front-runners were groups associated with the David Sarnoff Research Center (ACTV), the New York Institute of Technology (Glenn), Philips of North America (HDNTSC), and the Del Rey Group (HD-NTSC). US electronics industry and broadcasting company leaders successfully lobbied the Federal Communications Commission (FCC) to set an independent US standard for HDTV. This the FCC duly did in September, 1988, when it announced preliminary technical guidelines requiring any HDTV system to be compatible with existing receivers. This meant that conventional TVs would not suddenly become obsolete and that any changeover to HDTV would be orderly, akin to the changeover to color from black and white. It also effectively destroyed NHK's chances of getting MUSE adopted in America. And in a fairly obvious effort to play for time, the FCC further announced that detailed technical standards would not be determined for a year or so.

Meanwhile, the American Electronics Association (AEA) began to rally its troops, issuing a trenchant report on the strategic significance of HDTV and opening an HDTV lobbying/information center in Washington, DC. The report, published in November, 1988, warned that the US semiconductor, personal computer, office equipment, and manufacturing systems industries would all be endangered if America failed to develop a capability in HDTV. The AEA described HDTV as a "fundamental technology" which would be the "lifeblood" of future information technologies.

Soon after, the military significance of HDTV was implicitly recognized when, in early 1989, DARPA (the Defense Advanced Research Projects Agency) announced a three-year $30 million HDTV research program (this was later boosted to $75 million in fiscal 1990–1). As part of the AEA campaign to get HDTV on the political and industrial policy agenda, the chairman of Zenith Corp. told a House of Representatives committee that the US was also falling behind in areas such as air traffic control systems because it lacked HDTV technology.[20] Further reports in 1990 from the Office of Technology Assessment (OTA) and MIT's Sloan School of Management testified to HDTV's strategic importance.

Proponents of HDTV in America, like the AEA, argued that HDTV represented a heaven-sent opportunity for the US consumer electronics industry to "get back in the game." HDTV would enable them to "leap-frog" the existing TV production technology and revive the American TV industry, which was by now virtually extinct. But critics pointed out that the loss of TV manufacturing expertise was so severe that it would make recovery very difficult. They also pointed out that the vast sums of capital required to start HDTV production were not likely to be forthcoming because few US investors would be prepared to take on the Japanese in consumer electronics, knowing their ruthless record of domestic protection combined with predatory overseas pricing.

Other HDTV skeptics – such as Steve Jobs of Next Inc. and Nicholas Negroponte of the MIT Media Lab – argued that there was too much hype and hot air being generated about HDTV. Despite all the headlines in 1989 about the "High Stakes" and "High Risks" of "High-Tech TV," they argued that HDTV was not really that important. As a technology, it would soon be superseded by digital TV transmission and developments in computer screen displays were rapidly catching up. Further, there was doubt that consumers would be prepared to pay much more for what was only a sharper picture and there would be a severe shortage of HDTV titles – or the "software" to go with the HDTV "hardware." As if in response, Japanese giant Sony announced in October, 1989, that it had purchased Columbia Pictures, giving it access to a massive library of film treasures which could be converted for HDTV.

In March, 1990, the FCC – while postponing a final decision on technical standards for HDTV until mid-1993 – indicated a preference for a digital simulcast system. This meant that HDTV programs would be broadcast on channels separate from conventional programs. It also meant that viewers who did not wish to buy expensive HDTV sets would still be able to watch their favorite TV programs on their old sets. Since just such a simulcast system was being developed by Zenith Corp. of Illinois, the FCC decision was seen to favor America's sole remaining TV manufacturer. There were now four US systems left in the HDTV race: the Zenith-AT&T system, two systems developed by a General Instrument–MIT team, and a system from the consortium formed by Philips, Thomson, NBC, and Sarnoff.

The FCC had also ruled out so-called enhanced or augmented systems, which simply enhance the existing broadcast signals. Some groups such as Philips, NBC, the New York Institute of Technology, and the David Sarnoff Research Center had been working independently on enhanced systems (or EDTV), but the FCC decision meant that they would have to focus on full-blown HDTV. This proved somewhat ironic as the failure of HDTV sets to sell in Japan in 1991–2 led the Japanese to turn their attention back to EDTV and in particular the "wide-vision" system. Wide-vision sets were selling in Japan for little more than the price of a conventional TV rather than 50 times as much, which was the case with HDTV sets.

One important fact overlooked in all this is that NHK's long-established MUSE system is only analog, while the four contending American HDTV systems are digital. This might look like all the delays have been worth it for US broadcasters and viewers: the Japanese are saddled with a huge investment in outdated technology, while the US might end up with the best system in the world – and one which is home grown. However, digital TV is still something of an unknown quantity. Digital signals have never been transmitted over the air and they may well suffer from interference from moving objects, electrical storms, and other TV channels. Compressing the signals so they are suitable for broadcasting will also pose major problems. In short, digital HDTV is untried and untested and the FCC's Advanced Television Test Center in Alexandria, Virginia, will have great difficulties in determining which of the four competing American systems will work best in the crowded US airwaves.

Moreover, the fact that the American FCC is taking its time to choose the best digital HDTV system in the world does not necessarily mean that the US will win back the TV industry from Japan. Japanese TV manufacturers will be able to quickly license the new technology from the winning US consortium and will rapidly put the new designs into production. In fact, given their huge manufacturing resources and current stranglehold on TV production equipment, on screens, and on other key components, the Japanese are almost bound to triumph. Already, US companies like General Instrument, Motorola, Texas Instruments, and LSI Logic have entered into alliances with the Japanese to do joint work on HDTV and more tie-ups will follow. Japan's mastery of manufacturing know-how and the ability of Japanese companies to supply key components at below-cost prices will ensure that they have American firms beating a path to their doors.

It is also interesting to note that while broadcast HDTV has been on hold in the West, Japanese companies have been developing lucrative niche markets for HDTV equipment in industrial TV systems, film-making, electronic publishing, medical training, and supercomputer graphics. In science, engineering, and computer-aided design (CAD), Japanese HDTV systems are becoming an indispensable tool and are even threatening to replace conventional workstations, a market in which US firms like Sun have been notably successful. In fact, if US companies don't get back into the TV game in a big way very soon, it will be game, set, and match to the Japanese.[21]

Staying Ahead: Multimedia, Screens and Things

The slow progress with DAT and HDTV has led some analysts to suggest that the consumer electronics market is running out of steam. In a sense, it is: most people who want and can afford the latest audio and video equipment now own it. The market is almost saturated. We are currently waiting for the next boom item or really revolutionary product – offering new and desirable functions – to come along. At the same time, we may be witnessing the *end* of "consumer electronics" as we know it, because technological convergence is blurring the boundaries between "home" and "office" products.

In response to these new realities, Japanese companies appear to have adopted a three-pronged strategy. First, they continue to extend the life of the home audio and video markets by launching an endless stream of new products or variants of existing products – such as Sony's Video Walkman and Data Discman – and by pushing into wholly new areas such as digital radio and home automation systems. Second, they are promoting portable pcs, personal organizers, answering machines, fax machines, and copiers in both the residential and commercial markets. The Japanese genius for miniaturization has created a whole range of compact products which can be used at home, in the office, on the factory floor, in an aeroplane, or on the beach. Third, and most important, in whatever direction the consumer electronics market goes, Japanese companies will be well placed to take advantage of it because they now have a stranglehold over key technologies.

Take screens or displays, for example, a $5 billion market which is expected to top $9 billion in 1995: Japanese companies already own 98 percent of it. Japan targeted screens way back in the early 1970s, recognizing they would be vital for the next generation of IT products. The demand for bigger, smaller, flatter, and brighter screens would be enormous. Japanese companies poured millions into researching liquid crystal displays (LCDs), electroluminescent flat-panels (ELs), plasma-based screens, vacuum microelectronics screens, and deformable mirrors. One such company was Sharp, who began work on LCDs in 1970 and two decades later were the No. 1 producer of optoelectronic devices, with 14 percent of the world market. In fact, by 1990 Sharp had 40 percent of the world LCD market and 60 percent of the world EL market – not to mention 40 percent of the world market for laser diodes, a key component in CD players, laser printers, and optical disk drives, and 35 percent of the world market for Mask-ROMs, the memory chips used in VCRs, video games, and microwave ovens (another Sharp speciality).

What is less well known is that virtually all of the key display technologies were first conceived in the USA. For example, color LCDs were invented in the laboratories of Westinghouse Electric, Pittsburgh. But despite filing patents and spending millions of dollars on LCD research, Westinghouse failed to make a useful consumer product out of LCDs and pulled out of the market in the early 1980s, just as Seiko, Sharp, and Matsushita moved in. In fact, no big US corporation seemed willing or able to make the kind of commitment to screens that was needed. That is still the case today, as a handful of small, innovative US companies struggle to survive against the might of the Japanese *keiretsu*. Without the massive manufacturing resources and accumulated experience of the Japanese to back them up, they are unlikely to survive in the long term. The Japanese have the displays market sewn up and even IBM and Apple are being forced into joint ventures with Japanese firms like Sharp and Sony in order to safeguard screen supplies.[22]

Japanese companies will also be in a strong position if, as many analysts suggest, we see a future merging of television and computer technologies in the form of "multimedia." Although definitions of multimedia tend to get a bit fuzzy, with other terms like "hypermedia," "telecomputer," and "video computer" being thrown around just to confuse us further, the essential notion is that a blending of the moving imagery of video and the number-crunching power of computers will enable us to manipulate pictures, sound, and text in interesting and informative ways. High-definition screens combined with CD sound quality and huge storage capacity will enable people to consult "living" encyclopedias and sales catalogs, prepare snazzy presentations and personal travelogs, and diagnose production and mechanical problems – all in stunning sound and color.

While there is some debate about whether multimedia will catch on and while there are many technical and standards problems to be solved before multimedia machines hit the market, when and if they do it will be the Japanese who will largely benefit. Japanese producers of memory chips, laser diodes, optical storage devices, and LCDs are much better positioned to supply the key components of multimedia systems. For instance, one of the first multimedia machines in the West, Steve Jobs's Next computer, contains an optical disk drive made by Canon, while both the high-resolution display and the sound system were supplied by Sony. The FM Towns – Japan's first multimedia product – is made entirely by Fujitsu.[23] Apart from being the dominant suppliers of key components, Japanese companies now have a great deal of accumulated knowledge of the consumer electronics market. This will give them the ability to sell cheap, reliable multimedia products on a massive scale. Judging by past experience, American and European firms will find it very hard to compete.

Notes

1 *Business Week*, February 29, 1988, pp. 44–5 and February 5, 1990, p. 39. William Spencer quoted in *Fortune*, May 6, 1991, p. 28.
2 Clyde V. Prestowitz, *Trading Places: How We Allowed Japan to Take the Lead* (Basic Books, New York, 1988), p. 201.
3 Quoted in *New Scientist*, February 24, 1990, p. 39.
4 Sheridan Tatsuno, *The Technopolis Strategy: Japan, High Technology, and the Control of the 21st Century* (Brady/Prentice-Hall, New York, 1986), pp. 7–8; Ian Mackintosh, *Sunrise Europe: The Dynamics of Information Technology* (Basil Blackwell, Oxford, UK, 1986), pp. 43–4; *Business Week*, March 25, 1991, pp. 42–8.
5 Prestowitz, *Trading Places*, p. 200.
6 Fred Warshofsky, *The Chip War: The Battle for the World of Tomorrow* (Charles Scribner's & Sons, New York, 1989), p. 154.
7 Prestowitz, *Trading Places*, p. 201.
8 Mackintosh, *Sunrise Europe*, p. 46. See also Warshofsky, *The Chip War*, pp. 155–6.
9 Prestowitz, *Trading Places*, pp. 202–6.
10 Mackintosh, *Sunrise Europe*, pp. 47–50.
11 Mark R. Levy (ed.), *The VCR Age: Home Video and Mass Communication* (Sage Publications, Newbury Park, CA, 1989).
12 Sheridan Tatsuno, *Created in Japan: From Imitators to World Class Innovators* (Harper & Row, New York, 1990), pp. 117–18.
13 Margaret Graham, *RCA and the Videodisc: The Business of Research* (Cambridge University Press, Cambridge, UK, 1986).
14 Tom Forester, *High-Tech Society: The Story of the Information Technology Revolution* (Basil Blackwell, Oxford, UK and MIT Press, Cambridge, MA, 1987), pp. 155–6.
15 *Fortune*, December 7, 1987, p. 8 and March 14, 1988, p. 6; *The Australian*, March 22, 1988.
16 *Business Week*, July 30, 1990, pp. 43–4; *Fortune*, November 5, 1990, pp. 69–72.
17 *Business Week*, September 16, 1991; *Fortune*, December 16, 1991; *The Economist* report in *The Australian*, February 4, 1992.
18 Tatsuno, *Created in Japan*, pp. 81–5.
19 *Business Week*, February 16, 1987, p. 73; *The Australian*, February 24, 1987.
20 *Business Week*, September 19, 1988, p. 35; *Fortune*, October 24, 1988, pp. 113–17; *High Technology Business*, April 1988, pp. 25–9; *The Australian*, November 29, 1988 and March 27, 1989.

21 *Fortune*, March 26, 1990, p. 87 and April 8, 1991, pp. 46–50; *Business Week*, October 16, 1989, p. 24, December 10, 1990, p. 55, and April 1, 1991, pp. 52–3.

22 *New Scientist*, April 7, 1988, p. 32 and February 24, 1990, pp. 38–40; *Business Week*, February 26, 1990, pp. 55–7 and April 29, 1991, pp. 52–3; Richard Florida and David Browdy, "The invention that got away," *Technology Review*, 94, no. 6 (1991), pp. 43–54.

23 *Fortune*, November 20, 1989, pp. 69–74; *Business Week*, October 9, 1989, pp. 38–44; *Communications of the ACM*, 32, no. 7 (1989), pp. 794–882; *New Scientist*, September 21, 1991, pp. 25–9; AFP report in *The Australian*, May 26, 1992.

3
Semiconductors: How Japan Captured the "Rice" Industry

Silicon Valley: Home of the Microchip – Life in the "Wild West" – More Problems in Paradise – Sayonara, Silicon Valley: The Rise and Rise of Japanese Chips – From California to Kyushu: How the West was Lost – Small Is No Longer Beautiful – Can the US and Europe Catch Up?

Semiconductors or "microchips" are the basic building blocks of all electronics, computing, and telecommunications systems. They are what the Japanese call the "rice" of industry. A strong national semiconductor industry underpins a country's competitiveness across the entire IT sector. A state-of-the-art semiconductor capability is also vitally important for national security, because modern military systems are now wholly dependent on semiconductor technology. For instance, it is said that when US forces went to war in the Gulf in 1991, they did so largely on Japanese-made chips.

The Japanese government targeted electronics and what was to become known as "microelectronics" back in 1957, when it passed the Electronics Industry Promotion Law. Under the law, the Ministry of International Trade and Industry (MITI) was given extraordinary powers to direct electronics research and development, to provide subsidies and to ensure bank loans for producers, to select promising new products, to set production quantity and cost targets, even to create cartels and to do whatever else was necessary to enable the Japanese electronics industry to "catch up" with the United States. At the time, few in the US seemed bothered: innovative US electronics companies reigned supreme with vast assets and a huge domestic market. Because of their success, the culture and management style of US companies was never questioned. Besides, everyone knew that the Japanese were just a bunch of third-rate "copy-cats."

That sort of complacent misjudgment has clearly cost America dear. The Japanese did more than merely "catch up" with the US. Exactly 30 years later, in 1987, a definitive report from the Defense Science Board, commissioned by the United States government, confirmed the West's worst fears: Japan had *overtaken* the US in key areas of semiconductor technology and had become the world's No. 1 producer of semiconductors. By controlling Japanese chip production, their prices and the availability of critical devices, mighty MITI was in effect the arbiter of the $38 billion world semiconductor industry. American companies who had once been pioneers of the semiconductor industry were now reduced to begging MITI to let Japanese companies supply them with key devices which were no longer available in the US.[1] The tables had been turned – and how.

Even in 1977 – two decades after the Japanese government had promulgated its Electronics Industry Promotion Law – the Japanese were still minor players in microelectronics, with less than 20 percent of the world semiconductor market. But in the following

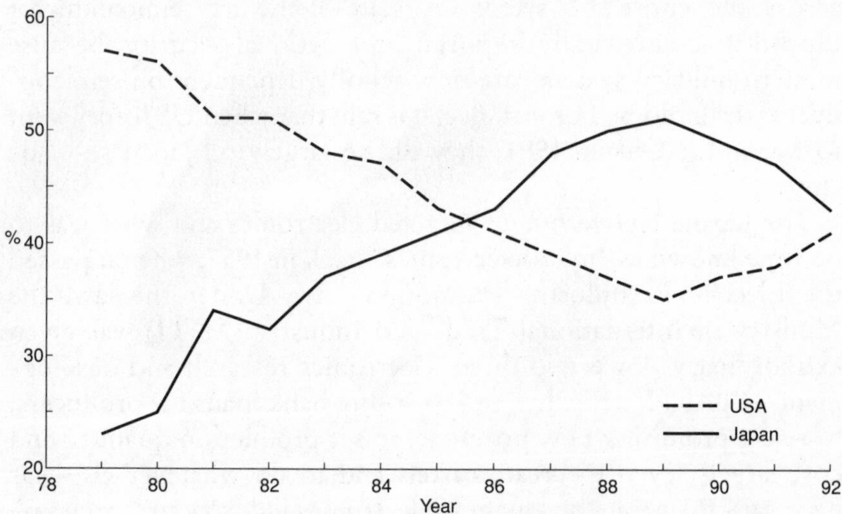

Figure 3.1 Percentage share of world chip market.
(*Sources*: Dataquest, International Data Corporation, Semiconductor Industry Association)

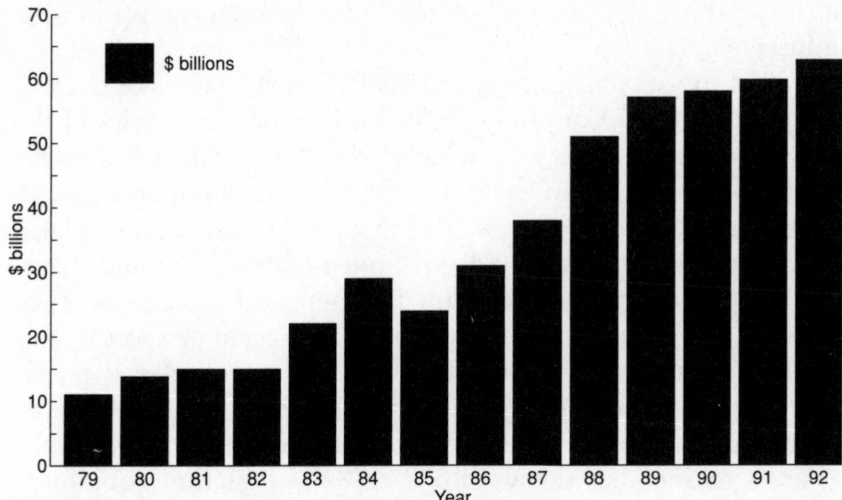

Figure 3.2 Total world chip sales ($ billions).
(*Sources*: Dataquest, International Data Corporation, Semiconductor Industry Association)

decade, Japanese companies rapidly boosted their share of the world market, actually overtaking the US in 1985–6 (see figures 3.1, 3.2). From a 2 percentage-point (43 percent Japan, 41 percent US) lead in 1986, Japan surged to a 9-point lead (48 to 39) in 1987, a 13-point lead in 1988 and a 16-point lead in 1989. Although Japan fell back two points and the US gained two points in 1990, 1991 and 1992, Japanese companies continued to hold a slight edge in the world semiconductor market. What's more, of the top ten semiconductor companies in the world in 1990 in terms of revenues, no less than six – NEC, Toshiba, Hitachi, Fujitsu, Mitsubishi, and Matsushita – were Japanese.[2]

Japan's conquest of the microchip industry followed the familiar pattern of Japanese companies importing and creatively refining key semiconductor technologies from the West; building up production and experience in a protected domestic market in which consumers were made to pay high prices for their chips; attacking overseas markets by cutting the prices of key components and commodity chips and by absorbing losses until the competition surrendered; and finally raising prices for overseas consumers on key components and more sophisticated products in order to reap healthy profits which could be used to help keep the lead in the industry.

Within this overall game-plan, MITI and the Japanese electronics companies had carefully studied the specific dynamics of the US microchip industry – mainly based in "Silicon Valley," California – and had tailored their semiconductor strategy accordingly. Safe in the knowledge that patient, low-cost capital, a secure domestic market, and government backing would prove more than a match long term for the mercurial entrepreneurs of Silicon Valley, the Japanese systematically targeted one sector after another: first, it was basic memory chips, especially the 64K DRAM, which the Japanese correctly viewed as the "technology driver" of the industry; next, it was chip-making equipment, for the obvious reason that those with the best production equipment would produce the best chips; and finally it was actual microprocessors ("computers on a chip"), because there was more profit to be made from these multi-functional devices.

But the Japanese have not stopped there: even now, Japanese companies are determined to win the race for 64-megabit chips, the next generation of memory devices due in 1994. Most analysts are agreed that only six firms are left in the race: five are Japanese and the other is IBM. The first five companies to announce 64-megabit prototypes in 1990–1 were Hitachi, Toshiba, Matsushita, Fujitsu, and Mitsubishi.

Silicon Valley: Home of the Microchip

At the south end of San Francisco Bay, some 50 miles from downtown San Francisco, lie the fertile flatlands of Santa Clara County, sandwiched between two ranges of low hills (see figure 3.3). The area was known as recently as 1950 as the "prune capital of America." Today the fruit orchards are mostly gone, replaced by a gridiron of futuristic factory units, new freeways, and rows of new apartment blocks which march toward the shimmering horizon. This is "Silicon Valley," home of the microchip – and a lot more besides: according to a recent publicity handout from the "capital" of Silicon Valley, the City of San Jose, the Valley is also the home of the vacuum tube, the transistor, the personal computer, the VTR, the video game, the hard disk drive, the workstation, the mouse, the laptop, the music synthesizer, nuclear body imaging, contact lenses, gene splicing, and the Koosh ball.[3]

"Silicon Valley," as it was first dubbed by local news-sheet editor Don C. Hoefler in 1971, rapidly rose to prominence in the late 1970s and early 1980s. By 1985, more than 600 of the companies in the American Electronics Association were located in Silicon Valley. Massachusetts trailed in second place with just 112 firms. By 1990, some 1,500 of the 2,500 electronics companies in the US with more than 500 employees could be found within a 30-mile radius of San Jose airport. A total of 2,600 high-tech firms directly employing in excess of 250,000 people were located in the Valley – and on average, 18 new companies were still being formed each week. Not

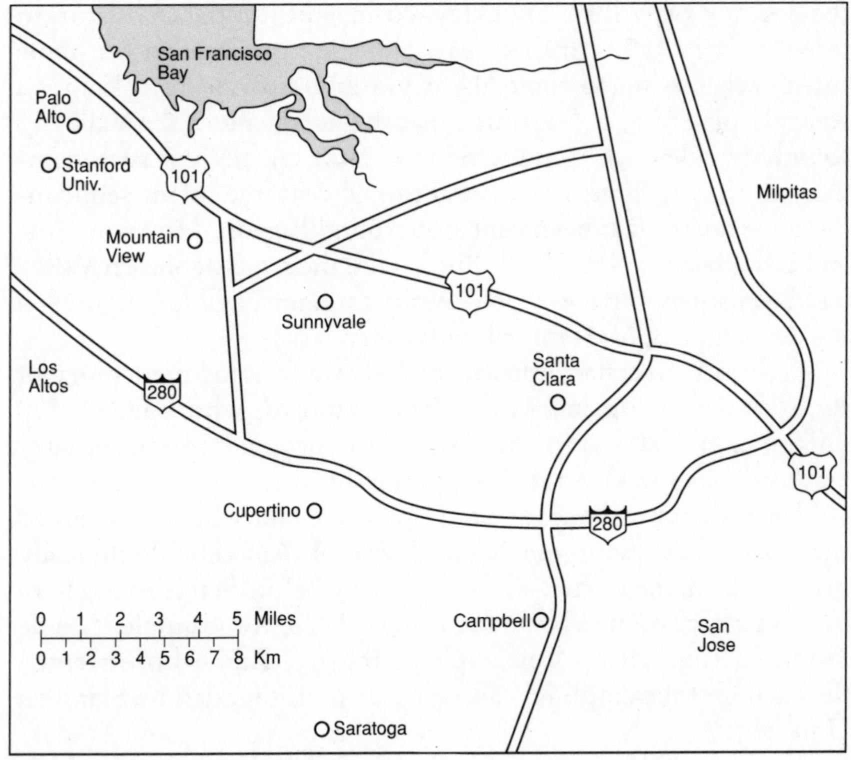

Figure 3.3 Silicon Valley.
(*Source*: Tom Forester, *High-Tech Society*, 1987, original drawing)

surprisingly, Silicon Valley has been described as a twentieth-century California "gold rush."

As the prune farmers moved out, the suburbs spread. San Jose, at the southern end of the valley, became America's fastest growing city. A small country town in 1950, it jumped from twenty-ninth place in the big-city league in 1970 to eighteenth in 1980 and eleventh in 1990. By then, San Jose had overhauled San Francisco itself to become the third largest city in California, behind Los Angeles and San Diego. With the highest median household income in the US, the second-highest level of educational attainment, 200,000 college students, over 6,000 PhDs, and more than 15,000 resident millionaires, Silicon Valley today would still appear to be the greatest concentration of scientific brainpower and new wealth in the US, if not in the world.

Most people trace the origins of this remarkable phenomenon to the decision of William Shockley, co-inventor of the transistor, to move west in 1955. In that year, Shockley returned to his home town of Palo Alto (so named by explorer Gaspar de Portolá after a scraggly pine tree, or "tall stick") at the north end of the Valley to found Shockley Semiconductor Laboratories, the first such company in the San Francisco area. Prior to that, the infant semiconductor industry had been centered around Boston, Massachusetts, and Long Island, New York. But in fact, the seeds of Silicon Valley had been sown much earlier – by the founders, and key figures in the development of, Stanford University.

Stanford University, opened in 1891, was created in memory of the son of Senator and Mrs Leland Stanford, who donated $20 million and 8,800 acres at Palo Alto for the project. Senator Stanford was the Central Pacific railroad magnate who drove the golden spike into the track near Ogden, Utah, which first linked the East Coast with the West Coast of America. Technically oriented from the start, it wasn't very long before Stanford began to have an effect on nearby industries: in 1912, for example, Lee de Forest of the Federal Telegraph Company, Palo Alto, invented the vacuum tube amplifier, his research partly funded by Stanford University.

A brilliant 1920 graduate, Frederick Terman, was also to play a vital role in Silicon Valley's development. Forced by illness in 1924 to forgo an MIT professorship and remain in California, Terman became Stanford's professor of "radio engineering." In the early 1930s, two of his students were one William R. Hewlett and one David Packard, later to become founders of Hewlett-Packard. Terman encouraged the duo, even to the extent of enticing them back from the East in 1938 with the help of fellowships, accommodation, and commercial work. By 1942 Hewlett-Packard employed 100 people, although it was 1950 before the firm added the next hundred. Rapid expansion followed in the 1950s and 1960s as the company moved from audio and electronic instruments into computers and microchips. By 1983 Hewlett-Packard had 68,000 employees and was ranked 110th in the *Fortune 500*. Dave Packard was worth over $2 billion and Bill Hewlett about $1 billion, making them the two richest entrepreneurs in America.

Another Terman brainwave was the Stanford Research Park, founded in 1951. This was the first such high-tech industrial park located near a university, an idea that has since been widely copied all over the world. By 1955 7 companies had moved into the park; by 1960 there were 32, and today there are 90 companies leasing all 655 acres. The revenue from leases and donations from Research Park companies has produced a handy income for Stanford over the years and has enabled it to become one of the world's best research universities.

Shockley Semiconductor Laboratories, the first actual semiconductor company in the Valley, was of course the brainchild of William Shockley. Shockley represented the new breed of postwar scientific entrepreneurs. Astute and determined to make a million, it was he more than anyone else who was responsible for originating the entrepreneurial tradition of Silicon Valley. Unfortunately for him, most of the brilliant young electronics engineers he recruited from the East had similar ideas: in 1957 eight of them, including Robert Noyce and Gordon Moore (later to found Intel), left to form Fairchild Semiconductor. People were shocked at the time by this seeming "betrayal" by the "Shockley Eight," but it became the pattern for future company development in the Valley.

Fairchild and the "Fairchildren" (people who worked for Fairchild in the early days) have had an even greater influence in the Valley in succeeding decades, as Michael S. Malone argues in his book, *The Big Score: The Billion Dollar Story of Silicon Valley* (1985). It is said that, at a conference of key figures in the semiconductor industry held at Sunnyvale in 1969, less than two dozen of the 400 people present had *not* worked at some time for Fairchild. By the early 1970s, it was possible to trace some 41 companies founded by former Fairchild employees. "There can be no doubt," write Ernest Braun and Stuart Macdonald in their book, *Revolution in Miniature* (1982), "that the location of Fairchild explains much of the present concentration of the semiconductor industry in California." But this was only part of the story. The San Francisco Bay area had other attractions . . .

The sunny San Francisco Bay area of northern California has a climate that many consider to be ideal. Proximity to the Pacific ensures that average temperatures remain within the 60–80°F range all the year round. Humidity is rarely high and damp almost unknown. When the inland temperature does rise on a hot summer afternoon, San Francisco's famous fog rolls in through the Golden Gate Bridge to cool things down. This refreshing daily occurrence has been described as "nature's air conditioning." San Francisco itself is one of the world's most beautiful cities. Quite unlike most of urban America, it elicits superlatives from all who visit it. The wider Bay area also seems to be everybody's favorite residential location. Parts of it are getting over-developed now and house prices are sky-high, but northern Californians still enjoy a much higher standard of living and quality of life than most other places in the world.

It's therefore not surprising that the Bay area has continued to attract young, well-educated Americans looking for the good life, as well as Hispanic migrants looking for good jobs. This has created a pool of highly skilled scientific and technical personnel – a vital requirement for a new, expanding industry like microelectronics – and a reservoir of unskilled labor eager for assembly-line work. With local universities cranking out science and engineering graduates who wished to stay in sunny California, entrepreneurs just setting up in Silicon Valley and firms relocating there in the 1950s and 1960s had a ready supply of locally available brainpower. Without it, say Everett M. Rogers and Judith K. Larsen in their book, *Silicon Valley Fever* (1984), Silicon Valley might never have got started.

Likewise, military funding played an important role in the early days of Silicon Valley. At one time in the 1950s and early 1960s,

Department of Defense purchases accounted for as much as 40 percent of total chip production. Firms like Transitron, for example, were wholly dependent on military purchases. Today the percentage is more like 7–8 percent and falling as military expenditure is slowly reduced. The change began in the late 1960s and 1970s as the computer and consumer electronics markets really took off. There is a continuing debate about the precise role of military purchases in the origins and growth of the US semiconductor industry, with the skeptics pointing out that much military research money was in fact wasted on blind-alley, ill-fated projects.

In addition to the meteorological climate, the Californian business climate proved especially favorable to the growth of the semiconductor industry – an industry in which most of the important innovations in the early days came in small firms, either in the form of spin-offs from established firms (like Intel, who gave us the first microprocessor) or "two-guys-in-a-garage" start-ups (like Apple, who gave us the first personal computer). Components of this business climate included a good communications infrastructure; ready supplies of venture capital; an abundance of skilled, mobile, and mostly non-union labor; and a high value placed on the individual, entrepreneurship, and money-making. Industry characteristics included a preponderance of small firms; high spending on R&D; a premium on being first with a new product; high rates of job mobility; networks of contacts between firms; and intense competition to attract and hold industry "stars." It is easy to see how these industry characteristics and the local business climate interacted to form a potent mix, to create a "synergy" in Silicon Valley which proved unique and unstoppable.

Many of the key individuals and companies in Silicon Valley came from the eastern USA or Europe. They came to escape the restrictions of hidebound cultures and companies, attracted by the opportunity and openness of Californian society. They were also the *type* of people who would be so attracted and repelled. As Valley venture capitalist, Don Valentine, put it, "The East is large companies and rigid structures. The individual doesn't fit well in them. California is the frontier: unstructured economically, socially and institutionally, and above all with a real commitment to personal net worth." Or as one Intel manager told me during a visit back in 1978, "It was something to do with the nine-to-five attitude and not feeling part of a team in the big corporations. In a small-team set-up, you don't have to refer things to some goddam committee all the time. You just get right on with the job yourself." In confirmation of the importance of this, it is interesting to note that the top three US electronics companies in 1950 – General Electric, Westinghouse, and RCA – completely missed out on the microelectronics revolution.[4]

From the beginning, the Silicon Valley semiconductor industry was seen as one of people rather than companies. Expertise was regarded as the property of individuals rather than companies. Skills required by companies were acquired by hiring key individuals. Company progress would then largely depend upon creating the conditions in which these "stars" would come up with ideas for new products. With this emphasis on individuals rather than companies, most electronics engineers had no qualms about "job-hopping" from firm to firm, taking with them their expertise. For example, one day in January, 1983, seventeen key employees of Intel quit to start their own company, Sequent. It was often said in Silicon Valley that if you wanted to change jobs you simply took a different exit off Highway 101 on the way to work in the morning. With annual turnover rates running at 30–50 percent at one stage, head-hunting agencies exacerbated the problem by enticing key workers away from firm A with offers of salary increases and better conditions at firm B.

A high degree of labor mobility and the cross-fertilization of ideas may have been good for new or expanding firms and for the Valley as a whole, but it was bad news for established employers who had to go to great lengths to hold on to the employees they'd got. So high pay, help with housing costs, sabbaticals, company gyms, swimming pools, saunas and hot tubs, free Friday-afternoon drinks, and frequent parties tended to become the norm in fast-growing Valley firms in the 1970s and early 1980s. Profit-sharing schemes and stock options also became widespread devices to entrap valued employees.

Networks of contacts were another important factor in the Valley's success – enabling firms to stay up with, or get one jump ahead of, the competition. In an industry based on rapid innovation, success was highly dependent on the exchange of information about how to solve problems, what techniques have already been tried, and so on. The close physical proximity of firms in the Valley made for the rapid transfer of information about developments in other firms through these informal networks. Information might be traded over the telephone between friends and ex-colleagues or exchanged more directly at one of the Valley's favorite watering holes.

Venture capitalists played a key role in the growth of Silicon Valley. Risk capital was always more plentiful on the West Coast – indeed, that's one reason why Silicon Valley got started where it did in the first place. But the semiconductor industry was largely responsible for creating a new breed of person, expert in both electronics and finance, whose job it was to assess the potential of proposed companies and products. Venture capitalists – or "vulture" capitalists, as they have been unkindly called – gamble by putting money into new or growing high-technology firms with the potential for rapid growth. They do this on the assumption that some will go bust and some will survive, but it's the spectacular Apple-style "winners" they're really after, because these can repay the initial investment many times over.

Finally, good marketing and public relations were vital ingredients in the success of individual Valley companies. Why should anyone buy firm A's widget rather than firm B's? Who was to know whether one was better than the other? This was a job for the PR men, such as Regis McKenna. McKenna had a knack of crafting compelling images for companies, and he played a key role in creating the reputations of National Semiconductor, Intel, and Apple – indeed, he is credited with inventing the Apple name and logo and the whole idea of a "personal computer." Apple later hired a marketing man from Pepsico, John Sculley, to further boost sales and he ended up running the company. McKenna worked at giving companies a "personality" and "positioning" them in the market. L. J. Sevin, whose failed Mostek company was once on a par technically with Intel, says he was "clobbered" by McKenna's campaign to position Intel as the market leader. He is quoted as saying: "I didn't realize PR mattered so much until it was too late."

Life in the "Wild West"

The early success of Silicon Valley created its own mythology and there have been many attempts to replicate the phenomenon around the world. But even in its heyday, critics pointed to various clouds looming in Silicon Valley and some industry analysts actually suggested that the Silicon Valley entrepreneurial model might contain the seeds of its own destruction.

During the 1980s, pressure on the environment resulted in serious air and water pollution, while there was growing concern over the occupational health and safety record of a supposedly "clean" industry. The social costs of high-tech success in terms of high divorce and death rates became more obvious. Crime soared and the Valley was rocked by a series of "spy" scandals involving the Soviets and the Japanese. The industry was further confronted with the problem of Pentagon-inspired high-tech export curbs, which reduced lucrative foreign sales. In addition, well-known Valley companies became locked in suits with domestic and overseas competitors alleging infringement of copyrights and patents on hardware and software. The industry continued to be plagued by runaway booms and savage slumps and there were some spectacular business failures. All this was duly noted by the Japanese, who earlier on had come to view Silicon Valley as the "Wild West" incarnate.[5]

Like most things that work in America, the Silicon Valley semiconductor industry was not planned: it just happened. But the choice of Santa Clara was unfortunate because a severe shortage of land soon developed. This pushed up land prices and thus the costs of new factories and housing. The unplanned way in which the Valley developed from north to south also allowed the more attractive North County communities of Palo Alto, Mountain View, and Sunnyvale to cream off the top microchip companies, with their profits and their large, landscaped sites. South County communities around San Jose, like Gilroy, were left to pick up what companies they could and to provide low-cost housing for the Valley's manual workers. Because of high housing costs in the north, manual workers faced a long commute every day on the Valley's overburdened freeways. In the absence of a public transportation system – over 90 percent of Valley residents go to work by car – photochemical smogs became commonplace. No one thought to plan a mass transit bus or rail network for Silicon Valley because nobody knew it was going to develop where it did in the way it did.

Car exhaust gases are one cause of air pollution; the large quantities of chemicals, toxic materials, and gases used in chip production are another. Every day about 9 tons of "reactive organic gases" are released into the atmosphere by Valley semiconductor companies, according to the Bay Area Air Quality Management Agency. In order to comply with the federal Clean Air Act, this figure will have to be reduced substantially – perhaps to 3 tons a day. In 1990, it was revealed that 3,000 US companies had admitted to pumping 200 million pounds of chlorofluorocarbons (CFCs) into the atmosphere in 1987, the last year for which figures were available. The single worst culprit was IBM's San Jose plant which generated no less than 1.47 million pounds of CFCs in that year. IBM, Apple, and Hewlett-Packard were pledged to phase out the use of CFCs by 1993–4, but progress appeared slow.

By far the most serious pollution problem in the Valley involved the contamination of groundwater by leaking underground chemical-storage tanks. In 1981, workers excavating near the Fairchild chip plant at South San Jose discovered chemicals in the soil. A subsequent check revealed that no less than 58,000 gallons of solvent had leaked out of a flimsy fiberglass underground tank. Some 13,000 of the missing gallons were the toxic solvent, trichloroethane (TCA). Less than 2,000 feet away was Well 13, an aquifer belonging to the Great Oaks Water Company, which had been supplying contaminated water to thousands of local residents in the Los Paseos area. About 400 plaintiffs began proceedings against Fairchild, alleging the company had caused miscarriages, the premature deaths of babies, birth defects, cancer, skin disorders, and blood diseases. The plant was closed down, and Fairchild spent $12 million on monitoring wells and soil replacement.

After the Fairchild leak, local officials throughout the Valley hastily drew up new ordinances to cover the underground storage of chemicals. Numerous leaks came to light elsewhere. In 1982, the California Regional Water Quality Control Board initiated an underground tank inspection program. Of the first 80 sites visited, 64 showed evidence of soil and/or water contamination by solvents, acids, metals, resins, and fuels leaking from tanks, sumps, and pipes. The Environmental Protection Agency (EPA) also began a study of air and water pollution in Silicon Valley, but even this did not cover potential hazards such as the accidental rupture of cylinders containing toxic gases like arsine, phosphine, and diborane: their release into the atmosphere could result in poisoning on a mass scale and yet the Valley was not equipped to handle such a disaster.

In 1987, Dr Kenneth McKay and colleagues at San Jose State University reported that the people of Silicon Valley were seriously endangered by the storage of toxic gases used in the production of microchips. Their study warned that accidents, acts of terrorism, and natural calamities such as Californian earthquakes could cause the release of such gases unless safety standards were greatly improved. In 1988, it was revealed that IBM was spending the staggering sum of $82 million to clean up a massive toxic chemical spill at one of their plants in the Valley.

Research by Dr Joseph LaDou of the University of California also showed the extent to which the "clean" image of the microchip industry is misleading: in fact, it appeared to pose far greater health and safety problems for its workers than manufacturing in general. Company records indicated an unusually high incidence of occupational illnesses in the semiconductor industry: 1.3 illnesses per 100 workers, compared with 0.4 in general manufacturing; 18.6 percent of lost work time in chip companies was due to occupational illness, compared with only 6.0 percent in all manufacturing; and compensation statistics showed that 47 percent of occupational illnesses among chip workers in California resulted from exposure to toxic chemicals – *twice* the level of all manufacturing.

A major study for Digital Equipment Corporation by the University of Massachusetts found that women production-line workers at Digital had significantly more miscarriages than the general population. While 18 percent of the pregnancies of non-production-line workers resulted in miscarriages (about the same as the general population), the miscarriage rate among production-line workers whose work involved photolithography using solvents was 29 percent and it rose to 39 percent among a group of workers who used acids in an etching process. After the study, Digital adopted a policy of transferring pregnant production workers to non-production work and offering transfers to any women production-line workers of child-bearing age. In 1987, AT&T followed suit, but one might ask why this had not been done earlier.

Silicon Valley people work hard – perhaps too hard. Engineers often put in fifteen-hour days and seven-day weeks. The competition between firms is so intense that survival may well depend on being first to market with a new product. Many are out to simply get rich quick. Competition encourages companies to indulge in marathon "pushes": these mammoth efforts usually involve close-knit teams of young engineers working day and night to get a new product ready for launch. At this inhuman pace, many engineers and executives "burn out" at an early age – rather like sports and pop stars. Indeed, many expect to do so, and this increases the pressure to "make a pile" quickly. One study found that many electronics whiz kids were "washed-up" by the time they were 35 or 40 and were "fighting a losing battle to keep from falling behind intellectually." Each year, about 10,000 electronics engineers – or 5 percent of the US total – transfer out of the field altogether. In Silicon Valley, this is called "dropping off the edge." It is little publicized, but it goes on all the time.

Because of the importance attached to work and an individual's work performance, Silicon Valley is more meritocratic than most industries. Electronics engineers get promoted if they can deliver the goods. In order to get the best out of people, Silicon Valley firms have developed a distinctive management style that tends to be informal, flexible, and egalitarian – the very opposite of the norms prevailing in traditional companies. As firms grow, managers go to great lengths to sustain the entrepreneurial spirit and to keep administrative units small. They might allow key employees to come and go as they please, to take the occasional paid sabbatical, and to use the company's free recreational facilities. Such a system works particularly well for the winners, but it can be cruel on life's losers.

The human and social cost of the Silicon Valley "gold rush" are most evident at home in the family. Workaholic electronics engineers see little of their wives and even less of their children. Husbands find it hard to explain to their families what they are working on, and wives are sometimes barred for security reasons from even visiting their husbands' workplaces. Partly in consequence, the divorce rate in Santa Clara County is the highest in

California, which itself has a divorce rate 20 percent above the nation's average. Further, there are worrying reports that the neglected children of electronics superstars are turning to alcohol and drugs in increasing numbers. The pressures can be particularly strong on the children in two-career households.

Rogers and Larsen say the model 1950s employee, "Organization Man," has been superseded by "High-Tech Entrepreneur." Organization Man worked for a large corporation, kept regular 9-to-5 hours and was family-oriented, returning home for dinner every night with the wife and kids in the suburbs. Organization Man was a contented conformist, conservatively dressed and dedicated to serving the organization. High-Tech Entrepreneur, on the other hand, is more likely to be divorced and living with someone else in a condo. He rarely sees his kids. This high-tech man is a high achiever: he prefers to work in a small outfit and shows no loyalty to any company, only himself. Indeed, he is secretly planning his own start-up, and hopes one day to join the galaxy of Silicon Valley "superstars" or "living legends" who love to flaunt their new-found wealth in the form of white Rolls Royces, Ferraris, and Porsches – not forgetting the private planes, helicopters, luxury sailboats, and girlfriends.[6] But critics point out that life for 99.99 percent of the people in Silicon Valley was never anything like that.

More Problems in Paradise

In recent years, the "Wild West" of electronics has been plagued by the problems of theft, counterfeiting, and espionage. Chips are small and easily pocketed. Their origins can be disguised, and they can be copied. The result is that millions of stolen, counterfeit, and even defective chips find their way on to the "gray market" every year and into the hands of competitors, unsuspecting customers, and foreign governments. Since many crimes go unreported, nobody knows the true extent of the problem. But it is a problem that can be deadly serious, as became clear in 1984, when it was revealed that thousands of potentially defective Texas Instruments chips had been used in advanced US nuclear weapons systems.

Throughout the postwar era, the Soviets maintained a massive worldwide intelligence-gathering operation because they were desperate to keep pace with US technology. In his book, *High-Tech Espionage: How the KGB Smuggles Nato's Strategic Secrets to Moscow* (1986), Jay Tuck estimates that the USSR had no less than 20,000 agents trying to obtain US high-technology secrets through such tried-and-tested techniques as dummy companies and bogus research institutes. Fully two-thirds of major Soviet weapons systems were said to be based on US technology. The KGB even had its own "wish list," a thick catalog of high-tech items – called, appropriately, *The Red Book* – which it would like to acquire. A captured KGB report boasted of Soviet agents obtaining no less than 111,396 documents and 15,072 samples from high-tech companies in just three years, 1978–80. The KGB further boasted of tremendous "savings" made by Soviet civil industry and the Soviet military, thanks to the efforts of KGB "collection teams."

California, with its high concentration of defense, aerospace, and communications firms, was a prime target for Soviet industrial espionage, and Silicon Valley, with its hundreds of leading-edge electronics firms, became the bull's-eye in the 1980s. Soviet espionage operations were directed from the Soviet consulate on Green Street, San Francisco, a building that appeared to be over-staffed, with about 70 personnel, and had a roof which bristled with antennae, all pointing in the direction of Silicon Valley.

In 1982 the Reagan administration became concerned about the extent of the Soviet intelligence effort after a sophisticated Soviet marker buoy was picked up in the Pacific and found to contain chips made by Texas Instruments. The previous year, a Soviet spy named Kessler was stopped boarding an aircraft at Los Angeles with two suitcases containing $200,000 worth of secret radar equipment taken from the Hughes Aircraft Corporation. Reagan announced Operation Exodus, designed to halt the flow of high-tech goods abroad, and US negotiators were instructed to take a tough line at the 1984 talks of COCOM (Coordinating Committee for Multilateral Export Controls), the Paris-based committee of 15 Western countries which agreed embargoes of sensitive technologies that might reach the Eastern Bloc.

In subsequent months, a fierce tug-of-war developed between the Department of Defense (backed by the President) and the Department of Commerce (largely echoing the views of the US semiconductor industry) over a proposed tightening up of the

Export Administration Act, 1979. But the Defense Department's case was immeasurably strengthened by the dramatic seizure, in Sweden in November 1983, of a sophisticated Digital Equipment Corporation VAX computer, en route to the Soviet Union. It had originally been sold to a phoney South African company, who had exported it to West Germany and thence to Sweden. Similar seizures took place in Vienna, Austria, and in Luxembourg. Tighter export control regulations came into force in 1985.

Renewed evidence of the activities of "techno-bandits" emerged in 1986. In Derbyshire, England, a computer dealer by the name of Michael Ludlum was jailed for six months after it was revealed that he had exported PDP and VAX machines to Bulgaria without a license. A West German by the name of Wolfgang Lachmann purchased $11 million worth of workstations and disk drives from Tektronix and Control Data, ostensibly for the West German auto industry. But in fact most of the gear ended up in the Soviet Union via Belgium and Austria. Another West German, Levente Laszlo, was arrested at Chicago's O'Hare airport with part of a haul of $250,000 worth of restricted Digital Equipment hardware destined for Hungary.

The US government was further stunned to learn, in 1987, that a subsidiary of Toshiba had sold highly sensitive propeller-milling equipment to the Soviets, to be used in the construction of state-of-the-art "silent" submarines which couldn't be detected by conventional listening devices. Toshiba had not only set out to evade the COCOM export controls, but had subsequently tried to cover up the scandal by consistently lying about the case. While some US congressmen called for stiff sanctions against Toshiba, the company embarked on an expensive damage-limitation campaign using PR consultants and Washington lobbyists. Fingers were also pointed at other Japanese companies, especially after a report by Japanese journalist Bungei Shunju revealed some of the techniques (like dummy companies, disassembling large pieces of equipment and "masking" the origin of parts) used to outwit COCOM. The Toshiba case, he said, was just the tip of the iceberg.

In the same year, the head of the Soviet space agency, Roald Sagdeyev, was linked with a plot to steal a US supercomputer to be used for tracking submarines and incoming missiles. The leader of the plot, Charles McVey, was described as America's top techno-bandit and was wanted in Los Angeles on charges relating to 29 illegal shipments of computers to the Soviet Union. Meanwhile, the Pentagon put renewed pressure on COCOM not only to ban the export of supercomputers to the Soviet Union but also to prevent Soviet researchers from using supercomputers located on US campuses.

The feud between the Departments of Defense and Commerce reached a new intensity with the publication in 1987 of a National Academy of Sciences report claiming that the COCOM high-tech export curbs had cost the American IT industry $17 billion in lost sales in 1986 alone. As many as 180,000 jobs were at stake. Commerce officials further pointed out that a US trade surplus in high-tech goods of $27 billion in 1980 had been transformed into a $2.6 billion deficit in 1986. While some export controls might be justified on national security grounds, the existing COCOM regulations extended to many items such as standard pcs which had no military or strategic value and also to items which were already sold by other nations on the international market.

In Europe, the impact of the COCOM rules on local companies came in for savage criticism from industrialists and politicians. Angry debates on the role of COCOM were held in the British and European parliaments. Many European commentators argued that COCOM had allowed the US to exercise control over its allies and to give itself a trading advantage. The mounting pressure for a relaxation of the COCOM restrictions coincided with the rise of Gorbachev in the Soviet Union and the official ending of the Cold War. In 1990, COCOM members finally agreed a partial lifting of controls, particularly those relating to the nations of eastern Europe. AT&T, for example, was allowed to sell a $7 million digital switching system to Poland and US West allowed to sell cellular phone technology to Hungary. Digital set up shop in Hungary and Computerland opened its first store in Moscow. The US government also approved the sale of six CDC Cyber 960 machines, valued at $32 million, to the Soviet Union, to be used in monitoring the performance of nuclear power stations.

While the Silicon Valley semiconductor industry has seen output growth average 10 percent per year, progess has usually been in fits and starts, with spectacular booms being followed by disastrous slumps. The demand for microchips is largely dependent on the demand for chip-using products and is therefore greatly affected by changes in the US and world economies. Thus, the 1974–5 chip industry recession ended with the late 1970s boom, which in turn came to an end with a slump in 1980–2. The demand for personal computers and VCRs created boom conditions in 1983–4: worldwide semiconductor shipments in 1984 were up an incredible 46 percent to about $27 billion and some Valley firms notched up sales growth of 70–80 percent.

But behind the euphoria, there were fears that the industry was simply into another phase of its familiar "boom–bust" cycle, based on a failure to balance supply and demand. The cycle works like this: worried about reported shortages and long order books, chip users place extra orders with different suppliers. The suppliers simultaneously lay down extra capacity in response. But because of long "lead times" (maybe two years), when the new production lines finally come on stream there are too many chips on the market chasing too few buyers. The order book, or the "book-to-bill ratio" – a measure of orders received over orders shipped – declines and new investment is postponed. As Intel's Gordon Moore once put it, "The balance of supply and demand in this industry lasts for about 35 minutes."

And so it was that, toward the end of 1984, the familiar warning signs of canceled orders and a decline in the industry's book-to-bill ratio appeared. From an all-time high of 1.65 in December 1983, the book-to-bill ratio plunged to 0.67 in November 1984, meaning that orders in hand amounted to only two-thirds of recent sales. In early 1985, there was a distinct change of mood in the Valley as the full implications of the downturn in the pc market sank in. Some companies had started to defer capital projects and had stopped hiring new workers, but many were taken completely by surprise. No one had foreseen the depth of the slump that was to come in 1985. Rampant over-capacity produced a sudden glut of chips which sent prices tumbling.

Chip prices tumbled 40–50 percent, and by April 1985, industry spokesmen were talking about a "bloodbath" as the accountants' red ink flowed. Standard 64K DRAMs were selling for $0.75, down from $3.50 a year earlier (they finally bottomed out at $0.30). While the Japanese continued to add capacity, the surge of cheap Japanese imports led to growing calls for protection and pressure for action against unfair trading practices. The first ray of hope appeared in October in the form of a small rise in the book-to-bill ratio to 0.82, but the overall balance sheet for the industry in 1985 went like this: 64,000 workers laid off (nearly 20 percent of the workforce); worldwide sales down 17 percent, US sales down a massive 31 percent.

In January 1986 the book-to-bill ratio rose above unity to 1.04 for the first time in 17 months, although overall sales for 1986 were only slightly up. But by early 1987 the good times were well and truly rolling again in Silicon Valley. The book-to-bill ratio soared, the prices of standard chips firmed and then rose rapidly, and company profits jumped. The same rate of growth was maintained in 1988, fueled by strong sales of pcs, but already questions were being asked about whether the boom could continue. Apart from the danger of over-investment by Valley companies leading to excess capacity in the industry, concern was being expressed about Japanese inroads into the commodity chip business. But although sales growth was down to about 10 percent in 1989, the Valley experienced nothing like the great slump of 1985.

Rising investment costs and over-expansion are the bane of the semiconductor industry. As production technology becomes more sophisticated, costs rise steeply. For example, a standard chip production line might now cost $100–200 million, anything from four to eight times what it cost only a few years ago. A state-of-the-art 16-megabit chip line now costs around $400–500 million to set up. Some esoteric devices used in chip production have gone up 20 times in price. Yet firms are forced to invest heavily in the latest equipment because the "experience curve" dictates that production costs drop roughly by 30 percent for every doubling of volume.

Chip firms have coped with the problem of the boom–bust cycle and rising investment costs in different ways. Some have diversified out of semiconductors into products like laser-scanners, automated teller machines, and specialist medical equipment. Others have concentrated on proprietary designs or have gone in for "nichemanship" – finding small niches in the market which provide regular sales and above-average profits. Application-specific custom and semi-custom chips (ASICs) also provide some protection from violent swings in demand for standard or commodity chips.

While media coverage of the Valley has tended to focus on individual success stories and "living legends," a University of Santa Clara study found that 69 percent of Silicon Valley start-ups go bust or get taken over in their first eight years. There have also been some spectacular failures in recent years, mostly connected with pcs and video games. Osborne Computer, for example, had all the ingredients of success and one of the first portable pcs on the market in 1981. Huge sales were recorded in 1982, but by September 1983 founder Adam Osborne had to file for protection under chapter 11 of the US Bankruptcy Code. In the same year Victor Technologies crashed, Atari was in deep trouble, and Texas Instruments had to pull out of pcs altogether. In 1984 it was the turn of Gavilan and Convergent to go bust. Eagle Computer, TeleVideo, Trilogy, and Diasonics also ran into trouble. As one Valley wit put it, "The personal computer industry has reached a new chapter in its history: Chapter 11."

Apple, the very symbol of Silicon Valley success, ran into serious trouble in 1985: the company's earnings growth stopped, its share price declined, executives left ("Apple Turnover" according to one headline), and new products were delayed. Co-founder Steve Wozniak left to form a new company called CL9 (as in "cloud nine"). Apple then closed two out of its three US factories, cutting 1,200 jobs. Co-founder and main driving force Steve Jobs first gave up responsibility for day-to-day operations and then in September 1985 resigned as chairman and left the company altogether. Summing up his career, *Time* magazine described Jobs as "the brash, brilliant and sometimes bumptious brat of Silicon Valley, a symbol of its high-tech genius and fabulous sudden wealth . . . Jobs was the prototype of a new American hero – the irreverent and charismatic entrepreneur." With his departure from Apple, the days of the two-guys-in-a-garage entrepreneurs seemed to be over. The golden era of Silicon Valley had passed.

Sayonara, Silicon Valley: The Rise and Rise of Japanese Chips

The first Japanese chips arrived in the US in significant numbers in 1978. American chip firms could not keep up with demand because they had reduced investment during the 1974–5 recession. They were caught off guard, so much so that by the end of 1979 it was revealed that the Japanese had walked in and grabbed an amazing 42 percent of the market for 16K DRAMs, the current generation of memory chip.

Then came a further bombshell. Richard W. Anderson, a general manager at Hewlett-Packard, made a presentation to a Washington conference in March 1980 in which he reported Hewlett-Packard's findings on the comparative quality of US and Japanese chips. During 1979 the firm had purchased 16K DRAMs from three US and three Japanese producers: they found that the best of the American products had a failure rate *six times* that of the lowest quality Japanese firm. Industry observers were amazed. Even though Anderson was to report a dramatic narrowing of the quality gap two years later, his initial presentation sent shock waves through Silicon Valley. American producers suddenly realized they had a fight on their hands.

Worse was to follow in 1981. The 64K DRAM, successor to the 16K DRAM, was widely seen as the new workhorse of the computer industry, the standard memory chip of the future. Potential sales were enormous. A 64K DRAM contains 65,536 memory cells, each of which can be reached independently, rather like a telephone network. Being a DRAM (dynamic random access memory) rather than a ROM (ready-only memory), the new chip could be erased like a miniature blackboard and re-used. The 64K DRAM was destined to become the basic building block of computers, telecommunications systems, and a vast array of electronic products – and by the end of 1981 the Japanese were producing no less than 70 percent of them. Influential industry figures started to panic. Even the then Governor of California, the quixotic Jerry Brown, was moved to warn that Silicon Valley "could become the next Detroit."

The Valley had certainly been surprised by the suddenness of the Japanese assault. Intel had produced the first 1K DRAM only in 1970, and throughout the 1970s US firms like Intel, Mostek, Texas Instruments, and Motorola had continued to lead the world in memory devices, through the 1K, 4K, and 16K generations. But, while they were struggling to execute complicated new designs for packing 64K of memory into a tiny chip, the Japanese chose a simpler and more conservative approach, which basically meant doing a bigger version of the 16K DRAM. Its simplicity meant fewer problems, cheaper production, and greater reliability. In one fell swoop, the Japanese "leap-frogged" the US industry, and their policy of rapid price cutting in order to buy market share (prices for 64K DRAMs fell from $28 to $6 in one year) enabled them quickly to grab a huge slice of this key market.

Price cutting deprived US producers of the early profits they had expected to make on their first 64K DRAMs and wrecked their long-term plans. And by gaining early experience with 64K DRAMs, the Japanese were in a far better position to tackle the 256K DRAM market. Their domination of the memory market allowed them to set industry technical standards not just for memory chips, but for other chips as well. As Jerry Sanders, chairman of AMD, put it, "Memories are where we learn the technology for all the other semiconductor devices. If you're not in memory, you're at a big disadvantage." Whereas around 15 US producers were in memories up to the 16K level, only 5 stayed the course with 64K – although IBM and Western Electric produced large numbers of them for their own use.

American firms began to fight back and in 1984, for example, major chip user Sperry announced that only three firms had made the grade into its "100 PPM Club" for suppliers of chips with less than 100 defective parts per million: Intel, National Semiconductor, and Motorola. The US share of the world memory market in 1984 actually rose to about 35–40 percent. With growing sophistication in the chip market – and customers demanding special kinds of memory rather than just more memory – it was argued that US firms would benefit from being nearer in geography and language to the big customers. This would enable them to find lucrative "niches" in the market. Moreover, although the Japanese were strong in memory chips, they had yet to break into the more lucrative market for microprocessors.

In 1985, continuing Japanese success in the midst of the most serious slump in Silicon Valley's history led to renewed pressure on the US government. Final figures for 1984 showed that the US share of the world market for chips was falling, while Japan's was rapidly rising. From a chip trade surplus with Japan in 1980, the US had run up a trade deficit of $800 million in 1984. Despite calls by

Japan's prime minister, Yasuhiro Nakasone, for trade liberalization – and his allegedly close relationship with President Reagan (this was the "Ron and Yasu" era) – it was pretty obvious that Tokyo had no intention of opening up its home market to US chip companies.

The fear that the Japanese would dominate the emerging market for 1-megabit memory chips, following their successes with 64K and 256K DRAMs, led the Semiconductor Industry Association (SIA), in June 1985, to file a complaint under section 301 of the 1974 Trade Act with the International Trade Commission (ITC) and the US Department of Commerce. In response to an earlier complaint from memory maker Micron Technology of Boise, Idaho, the ITC ruled in July 1985 that Japan was indeed dumping 64K DRAMs – and this was later confirmed by the Commerce Department. Intel, AMD, and National Semiconductor all filed antidumping petitions over the pricing of Japanese EPROMs – and their complaints were also upheld. In January 1986 the ITC ruled against the Japanese once again, charging this time that they had dumped 256K DRAMs.

Friction grew between Washington and Tokyo and in March 1986 talks between US and Japanese government officials broke up in disarray. With the Japanese by then controlling 90 percent of the memory market, the Commerce Department ruled in April 1986 that the Japanese were illegally dumping memory chips and announced the imposition of import duties. Under growing pressure, the Japanese government finally signed the US–Japan "chip accord" in July 1986, by which they agreed to raise the prices of devices made in Japan – with the intention of reducing Japanese imports into the US – and they apparently agreed to allow US companies a larger share of the Japanese market.

But within months there was concern in the US that the chip accord was not working. First, prices of memory chips rose rapidly – in fact they doubled – thus creating windfall profits for Japanese companies: according to one industry analyst, Japanese DRAM producers extracted over $5 billion in excess profits from the US computer industry in the two years following the accord. This neatly covered the $4 billion in losses that Japanese companies had allegedly absorbed over previous years in "buying" the American DRAM market.[7]

Second, there was evidence that the accord, in forcing MITI to curtail Japanese chip production, was actually conducive to the formation of a price cartel by Japanese memory chip producers. Third, US companies were not re-entering the memory chip business on the scale that had been hoped. Fourth, the US share of the Japanese chip market remained stuck at around 9–10 percent, instead of the 20 percent envisaged in the accord. Finally – as if to add insult to injury – American computer company executives were now being forced to fly to Japan in order to plead with Japanese companies to increase supplies of vital memory chips. The DRAM accord had been a disaster.

When the news broke early in 1987 that the Japanese had for the first time in 1986 taken the largest share of the world semiconductor market (38 percent versus 36 percent for the US), there was pandemonium in Silicon Valley. The SIA hurriedly announced the formation of Sematech, a consortium of 14 leading US chip companies to be based in Austin, Texas – even though CEO Bob Noyce would not be appointed for another 18 months. Under pressure from the chip industry, the US government and the American public, Schlumberger was forced to drop its plan to sell Fairchild to the Japanese firm Fujitsu. National security concerns (Fairchild was the second largest supplier of chips to the US military) were cited. At the same time, both the National Security Council and the Defense Science Board produced reports on the dire consequences of military dependence on Japanese chips – although some argued that national security would not be compromised by the foreign sourcing of standard chips and that "national security" was being used as a convenient cover for protectionism.

In early 1988, the world semiconductor market share figures for 1987 came as an even bigger shock: the Japanese had stormed to a 48 percent versus 39 percent lead over the US. There were now five Japanese companies in the world top ten chip producers: Hitachi, NEC, Fujitsu, Toshiba, and Matsushita. The 1988 figures, released in early 1989, showed that Japan had again increased its share of the world semiconductor market, to exactly 50 percent, while the US had slipped again to 37 percent and Europe trailed on just 10 percent. As Sematech struggled to get going, there was renewed criticism in the US Congress of what were seen as taxpayer-funded attempts to bail out the ailing American chip industry – although a major GAO (General Accounting Office) study concluded that Sematech represented money well spent. Indeed, a further cooperative venture, US Memories, was launched with the intention of getting the US back into memory chips.

In January 1990, US Memories collapsed through lack of support. At the same time, it was revealed that the Japanese had again widened their lead in the world semiconductor stakes in 1989 to 51 percent versus 35 percent for the US. Europe had held on to a 10 percent market share, while South Korea on its own had taken 4 percent and Taiwan had entered the ratings on about 1 percent. The top five semiconductor companies in the world were now NEC, Toshiba, Hitachi, Motorola, and Fujitsu, in that order. Texas Instruments had dropped to No. 6. When – to many people's surprise – the five-year-old US–Japan chip accord was renewed in June 1991, there was widespread skepticism that US firms would ever be allowed to gain significant market share in Japan. The foreign share of the Japanese chip market stood at just 12.3 percent in 1990 and 14.3 percent in 1991 – half a decade after the first accord had set a goal of 20 percent.

The Japanese were also consolidating their position in chip-making equipment, aided by the sudden collapse of the leading US company and former world leader, Perkin-Elmer. The top two chip equipment makers in the world, Nikon and Tokyo Electron, were now Japanese – ten years earlier, the best that any Japanese company could manage was fifteenth place. Sony had also bought out a promising US maker of chip-making gear, Materials Research Corp., while Nippon Denso moved to buy its main American competitor, Semi-Gas Systems, a very successful producer of gases needed to make semiconductors. AT&T was forced into a joint venture with Japan's Hoya Corp. As Japanese suppliers of chip-making equipment gained the whip hand, Silicon Valley executives were already grumbling that the Japanese were holding back on the latest gear, thus giving Japanese chip producers a head start.[8] This was confirmed by a GAO study, released in 1991. Not only had the Japanese captured the market for the "rice" of industry, they were now moving to control the means with which to produce industry's new staple diet.

From California to Kyushu: How the West was Lost

One day in June 1982, Silicon Valley was stunned to learn of the arrest in Santa Clara of six senior executives of the Japanese firms Hitachi and Mitsubishi, for conspiring to steal documents, parts and software from IBM. They and 14 others were subsequently accused of paying a total of $648,000 to a firm of consultants called Glenmar Associates for material and trade secrets they knew to be the property of IBM. It turned out that Glenmar Associates was an FBI front – and the luckless Japanese with their "shopping list" of secrets had been entrapped in a "sting" operation that later became known as "Jap-scam."

When the Hitachi people came to trial on criminal charges in San Francisco in early 1983, they all pleaded guilty. The company was fined the maximum $10,000 and two employees were fined a paltry $14,000. IBM's civil suit against Hitachi was finally settled out of court in October 1983. Hitachi agreed to pay IBM substantial damages and all of IBM's legal costs (estimated at several million dollars). IBM also won the right to inspect all of Hitachi's new products for five years to ensure that they were not using IBM designs.

"Jap-scam" and related events shocked many in the Valley who were still unaware of the extent of Japanese industrial espionage. But industrial espionage was hardly a new phenomenon in the "Wild West" of northern California. The Soviets had been at it for years, as had the French – and after all, the creation of "spin-off" companies by former employees taking away secrets was one of the factors that allegedly helped make the Valley great in the first place. One could even say that this milder form of industrial espionage was part of the industry's way of life. Yet there was still an important difference between legitimate business activity and illegal behavior.

In their efforts to "catch up" with the US in semiconductor technology, various well-worn intelligence-gathering techniques were used by Japanese and other industrial spys. Many were perfectly legal, such as monitoring academic journals, attending industry conferences and even taking jobs in leading research laboratories. Japanese firms also learned a lot about their American competitors by gaining access to public records using the 1966

Freedom of Information Act. A less ethical but nevertheless still legal form of stealing ideas was the phoney employment ad. A firm advertises and interviews prospective employees from other firms about their work, maybe even getting them to produce samples. More often than not, no job offer materializes. Bogus companies were also set up to offer collaboration or to elicit information through proposed joint-venture partnerships, or – in the case of some Japanese firms – simply to buy the latest equipment or products for "reverse engineering" back home. When such "legitimate" means were exhausted, more questionable tactics such as bribery, blackmail, sexual favors, outright theft in the form of pilfering, and even break-ins were used to obtain vital secrets.

Japanese companies were also accused of infringing copyrights and patents. This usually arose when US companies licensed their original designs to a Japanese "second source." For example, in 1984 Intel and Japan's NEC became embroiled in legal action over Intel's claim to hold the copyright to the microcode (the software embedded in a microprocessor) in one of its chips. NEC tried to claim that microcode could not be copyrighted, while Intel claimed that NEC had plagiarized large chunks of it. The case dragged on through the US courts for five years, with both sides claiming victory from time to time.

Finally, in February 1989, district court judge William P. Gray, sitting in San Jose, ruled that Intel did hold a copyright on its microcode but that it had forfeited that copyright (and any hopes of compensation) because the company had omitted to attach copyright notices to the millions of chips which it had shipped! Although this landmark decision turned out to be something of a hollow victory for Intel, it did at least establish that microcode was copyrightable. In 1990, a similar dispute between Motorola and Hitachi over a chip design patent was resolved with an out-of-court settlement. Meanwhile, it was revealed that Texas Instruments had picked up hundreds of millions of dollars in license fees from Japanese, US, and Korean competitors it had threatened to sue for infringing chip patents.

Aside from less savory tactics such as industrial espionage and patent infringement, Japanese companies, guided by MITI, deployed a whole variety of "catch-up" techniques and "take-lead" strategies as part of their campaign of conquest in the semiconductor industry. These included targeting key technologies, government subsidies in the form of cheap loans to producers, the direct acquisition of foreign competitors where necessary, and the intelligent use of partnerships or strategic alliances in order to obtain technology, distribution channels, and market share. Generally speaking, the Japanese wished to emulate Silicon Valley's success, but wanted to avoid its downside and its internal contradictions. They also realized that building the Japanese semiconductor industry would require a wholly different approach from that used in the building of Silicon Valley.

In the 1950s, the Japanese electronics industry mainly produced germanium-based transistors for consumer products. It was less advanced in silicon-based integrated circuits (ICs). Indeed, MITI was alarmed to learn that US firms like Texas Instruments had a big lead in IC technology, especially planar techniques. ICs were seen as central to the future of microelectronics and microelectronics was seen as the key to the future of computing. Although MITI had originally targeted electronics in 1957 with the Electronics Industry Promotion Law, in 1964 MITI specifically targeted microelectronics, establishing promotion agencies, data centers, and research institutes. Direct funding and low-interest loans were made available for approved projects and MITI further engineered a series of mergers and agreements between existing firms so they could pool their resources in the struggle to "catch up" with America.

More MITI-inspired plans, promotion laws, research initiatives and funding schemes followed throughout the late 1960s and early 1970s. But by far the most significant event was the launch, in 1975, of the Japanese VLSI (very large scale integration) Project. The VLSI Project brought together the five leading computer companies in Japan: Fujitsu, Hitachi, Mitsubishi, NEC, and Toshiba. Capital spending by the companies surged as six major VLSI research labs were opened. MITI supplemented these corporate investments with interest-free loans and ensured that major chip buyers like NTT would give preference to Japanese chips.[9] Within 2–3 years, results were already being seen in terms of patents issued, research papers published – and most important, a rapidly rising world market share for Japanese companies.

The success of the VLSI Project caught American and European companies by surprise. They blundered badly by underestimating Japan's existing strengths in consumer electronics and its determination to succeed in semiconductors. Another error was to stick with cumbersome NMOS technology rather than go over to the more compact CMOS, as the Japanese did. CMOS (complementary metal-oxide semiconductor) chips use only 10 percent of the power of an NMOS chip, can be run off tiny batteries and generate less heat. They are also better able to cope with rough conditions, such as portability. The Japanese soon demonstrated the advantages of CMOS, when they flooded the market with battery operated digital watches, calculators, and other consumer products containing low-power CMOS chips. George Gilder, author of *Microcosm* (1989), argues that American firms failed to see the centrality of CMOS in the process of "collapsing the computer" and what he calls "the CMOS slip" enabled the Japanese, among other things, to capture the emerging market for laptop computers.[10]

A major reason for Japan's success in semiconductors was the structure of Japanese industry. Leading Japanese companies belong to *keiretsu*, or large families of companies linked together financially and as mutual suppliers. These long-term, supportive arrangements, combined with easy access to cheap, patient capital meant that Japanese companies were ideally placed to "hold their breath for a long time" while waiting for returns from their massive investments in VLSI technology. Stable, homogeneous workforces, experience with teamwork, cleanliness and meticulous attention to detail, excellence in automating manufacturing for maximum quality and reliability, the sharing of research results, and strategic coordination against foreign rivals in domestic and overseas markets were other "secrets" of Japanese chip success.

When Japanese firms could not win through the "normal" operation of the market, they resorted to the direct acquisition of foreign rivals. Although Fujitsu's purchase of Silicon Valley legend Fairchild was blocked by the US government in 1987, nobody stopped the subsequent sale to Japanese interests of about 30 US companies involved in semiconductors. Indeed a 1991 survey found that two out of three US semiconductor companies expected to be bought out by 1995 – and half of them expected the buyers to be Japanese.[11] Although US firms were learning to fight back better against the Japanese, there was deep concern in Silicon Valley that the Japanese were now wealthy enough to pick off any US company that stood in their way.

When complete takeover was not desirable or possible, Japanese companies would offer joint-venture partnerships or strategic alliances to their competitors. This would often appear attractive to US firms, who found it hard to raise the capital needed to start new chip production lines. For example, Texas Instruments entered into an arrangement with Hitachi in 1989 and Intel announced a joint venture with NMB Semiconductor of Japan in 1990. The usual pattern was for US firms to trade their design and software skills for Japanese manufacturing skills or production technology. A dense network of such strategic alliances was in place by the early 1990s. American executives argued that they had no alternative, but past experience of technology transfer across the Pacific to Japan suggested that the Japanese would once again wind up the winners.

Today, much of Japan's semiconductor industry is located on the southern island of Kyushu (see figure 3.4). According to Tatsuno, this region of 13 million people has attracted over 190 electronics companies in recent years, giving it the title of "Silicon Island." They were attracted, it is said, by clean air and water, cheaper land, industrial parks, airports, and beautiful scenery.[12] Even by the mid-1980s, Kyushu had over 70 chip-manufacturing plants producing 40 percent of Japan's semiconductor output or 10 percent of the world total. Unlike Silicon Valley, Silicon Island is primarily a manufacturing base. Most semiconductor R&D takes place elsewhere in Japan. But that is changing as communications improve and more and more high-tech firms relocate out of the mainland cities as part of the Japanese government's "Technopolis Plan."

Small Is No Longer Beautiful

As Japan's success in semiconductors became more apparent, many people back in Silicon Valley were starting to seriously question the continuing validity of the entrepreneurial model. Some even argued that this early ingredient of the Valley's success had now become its Achilles' heel.

In this context, it's worth recalling the origins of Apple, for it was

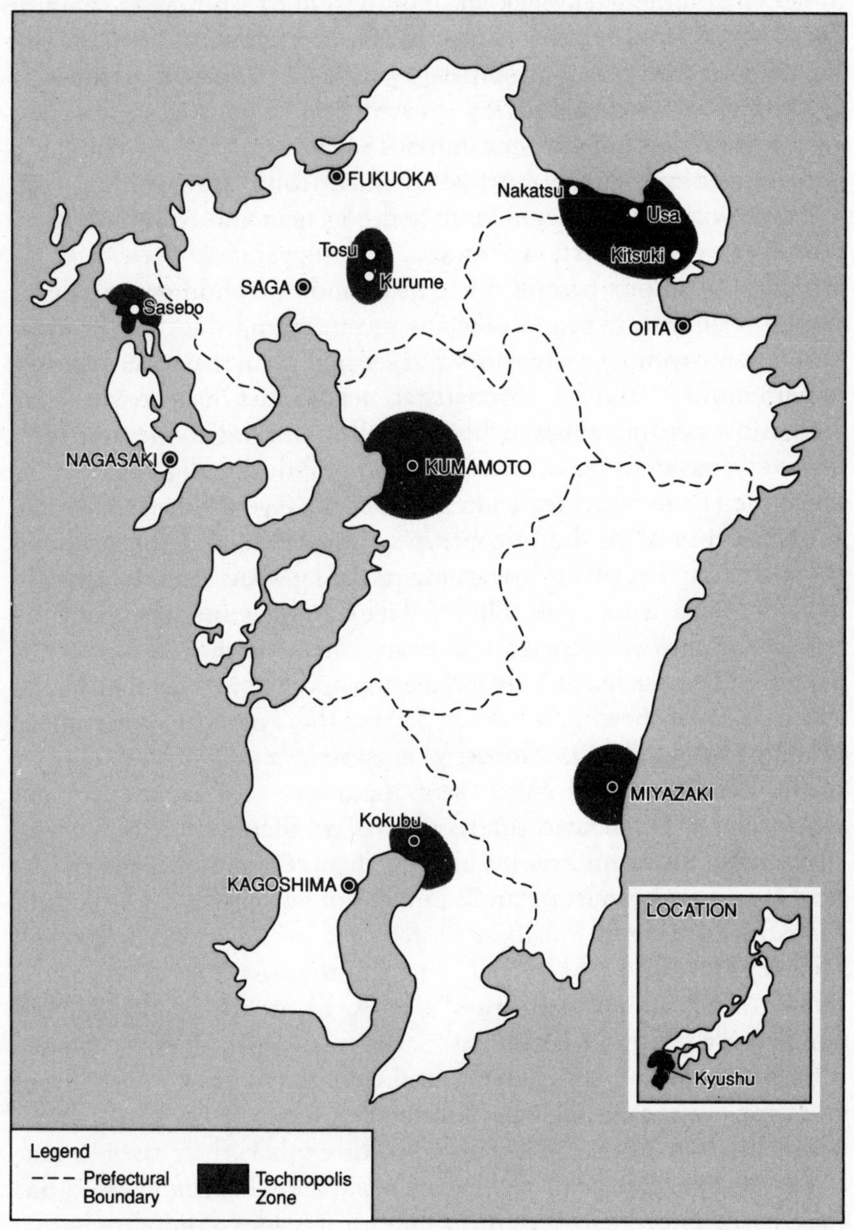

Figure 3.4 Kyushu: Japan's "Silicon Island."
(*Source*: Ministry of International Trade and Industry)

the Apple/two-guys-in-a-garage legend more than any other which influenced US and European thinking about high-tech industry for more than a decade. Back in 1975, a young computer whiz at Hewlett-Packard by the name of Stephen "Woz" Wozniak put forward the idea of selling something called a "personal" computer. Hewlett-Packard management turned him down flat, saying that such a product would never catch on. So Wozniak left the company and teamed up with a guy called Steve Jobs, who sold his old Volkswagen so they could start building personal computers in a rented garage. The rest, as they say, is history.

"Woz" was only doing what thousands of budding computer entrepreneurs have been doing for years: taking their bright ideas out of the corporate glass doors and setting up on their own – partly to gain more freedom, but mostly to make a fast buck. As we have seen, most entrepreneurs in Silicon Valley worked at one time for a few well-known large companies – and practically all of these were descended from Shockley and Fairchild, the big names of the 1950s. With the arrival of the microchip in the 1970s and the personal computer in the 1980s, governments and policy-makers actually looked to the Apple and Silicon Valley models for lessons about how to develop a more entrepreneurial culture in the rest of society. President Reagan lauded the pioneering spirit of entrepreneurs, the new American heroes, while in Britain the Thatcher government launched a "Small Firms Strategy" to save British industry.

The case for small firms was apparently backed up by the research of MIT's David Birch, who found that in the US between 1981 and 1985, firms employing less than 20 people were responsible for creating no less than 88 percent of new jobs. In *The Second Industrial Divide: Possibilities for Prosperity* (1984), authors Michael Piore and Charles Sabel argued that small firms were best suited to "flexible specialization" – using IT to quickly switch from one product design to another. Economist/writer George Gilder argued that most of the energy and dynamism in economies and most innovation in high-tech industries came from small firms, while Eli Ginzberg and George Vojta explained in their book, *Beyond Human Scale: The Large Corporation at Risk* (1985), that large companies had been in decline for decades. They bred conformism and stifled creativity.

In response to this new orthodoxy, some companies decided to go in for "Intrapreneuring." Intrapreneurs were go-ahead employees who didn't get on by getting out. Instead, intrapreneurs were encouraged to stay in the firm and were given more freedom, resources, and rewards to operate *as if they were entrepreneurs.* They were promised no more stifling bureaucracy, endless meetings, and incessant office politics. Intrapreneuring was heavily promoted by one Gifford Pinchot III, author of a book of the same name, and it became flavor of the month. Two of the best-known examples were IBM's decision to develop its PC at an autonomous plant at Boca Raton, Florida and GM's decision to launch the independent Saturn Corp. Many computer firms – including Hewlett-Packard – made renewed efforts to hold on to valued employees.

But as the Japanese, with their *keiretsu* and their huge, vertically integrated conglomerates, captured a larger and larger share of the semiconductor market, a growing number of academics and businessmen began to question the small-firms orthodoxy. Small was no longer seen as efficient. Small companies did not appear to have the resources to compete with the Japanese corporate giants. The constant exodus of talent to start-ups was surely sapping their strength. Even worse, cash-strapped small firms were being forced to sell their ideas to foreigners, mainly the Japanese. It seemed that high-tech entrepreneurialism was on the way out: big was back in again.

More evidence emerged to suggest that small was no longer beautiful. First, the accuracy of David Birch's findings, upon which much of the small-firms fever was based, was challenged by new research from the US Small Business Administration which showed that only 36.5 percent of new jobs – not 88 percent – were created in the early 1980s in the US by firms with less than 20 employees. Second, Maryellen Kelly and Harvey Brooks of Carnegie-Mellon University claimed that Piore and Sabel's "flexible specialization" thesis was flawed: big firms, not small firms, they said, were most likely to adopt flexible manufacturing systems (FMS). Harvard economist Robert Reich claimed that American high-tech industries were suffering from "chronic entrepreneurialism" and this was undermining US competitive strength. The flight of budding entrepreneurs from large corporations was wounding the very companies most able to compete with the Japanese monoliths.

In a particularly cogent analysis, semiconductor industry expert Charles H. Ferguson argued that the American microchip industry had become too fragmented to compete as a result of defections; that its smaller companies were unable to achieve economies of scale; that the loss of continuity caused by staff defections or "spin-offs" led to under-investment in the "mother" companies; and that small, entrepreneurial firms were being forced to raise capital by trading vital technology for production equipment with overseas competitors. For example, LSI Logic, a 7-year-old leader in semi-custom chips, allegedly gave away its software secrets to Toshiba in return for the manufacture of some other chips it needed but could not get made in America. VLSI Technology of San Jose did much the same with Hitachi.

Ferguson further argued that the cost of setting up a chip production operation, with its associated R&D facilities, flexible manufacturing systems, and worldwide marketing and customer support, was so enormous by the late 1980s that only very large companies could even contemplate it. America's consistently most successful industries, he said, had been aerospace and chemicals, where big firms predominated. Large companies were often best at long-term R&D, at manufacturing, and at marketing.

Although entrepreneurialism may have suited an earlier stage in the growth of the US semiconductor industry, this model was no longer appropriate: "Making yourself or a small number of managers rich is very different from contributing to the long-run growth of an industry," he wrote. "In semiconductors, a combination of personnel mobility, ineffective intellectual property protection, risk aversion in large companies and tax subsidies for the formation of new companies contribute to a fragmented 'chronically entrepreneurial' industry. US semiconductor companies are unable to sustain the large, long-term investments required for continued US competitiveness."[13]

Silicon Valley's entrepreneurs had been lionized, but the US semiconductor industry was now being forced to reconsider its obsession with individualistic entrepreneurialism and to study how the Japanese had succeeded so well with a very different model. Silicon Valley was not yet dead – indeed, rumors of its death may have been exaggerated. But the successful industry figures of the 1990s would not be those "two-guys-in-a-garage." Rather, they would be sort of high-tech diplomats working for large companies, negotiating strategic alliances and licensing deals involving huge sums of money, and snapping up the small fry before they get a chance to grow into sizable fish.

Can the US and Europe Catch Up?

One American response to the rise of Japanese chips was an increasing number of tie-ups, mergers, and alliances between US suppliers and end-users. This trend toward "vertical" or "backward" integration had actually started some years earlier with Schlumberger's purchase of Fairchild (generally considered to have been a disaster), Xerox's purchase of SDS, and the absorption of Mostek by United Technologies. Gould also took over American Microsystems Inc. (AMI), while Intel signed a collaboration agreement with Advanced Micro Devices (AMD).

In the 1980s, the trend became a scramble as firms rushed to form partnerships and to broaden their range of products. Thus IBM purchased 20 percent of Intel, a leading chip maker (although it sold some on) and 100 percent of Rolm, which made telecommunications equipment. Wang bought into VLSI Technology, NCR into Ztel, Sperry into Trilogy, Magnetic Peripherals into Centronics, and Control Data into Source Telecomputing. Western Union bought into Vitalink, while AT&T went overseas to purchase 25 percent of Olivetti, the Italian office equipment maker. RCA teamed up with Toshiba – together, they ranked eleventh worldwide in chip sales in 1985 – although later in the same year, Toshiba reached a wide-ranging agreement to cooperate in semiconductors with Siemens of West Germany.

With the technology moving fast, product lives shortening, and the cost of developing new products increasing, not even giants like IBM could afford to develop and produce a full range of products. Accordingly, in 1986 IBM and Intel forged a five-year technology-sharing agreement which, among other things, gave Intel the right to customize for others some of the 15,000 chips IBM had developed for its own use. In 1987, National Semiconductor purchased Fairchild from the luckless Schlumberger, after the proposed buy-out by Fujitsu had been quashed through security fears.

In fact, a wave of acquisitions and hostile takeovers took place in 1988 as the price of high-tech stocks fell and more companies became tempting targets.

However, security fears were not enough to halt in 1989 the announcement that leading US chip maker Texas Instruments was to cooperate with its Japanese arch-rival Hitachi in the design and production of the next generation of superchips such as high-performance microprocessors and the 16-megabit DRAM. More foreign liaisons followed: Hewlett-Packard signed technology and marketing agreements with both Hitachi and Samsung of South Korea; Sun teamed up with Fujitsu and Philips for technology-sharing and Tatung, Matsushita, ICL, and Toshiba in marketing; MIPS signed with Siemens, NEC, Sony, and Sumitomo. In 1990, Intel teamed up with NMB Semiconductor of Japan to jointly produce DRAMs, AT&T signed a technology-sharing agreement with Olin Corp., and IBM entered a joint venture with Germany's Siemens to develop commercial 64 megabit chips by 1995. In 1992, IBM teamed up with Toshiba to develop "flash" memory chips.

The convergence of electronics, computing, and telecommunications meant that firms who once thought of themselves as just being in semiconductors or mainframe computers or software or telecommunications now found that they were all part of the same IT industry. They were expected to offer a complete range of IT equipment – this is known as "one-stop shopping" – and teaming up allowed them to do this. Thus Burroughs, even before its merger with Sperry in 1986, already supplied small computers, medium computers, software, telecoms equipment, and peripherals – all of which had been made by someone else. This increased collaboration reflected concern about IBM's entry into every sector of the market and more especially fear of Japanese competition. With the chip industry firmly incorporated into the much larger IT industry, analysts predicted that we might end up with a few giant-sized, vertically integrated suppliers like IBM and Fujitsu.

The second major response to Japan's progress was the formation of research consortia. Starting with the Microelectronics and Computer Technology Corp. (MCC), a grouping of 19 US computer companies based in Austin, Texas, in 1983, this was followed by Sematech in 1987 and the short-lived US Memories in 1990. While MCC's performance has been somewhat disappointing, Sematech faced an uphill battle to gain acceptance among major chip makers. Its first CEO, Intel's Robert Noyce, found it hard to persuade egotistical Silicon Valley entrepreneurs to put cooperation before competition. He also had great difficulty persuading key members of the Bush administration to back anything that smacked of "industrial policy" rather than leaving everything to the workings of the "free market." Sematech was not helped by Noyce's untimely death in late 1990.

Meanwhile in Europe a similar pattern of alliances and consortia emerged as the Japanese began making inroads into the European chip market. In 1985, Germany's Siemens and Holland's Philips teamed up to start their "Megaproject." They were later joined by the Franco-Italian joint venture, SGS-Thomson, the only other major European player in microchips. The Megaproject was superseded by JESSI (Joint European Submicron Silicon) in 1989, but Philips was forced to pull out for financial reasons in the following year. At the same time, the European Community (EC) had sponsored a custom chip venture in the form of European Silicon Structures (or ES2). Amid accusations of Japanese dumping (despite a 14.9 percent tariff) and concern over Europe's growing chip trade deficit, more alliances were hastily formed between, for example, Plessey and Nixdorf and IBM and Siemens in 1991.

The pathetic demise of US Memories – which collapsed through lack of support from American chip companies in January 1990 – helped spark a furious debate in Washington over the merits of having a high-tech "industrial policy." Throughout 1990 a chorus of Silicon Valley executives called for a new agenda to tackle the Japanese threat. This included the creation of venture funds of "patient" capital, relaxing antitrust regulations, giving more R&D tax credits, federal aid for critical technologies, and enforcing existing antidumping laws. Sematech's Robert Noyce and industry analyst Charles H. Ferguson warned in no uncertain terms that the US semiconductor industry was doomed unless immediate action was taken. In particular, Silicon Valley had to abandon its "obsession" with entrepreneurialism and Washington had to replace its blind faith in the market with a more sophisticated, strategic approach to government–industry relations, as existed in Japan.

Yet there were still voices in America – notably those of economics writer George Gilder, T. J. Rodgers, outspoken CEO of Cypress Semiconductor, and White House advisers Richard G. Darman and Michael J. Boskin – who remained vigorously opposed to the US government doing anything to "save" the US semiconductor industry. In their view, it didn't need saving and everything would work out alright in the end if the market was left to its own devices. Others challenged this free-market "fanaticism": Andrew S. Grove, president of Intel, even sent a violin to the White House, suggesting that budget director Richard G. Darman might do some more fiddling while the American high-tech industry burned![14]

While Washington continued to reject intervention to assist the US semiconductor industry – preferring instead to spend its R&D dollars in 1992, for example, on "big science" projects like the Superconducting Supercollider ($534 million) and the NASA space station ($2 billion) – there was both good and bad news about American attempts to get back into the chip race. IBM and Texas Instruments appeared to be quite well placed in megabit memory chips, even though the top five Japanese companies had pipped them to the post with prototypes. The US still held a comfortable lead in state-of-the-art microprocessors. There were also persistent reports that US companies were doing nicely in highly profitable specialist or custom chips, EEPROMs or "flash memory" chips and DSP (digital signal processing) chips, although there was no suggestion that the US was about to reclaim the lead in standard memory chips. In terms of overall market share, US chip makers were getting back on more equal terms with the Japanese in the early 1990s – which was a lot better than the rapid decline in market share that had occurred in the 1980s.

Even so, Japanese companies are not about to give up their hard-won gains easily and their capture of the semiconductor equipment industry is a particular cause for concern. In addition, Japan has now emerged as the world's biggest consumer of chips, taking about 40 percent of the world's supply, compared with about 30 percent for the US. Among other things, it will make life harder for US producers of custom chips. The cost of setting up new production lines is becoming prohibitive for most US and European companies and the Japanese are already targeting next-generation semiconductor technologies, such as gallium arsenide and superconducting chips. It is hard to see how anyone can now take the "rice" industry back from the Japanese.

Notes

1 Clyde V. Prestowitz, *Trading Places: How We Allowed Japan to Take the Lead* (Basic Books, New York, 1988), pp. 32–3 and p. 68.
2 Wire service report in *The Australian*, January 8, 1991.
3 Parts of this chapter have been revised and updated from my earlier book, *High-Tech Society: The Story of the Information Technology Revolution* (Basil Blackwell, Oxford, UK and MIT Press, Cambridge, MA, 1987), pp. 50–80.
4 Simon Ramo, *The Business of Science: Winning and Losing in the High-Tech Age* (Hill and Wang, New York, 1988), p. 256; and Forester, *High-Tech Society*, p. 55.
5 Sheridan M. Tatsuno, *The Technopolis Strategy: Japan, High Technology, and the Control of the 21st Century* (Brady/Prentice-Hall, New York, 1986), p. 51.
6 Everett M. Rogers and Judith K. Larsen, *Silicon Valley Fever: Growth of High-Technology Culture* (Basic Books, New York, 1984).
7 Charles H. Ferguson, "Computers and the coming of the US keiretsu," *Harvard Business Review*, July–August 1990, p. 64; *Business Week*, July 4, 1988, p. 38.
8 *Business Week*, May 29, and September 4, 1989; *New Scientist*, October 20, 1990.
9 Tatsuno, *The Technopolis Strategy*, pp. 11–20.
10 George Gilder, *Microcosm: The Quantum Revolution in Economics and Technology* (Simon and Schuster, New York, 1989), pp. 144–9.
11 *New Scientist*, October 20, 1990; *The Australian*, May 21, 1991.
12 Tatsuno, *The Technopolis Strategy*, pp. 173–97.
13 Charles H. Ferguson, "From the people who brought you voodoo economics," *Harvard Business Review*, May–June 1988, pp. 55–62. See also reports in *The Australian*, September 13, 1988 and April 2, 1991; and Scott Brown, "How gray is my valley," *Time*, November 18, 1991.
14 *Business Week*, February 5, 1990, pp. 36–42; *Fortune*, May 6, 1991, pp. 60–3.

4
Computers and Software: Up the Technology "Food Chain"

Personal Computers and Workstations: Born in the USA, Made in Japan? – Here Come the Software Factories – Japan's March on Mainframes – The Search for Supercomputer Supremacy – AI and the Fifth Generation: The Limits of Hype – Computing in the Future: Japan Takes the Next-Generation Initiative

Japan's move up the technology "food chain" from consumer electronics and semiconductors into the heartland of computers has long been predicted and often delayed. Some say that the Japanese have deliberately held back, not wishing to unduly alarm the West, whilst making quiet progress in critical, related areas like screen technologies, computer peripherals, image-processing, and robotics. It's also pretty clear that sometime in the 1970s Japan's computer companies decided not to take on US vendors in finished products, but to target computer components instead.

Observers also frequently pointed to Japan's continued weaknesses in pcs, software, and workstations, and in particular the apparent failure of the much publicized "Fifth Generation Computer Project" to come up with the next generation of computers. Despite many other such projects and plans, it was clear that American researchers still had the leading edge in computer science, artificial intelligence, and distributed systems right through the 1980s. By 1990, the US still held a comfortable 60 percent of the world computer market – albeit down from around 70 percent in 1980.

But many analysts believe that the 1990s will be different. They say that the US computer industry has reached a turning point and that the Japanese are poised for a major assault in hardware and in software. Market share figures are deceptive because they ignore the extent to which US computer companies are already dependent on the Japanese for supplies of components: for example, the US produced 66 percent of the world's floppy disks in 1978 but only 4 percent in 1988. "Hollowing-out" is further evident in the fact that the proportion of computers sold in the US which were actually produced in American factories slumped from 94 percent in 1979 to 66 percent in 1989. Moreover, it has been suggested that the popular notions that the Japanese "aren't creative" and "can't write software" and that "the Fifth Generation project was a flop" are simply comforting myths which obscure the fact that the Japanese are making massive gains in strategic areas.

Through their mastery of miniaturization and LCD screen technology, Japanese companies like Toshiba, NEC, and Sharp grabbed a big lead in the late 1980s in laptop computers, the fastest-growing segment of the pc market. Through their ruthless acquisition of American RISC (reduced instruction set computer) chip know-how, the Japanese may yet equal the US in workstations and they will also benefit from the worldwide move toward "open" hardware systems that run on standard operating systems like Unix.

In mainframes, Japan's Fujitsu is already No. 2 in the world to the fast-fading IBM and Hitachi Data Systems is posing a major threat to US producers. In supercomputers, it seems that NEC, Fujitsu, and Hitachi machines have already taken the world lead in terms of speed, while the Japanese have been first to commercialize AI applications like "fuzzy logic." Even in software, where Japan had just 13 percent of the $110 billion world market in 1990 compared with 57 percent for the US, the Japanese look set to catch up with their relentless drive to produce high-quality software in their so-called "software factories."

Japan's push into computers dates back to the early 1950s. But, as Marie Anchordoguy explains, it was not until 1959 that MITI really recognized the overall strategic importance of computers to the future of society and took decisive action. In one fell swoop, MITI raised tariffs on imported computers to 25 percent in order to protect the infant Japanese computer industry; launched a computer rental authority called Japan Electronic Computer Company

(JECC) that bought systems from Japanese suppliers and then rented them out to Japanese users at rates far below IBM's; sponsored a number of ambitious cooperative R&D projects designed to benefit Japanese computer vendors; and pumped huge, direct subsidies into the industry for R&D, new equipment, and working capital. This aid amounted to $6 billion between 1961 and 1981 alone.[1]

At the same time, Japanese computer companies spent millions on licensing technology from US vendors: "In almost every case, Japanese manufacturers copied the American products, then gradually added their own features," says Tatsuno.[2] When the Japanese couldn't develop the required technology themselves or obtain US or European technology through licensing deals, they began buying into or buying up US and European companies. For example, Fujitsu first bought into Amdahl Corp., the company started by Gene Amdahl, IBM's chief mainframe designer, and then took it over. Fujitsu purchased Britain's ICL for its systems software. The company also picked up Poqet Computer of California for its power technology secrets and Intellistor for its memory expertise. Japan's Canon bought a major stake in Steve Jobs's Next Inc., while Sony purchased Materials Research Corp., a maker of semiconductor manufacturing equipment. Even Japanese tractor maker Kubota and tire maker Sumitomo have bought US software and hardware companies in order to gain technology secrets.

Having played "catch-up" with the West in most areas of computing, the Japanese have now embarked on "take-lead" strategies they hope will ensure that Japan will inevitably become the undisputed No. 1 in computers. This is a matter of great concern because it is difficult to find an example of any American or European industry that has successfully fought back in a big way where the Japanese have decided to go for leadership. Tatsuno says that the Japanese are currently working on the next generation of machines, which will be compact, stylish, and user-friendly. Like the Powerbook 100, they will be more like consumer electronics toys than computers and they will slot neatly into the home, school, or office. Bill Totten says (with the authority of 20 years at the helm of Japan's largest distributor of independent software) that because US companies have ignored the needs of the Japanese market, the

Japanese have been forced to develop their own products and in particular their own software. He predicts that Japanese consumer electronics giants like Sony and Matsushita will move into the computer market and trounce the competition.[3]

On the surface, there is no crisis in the US computer industry, says MIT researcher Charles H. Ferguson. But beneath the surface, he says, the economic imperatives of modern mass production and the technology trends in the IT industry clearly suggest that the US and European computer industries should be put on the endangered list. In an important analysis published in *Harvard Business Review* in 1990, Ferguson argued that Japan's strength in components, its manufacturing expertise, its patient capital, and its cooperative industrial structures in the form of *kieretsu*, or families of companies, make it highly likely that Japan will eventually triumph in information technology. He predicted: "If US and European companies continue business as usual, they will either fail outright or become, in effect, local design and marketing subsidiaries of Japanese companies."[4]

Pointing out that America had become a net importer of computers in 1989 and already had a computer trade deficit with Japan of $6 billion, Ferguson argued that this could only get worse because computing is entering a new era of standardized, inexpensive personal systems assembled from low-cost, mass-produced components: "Companies with excellent process technology, capital-intensive components production, and flexible high-volume assembly will dominate the hardware value chain" – and these companies tend to be Japanese. Moreover, "The most profound advantages will go to companies that have access to patient capital, that maintain close links with component and equipment developers and that can afford huge, continuing expenditures for R&D and capital investment" – and these also tend to be Japanese.

All in all "These facts play directly into the strategic and technical strengths of Japanese companies . . . In contrast, US industry has superior design skills, but it is largely fragmented, undercapitalized and shortsighted. It has failed to develop the structures, strategies and operational techniques necessary for commercial success in the markets created by its own innovations. Many European companies have clearer strategic vision, but they are starting from far behind . . . As a result, Japan could dominate world hardware markets even though US companies, universities and standards organizations still define the state of the art in computer science, systems architecture, innovative design, networking, software and digital communications – even in semiconductor memories, a $10 billion world market the United States has all but lost."[5]

Ferguson has also written: "It is my own view . . . that US society is in systemic decline far more profound than is generally appreciated."[6] Clyde V. Prestowitz agrees wholeheartedly with Ferguson, stating bluntly: "With its present organization and attitudes, US industry cannot hope to survive." And as for the IT industry: "The Japanese are going to run away with the world computer market."[7]

Personal Computers and Workstations: Born in the USA, Made in Japan?

The personal computer was invented in America. Early in 1975, the electronics hobbyists' magazine, *Popular Electronics*, featured a strange rectangular box on its cover, which looked rather like a stereo. It was called the Altair "microcomputer," and a kit of parts could be ordered for $397 from an Albuquerque firm, Micro Instrumentation and Telemetry Systems (MITS). In made-up form, it cost $621. Based on the first 8-bit microprocessor unveiled by Intel in 1972, the Altair had no keyboard or screen, and so it wasn't exactly "user-friendly." Even so, it was popular with engineers and hobbyists, and MITS sold a respectable 2,000 machines by the end of 1975.

Among the electronics enthusiasts attracted to the Altair were a small group of youngsters in Silicon Valley who called themselves the Homebrew Computer Club. Homebrew members first met in a garage in March 1975, in order to discuss and tinker with the latest gadgetry. Excited by the Altair and the idea of "personal" computers, the more ambitious wanted to build their own. Homebrew included some pretty bright kids – among their number, Bill Gates, now billionaire boss of Microsoft, and Steve Jobs and Steve Wozniak, who went on to found Apple Computer, the company that introduced millions to personal computing and literally grew from a two-guys-in-a-garage operation to a billion dollar international corporation in just eight years.

Jobs and Wozniak ("Woz") couldn't afford an Altair, so they set out to build one. Woz was the technical wizard, while Jobs was the entrepreneur. Using parts from Hewlett-Packard and Atari – where Woz and Jobs worked – and ideas from Xerox's Palo Alto Research Center (PARC), they showed Apple I to the Homebrew Club in early 1976. Everybody wanted one. By selling Jobs's Volkswagen and Woz's calculator, the duo raised $1,300 and began production. Excited by the prospect of retailing "personal" computers, Jobs approached his boss at Atari, Nolan Bushnell, and Wozniak his seniors at Hewlett-Packard. They didn't want to know. Then Jobs and Woz were put in touch with A. C. "Mike" Markkula, a former marketing boss at Intel. Markkula joined forces as a third equal partner and set about raising more money, hiring key personnel and establishing a manufacturing facility. It was at about this time that the famous Apple logo (a rainbow-colored apple with a bite out of it) was created, with the advice of Valley PR whiz, Regis McKenna.

In April 1977, the Apple II was shown at a San Francisco computer fair and sales went through the roof. By the end of that year, Apple had sold $2.5 million worth of computers. Not only was the Apple II a great technical success, it was creating a mass market for personal computers. Its success encouraged thousands of software writers to create programs specifically for use on the Apple. This had the effect of boosting sales at a crucial time. In 1979 Apple's sales hit $70 million; in 1981, $335 million; and in 1982, $583 million, putting Apple into the *Fortune* 500 of top companies in just five years. By 1982, Apple had 4,000 employees and some 750,000 Apple IIs had been sold. A hundred or so Apple employees had also become millionaires when Apple went "public," and Jobs himself – just 28 years old and worth $300 million – even made the cover of *Time* magazine.

Although most accounts of the history of the personal computer (including this one) state that the Altair was the first one, researchers at Xerox's PARC had in fact demonstrated a pc called the Alto two years earlier in 1973. Keen to diversify out of photocopiers, Xerox president Peter McColough had correctly targeted computers as the next growth area – and the Alto was rapidly produced by PARC's talented researchers. But as Douglas K. Smith and

Robert C. Alexander make clear in their revealing book, *Fumbling the Future: How Xerox Invented, Then Ignored, The First Personal Computer* (1988), Xerox's management in the mid-1970s had their hands full with antitrusts suits and Japanese competition in the copier market. In addition, political infighting, bureaucratic inertia and an aversion to risk-taking within Xerox rendered the company incapable of capitalizing on its PARC inventions. Xerox even went so far as to advertise the Alto system in 1979, but it never plunged into the computer business.[8]

In August 1981, IBM had finally entered the personal computer business with its long-awaited PC. IBM's PC quickly grabbed a large slice of the market and PCs began appearing in offices everywhere. In the comparatively short space of a few years, the personal computer had been transformed from a hobbyist's toy to an all-pervasive working tool. Making personal computers, once the prerogative of amateur tinkerers, had become a multi-million dollar industry. In fact, it qualified as the fastest growing industry ever. Back in the 1960s, computers could be afforded only by large organizations; then, in the 1970s, departments or sections of organizations were able to buy them; in the early 1980s, personal computers came to be owned and operated by individuals. In offices, personal computers started a desktop revolution by putting 1950s mainframe computing power on the desks of millions. In homes, schools, and universities, they have been adopted faster than any other technology.

Sales of personal computers in the US rocketed from none in 1974 to 47,000 units in 1977, 500,000 in 1980, 750,000 in 1981, and 1.4 million in 1983. The launch of the IBM PC gave a tremendous boost to sales, while the arrival of the PC "clones" pushed pc sales into the stratosphere. Houston-based Compaq was by far the most successful of the clone makers, selling more than $100 million worth of computers in its first year. Founded only in 1982, Compaq specialized in producing machines that offered better performance and more convenience at a lower price than IBM. Despite IBM's frantic clone-busting efforts, Compaq's sales zoomed and the firm rapidly became America's fastest-growing company ever, entering the *Fortune* 500 in 1985, just three years after its birth. This even beat Apple's record.

Through various booms and slumps, personal computer sales

steadily grew in the US, reaching 6 million units sold in 1990. In 1991, the installed base of personal computers in the US alone was estimated to be about 66 million. Over the decade 1977–87, the world market for personal computers had grown in value from a few million dollars to $27 billion, equal to the world market for mainframes and overtaking that of minicomputers. By 1991, little more than a decade after the first volume shipments, personal computers accounted for $45.7 billion of the $110 billion US market for computers – mainframe sales were worth $26.9 billion. The vast majority of sales were of American brands.

Now America's hegemony in personal computers is under threat. After several false starts, such as the ill-fated MSX machines of the mid-1980s which were pronounced "dead on arrival," the Japanese are now pushing into the pc market through their strength in laptops, the fastest growing sector of the pc business, their grip on LCD screen technology and other key components such as semiconductors and disks, and their new-found expertise in producing RISC chips, which are the essential ingredient of the hugely popular workstations.

Japan's assault on laptops began in earnest in the late 1980s, after it was clear that Japanese companies had missed out on the PC clone boom and their attempt to introduce the MSX software standard for pcs failed. Some say that the Japanese deliberately steered clear of the PC clone market, fearing the power of IBM and realizing that a price-cutting war with low-cost clone makers like the Koreans and the Taiwanese would simply destroy profits. Building a beachhead in laptops would play to Japan's existing strengths in miniaturized manufacturing, help consolidate Japan's control over key components, and at the same time fit in with the predicted trend toward the convergence of computing and consumer electronics. In particular, the expected blending of the two in the form of multimedia had attracted the attention of Japan's enormously successful and fabulously wealthy consumer electronics giants.

In 1987, Toshiba launched its T3100 laptop, which weighed in at 15 lb. and featured a crisp, orange LCD display. Although it cost more than twice as much as IBM's clunky 25 lb. PC Convertible, introduced in 1986, the Toshiba machine was soon outselling IBM by five to one thanks to its compact size and superior screen. Other US companies with laptops included Zenith (although its best-selling Z-181 was in fact built in Japan by Sanyo), Tandy's Grid Systems, and Compaq. They found Toshiba to be a tough competitor in a market which was exploding: in 1986, 300,000 laptops were sold worldwide, in 1987 sales grew to nearly 500,000, and in 1988 reached 700,000, of which 500,000 were sold in America. At the end of 1988, Zenith still held the market lead over Toshiba in the US by a margin of 26 to 22 percent, with Grid, NEC, Datavue, and Sharp some way behind. But by 1990, Toshiba had zoomed past Zenith to take 21 percent of the US laptop market, with Zenith slumping to join Compaq on 10 percent and Grid/Tandy on 8 percent. Japan's NEC and Sharp had 9 and 8 percent respectively.

Laptop sales in the US totaled 830,000 in 1990, accounting for 19 percent of the entire pc market. Analysts were predicting that laptops would soon account for 35 percent of the pc market, especially with the arrival of new varieties of laptop, such as the smaller "notebook" computer, the even smaller "palmtop" computer and the so-called "pentop" (or "notepad" or "tablet" or "pen") computers that can read and manipulate handwriting. If, as expected, laptops do assume this level of importance in the overall pc market, then it will lead to an enormous expansion in Japan's role in the global computer industry. This is primarily because Japan controls the supply of the crucial laptop components – LCD screens, floppy disk drives, and memory chips. Moreover, Western firms simply do not have the miniaturized manufacturing expertise required to put their new designs into production, as Apple found with the Powerbook 100 and the Newton.

Some, like Apple and IBM, are trying to solve the problem by entering into partnerships with Japanese companies like Sony and Sharp, but past history would suggest that the Japanese will inevitably come out on top. This is not solely because the Japanese have a stranglehold over component supplies, but also because they have made the enormous investment in manufacturing technology that enables them to swiftly put new or updated products into production. Thus – just as happened in consumer electronics – Japanese producers will be able to maintain a constant flow of new models ahead of their Western rivals. With product life-cycles shortening, Japanese producers will be better able to reflect changing consumer tastes and to incorporate the latest technological innovations.

Ever since the introduction of NEC's 4 lb. Ultralite in 1989, the Japanese have been better placed in notebook computers. This was confirmed by Apple's surprise deal with Sony and IBM's partnership with Toshiba. Meanwhile, Japan's Sharp, Sony, Canon, and Casio look well placed with the new generation of 9 oz. palmtops and the new range of pen-using pentops. Although American firms like Hewlett-Packard, NCR, Grid, Go, and General Magic have designed and/or introduced innovative products in these markets, they are for the most part dependent on Japanese companies for supplies of memory chips and batteries – and for LCD screens, they are wholly dependent on the Japanese.

The story of how the US came to lose the "active matrix" LCD industry to Japan is a parable of the postwar era. As told by Richard Florida and David Browdy, it seems that the pioneer of flat-screen technology and active matrix LCDs in particular was one T. Peter Brody of Westinghouse Electric research labs in Pittsburgh.[9] As a result of Brody's research, Westinghouse had the thin-film transistor and flat-panel fields almost to itself in the early 1970s, but it lacked the capital or the courage to gear up for high-volume production. This was partly because Westinghouse had taken a bath in semiconductors and partly because it was at the time also being forced to liquidate its television division – due to the onslaught of Japanese competition. In 1979, Brody quit the monolithic Westinghouse, taking his ideas for flat-screen televisions and computers with him into a new entrepreneurial start-up called Panelvision.

Despite the excellence of its designs, Panelvision experienced manufacturing glitches and for five years was unable to raise the capital necessary to begin large-scale production. But just when in 1984 it looked like investors would stump up the money for volume production, the Japanese in the form of Seiko appeared on the scene with a color pocket television featuring an LCD screen – which incidentally infringed Westinghouse's original patents for active-matrix displays. According to Florida and Browdy, "Japan's entry sounded the death knell for Panelvision. Investors had already been hesitant about moving from R&D into volume production. Now they thought it utterly foolish to try to compete with the Japanese on their strong suit of manufacturing efficiency."[10] In 1985, Panelvision was sold to Litton Industries and Brody left the company. Brody later tried again with another company called

Magnascreen, but the same venture capitalists who built Silicon Valley now steered clear of such risky ventures. Neither Magnascreen nor the half-dozen or so US companies left in the screen-technology business were able to develop high-volume production.

Meanwhile by 1991 the Japanese had grabbed 98 percent of the world's LCD screen market and 100 percent of the fast-growing market for active-matrix LCDs. With Japanese companies – led by Sharp, Sanyo, Matsushita, Hitachi, Seiko Epson, Hoshiden, and Toshiba – planning to invest $2.35 billion in active-matrix display production alone in the next few years, it looks like the Japanese will completely dominate LCD technology for the foreseeable future. This will probably be the case even if, as some suggest, field-emission display (FED) technology eventually replaces LCD technology. US computer makers will be at the mercy of Japanese suppliers who are also their main competitors. This means that they are no longer assured of getting the latest technology and thus they will be at a perpetual disadvantage. The decision of the US government in August 1991 to slap a 63 percent tariff on imports of active-matrix LCDs from Japan was really a case of shutting the stable door, while the news that Europe's Philips would be spending large sums to get back into active-matrix LCDs was seen by analysts to be courageous but utimately doomed.

From laptop pcs, the next logical step up the technology food chain is to workstations – and sure enough, the Japanese seem to have targeted this sector of the pc market which has been growing at a very healthy 30 percent a year in the early 1990s. Workstations combine the power of a minicomputer with good graphics and the "open" operating system of Unix. Workstations for scientists were pioneered in America by the US firms Sun, Apollo, and Hewlett-Packard, who had the business pretty much to themselves as recently as 1988. When the US market grew to be worth $4 billion in 1989 and workstations started to move out of the lab and into the office, bigger US guns like DEC and IBM joined battle with their own products. But the big shock came when Sony and Oki appeared as if from nowhere with a range of workstations for the US market. However, these models were not a success and both firms quietly withdrew from the market.

The Japanese will probably mount a fresh assault on the workstation market for one very simple reason: there's no need to purchase microprocessor chips from America's Intel or Motorola, who refuse to license their chip designs. Workstations operate on RISC chips which the Japanese now make themselves, because the American RISC specialists Sun, Hewlett-Packard, and MIPS Computer Systems agreed in the late 1980s to license their designs to Sony, Fujitsu, NEC, Toshiba, and Hitachi. In addition, the Japanese already have the technical edge in key workstation components such as memory chips and high-resolution screens. As the workstation marketing battle hots up in the 1990s, Hewlett-Packard and Sun may rue the day they sold their RISC secrets to the Japanese. David L. House, head of Intel's microprocessor division, is quoted as saying: "Licensing those chips is one of the greatest crimes in American technology."[11]

Here Come the Software Factories

"OK, they can make the hardware, but they can't write good software," is the typical comment one hears about the Japanese IT effort from Western computer professionals. It's all rather reminiscent of 1970s claims that the Japanese might be able to make 4-cylinder cars, but "they'll never produce a BMW or a Jaguar." Try telling that to the millions of Acura, Lexus, and Infiniti owners. Besides, what do people think that faultless Japanese cameras, VCRs, camcorders, copiers, and faxes run on if it isn't Japanese software?

Like computers, software – the instructions that tell a computer what to do – originated in the USA, so the US software industry got something of a headstart. Most software in the 1950s and 1960s was used to run things like payroll, reservation, and billing systems and went into the big mainframes operated by big users like the banks, utilities, and government. The industry received a major boost when, in the late 1960s, IBM was made to "unbundle" – that is, stop providing software free with hardware. This opened the way for firms like MSA and Cullinet to set up as specialist "software houses" supplying new kinds of software. But the industry really took off with the advent of the personal computer, which created a mass market for software. The pc revolution put software into the hands of individuals for the first time and as the sales of pcs soared, demand for software packages soared with them.

The software industry in the early 1980s mushroomed almost overnight from a cottage industry of amateur programmers to a multi-million dollar business. Young computer nerds who were social rejects one day became millionaires the next. Freewheeling, creative individuals suddenly found themselves at the helm of major companies. New software distribution channels were opened up and the industry developed its own system of "stars" and pop "charts." US sales of software packages for pcs leapt from nothing to $2 billion by 1984, while the overall US software market shot past the $10 billion mark. Growth continued exponentially through the 1980s, so that by 1990 the US software industry had some 1.4 million people employed as programmers, engineers and salespersons. The world market for software in 1990 was worth no less than $110 billion, of which the US had a 57 percent share. Japan had 13 percent, followed by France (8 percent), Germany (7 percent), and Britain (6 percent).

Yet the software industry was not without its problems. The main problem was that developments in computer hardware were outpacing progress in the writing of software. This was (and still is) referred to variously as the software "crisis," "trap," "logjam," or "crunch."[12] The crux of the software crunch was that companies were demanding new and better software and programs were getting more complex. But this increased complexity was stretching out the software development process and holding back progress in the overall IT industry. Various suggestions were made for dealing with the software crunch and for improving programmer productivity: developing new techniques of "software engineering" such as the use of CASE (computer-aided software engineering) tools; developing new "object-oriented" software languages or OOPS (object-oriented programming systems); and improving the management of the software production process ("project management").

However, deployment of these techniques would not be that rapid and meanwhile US software was plagued with quality problems. Companies like Bank of America and Allstate Insurance were nearly brought to their knees by huge cost over-runs on failed software development projects, while software bugs were causing chaos in banks, insurance companies, utilities, government, and stock markets.[13] In fact, some US studies even indicated that failures in computer system development and use were not just commonplace: more often than not they were the rule. Even more worrying were the revelations that systems failure was a common problem in military systems and that in a number of well-documented military, aerospace, and medical accidents, faulty computer software could justifiably be accused of killing people.[14]

It did not take the Japanese long to realize that the US software industry was vulnerable on quality – just like every other US industry. American software entrepreneurs were good at pioneering new software ideas, but poor at attention to detail. Japanese software developers may be short on creative genius, but at least Japanese software tended to be delivered bug-free – and on time. What's more, most high-technology consumers were not demanding anything terribly fancy in the way of software products, just an "embedded" system which ran their pc, laptop, copier, fax, machine tool, robot, VCR, car, camera, or camcorder without any major hassles.

Accordingly, Japanese computer companies such as NEC, Fujitsu, Hitachi, and Toshiba have over recent years quietly developed a string of so-called "software factories" across Japan, with the express intention of beating the US and Europe on software quality. In order to produce high-quality software, the Japanese are using the same techniques of quality control and project management which have enabled them to become world leaders in manufacturing. Their avowed aim is to turn software production from being an art or a craft into a rigidly controlled, measured, and monitored process. MITI also launched in 1985 the $210 million Sigma Project, designed to find more efficient ways of producing software. Without rapid progress in software production, Japan will face a shortage of 1 million programmers by the year 2000.

In his major study of the Japanese software industry, published as *Japan's Software Factories* (1991), MIT professor Michael A. Cusumano found that leading Japanese firms had made significant progress in managing the process of software development and in many respects were now superior to US firms. For example, Japanese programmers produced about 70 percent more lines of source code than their American counterparts – 12,447 lines per man-year, as opposed to 7,290 per man-year for Americans. At the same time, Japanese-made programs had a failure rate of 1.96 per 1,000 lines of source code during the first 12 months of use, compared with 4.44 – more than twice – in the case of US-made programs. The Japanese were also more advanced in software standardization and reusability – that is, developing chunks of commonly used code for re-use later in new programs, instead of having to start from scratch every time.[15]

To a large extent, says Cusumano, the Japanese have merely continued and refined efforts to manufacture software first conceived in the US and Europe and progress has been fairly slow. The jury is still out on whether Japan will in fact succeed in transforming software production from an art or craft into a manufacturing science. In any event, he says, the software factory is still only a concept and not a thing, a state of mind rather than actual practice. Writing software has always been, and will remain, an extraordinarily difficult process.[16]

Apart from neglecting quality, the US software industry is also charged with neglecting the Japanese market. In his testimony on the networks in 1990, Japanese software distributor Bill Totten claims that American software companies have designed their products specifically for the US market and that they need substantial adaptation before they can be sold in Japan. American companies do not appreciate Japanese expectations of quality and do not provide documentation in Japanese. Worst of all, American software producers charge exorbitant prices for their products and impose exorbitant royalty rates on distributors. In other words, in the Japanese market – the second largest in the world – US software suppliers have been cutting their own throat.

Thus the Japanese software industry, says Totten, has been virtually forced by American neglect to produce its own products. These products are tailor-made for local markets, such as the huge, emerging Japanese office technology market. The latest Japanese software is now comparable in functional capability to US products, it is usually of much higher quality, it comes fully documented in Japanese and it is modestly priced to both the distributor and the final customer. In consequence, says Totten, whereas as recently as 1988 some 99 percent of his company's revenues in Japan came from imports and only 1 percent came from homegrown products, in 1990 the figures were more like 80 percent imports, 20 percent Japanese and the ominous trend was set to continue in the 1990s.

But while it seems likely that Japanese software producers will soon dominate their own market, the Japanese are still some time away from exporting much software to the US and European markets (aside from that embedded in Japanese goods). This is the view of Cusumano and it also finds an echo in the words of Kazuhiko Nishi, president of ASCII Corp., Japan's biggest producer of pc software. Nishi is quoted as saying: "We can't ship our product to the US because software is culture . . . Our only choice is to take a stake in established companies."[17] Accordingly, ASCII has bought into the US company Informix and has taken a controlling interest in Hyperdesk. Other Japanese companies such as CSK, Sumitomo, Kubota, Hitachi, and Japan Systems Engineering have bought shares or controlling interests in a variety of promising US software start-ups which have found it hard to raise capital. For the Japanese in computer software, it's very much a case of if at first you don't succeed, try and try again.

Japan's March on Mainframes

For three decades, from 1950 to 1980, America *owned* the computer industry, dominated as it was by mainframes and in particular by the American giant, International Business Machines (IBM). IBM and the second-tier US companies like Burroughs, Sperry, Control Data, Honeywell, and Digital Equipment lived high on the hog with steady domestic and overseas sales of (and 65 percent margins on) their mainframe "cash cows." Then, in the early 1980s, sales of personal computers began to explode and by 1987 pc revenues actually overtook mainframe revenues for the first time. Apart from IBM, the old mainframe companies were poorly represented in the pc market, while upstarts like Apple and Compaq rapidly became the new big names in computing.

Even worse, the long-awaited Japanese push into mainframes finally began. First, IBM-Japan was squeezed in the Japanese domestic market during the 1980s by the local *keiretsu* and in particular by the Japanese government's strong preference for local mainframe suppliers (in 1990, foreign suppliers were restricted to a mere 0.4 percent of the lucrative government market for computers in Japan). As a result, by the end of the decade, IBM-Japan was no longer mainframe market leader in Japan and had slipped to third place behind Fujitsu (23 percent) and Hitachi (19 percent). Moreover, Fujitsu and Hitachi were still growing in terms of sales and profits, while IBM-Japan was contracting and laying off workers. In the Japanese market – the second largest in the world – the trend was obvious and ominous.

In America, the world's largest mainframe market, IBM still held a commanding 65 percent market share in 1990, but it was under threat as never before from local competitors and the Japanese invaders. The Japanese were attacking by proxy through a series of stealthy acquisitions and "partnership" deals. They were thus not always easy to spot: for example, second-place Amdahl was in fact owned by Fujitsu, who had also quietly bought up Britain's flagship, ICL and Finland's Nokia Data. Hitachi in 1989 purchased National Advanced Systems from National Semiconductor – although it was renamed Hitachi Data Systems. HDS was described by its chief executive as a "vehicle for bringing other Hitachi products into the US."[18] This would include components like memory chips and disk drives. Meanwhile, over in Europe, Italy's Olivetti was already selling mainframes supplied by Hitachi and even France's Bull was selling mainframes made by NEC.

The story of America's decline in mainframes is mostly the story of the decline of IBM. All powerful in the 1960s and 1970s and seen as America's "defender" against the Japanese in the 1980s, IBM has continued to disappoint with its lackluster performance in recent years. From a high of 400,000 employees in 1985, successive waves of cut-backs have brought IBM's workforce down to 275,000. Profits have fallen and remained low. In January 1993, IBM announced an annual loss of $4.97 billion – the largest loss in US corporate history. A late starter in pcs, IBM's share of the US pc market fell from a peak of 27 percent to 16 percent in 1991. It has also missed important opportunities in laptops and workstations, the two growth areas of the pc market, and it has wasted millions on loudly trumpeted but ultimately abortive software development projects like OS/2 and SAA. Successive attempts to reorganize the company, chiefly by creating autonomous divisions, do not seem to have stemmed IBM's decline.

IBM is said to have become strangled by bureaucracy, with too many layers of management. The company still has great difficulty in commercializing its R&D, in getting new products to market and in responding swiftly to consumer trends. For example, IBM pioneered – but did not spot the potential of – RISC technology. Some say that IBM is stuck with its "mainframe mindset" and will never revive: only time will tell. Meanwhile IBM's mainframe business is looking distinctly shaky: competition from microcomputers and workstations is forcing IBM to cut prices, thus eroding profit margins. IBM benefited greatly from the age of proprietary software, but this has now passed and open systems are in. Most important of all, the hardware of mainframes today is becoming simpler to replicate, consisting as it does of sets of standard chips. This has halted revenue growth in mainframes and kept profits at rock bottom. This is good news for buyers, but is more bad news for IBM.

In contrast, Japan's main flag-carrier, Fujitsu, has grown steadily in recent years to become No. 2 in the world in mainframes. Despite some set-backs, like the aborted purchase of Fairchild Semiconductor in 1986, Fujitsu has progressed in America and Europe through buy-outs and partnerships. Some say that Fujitsu has been forced to make acquisitions because its corporate culture mitigates against creativity, while others point out that Fujitsu has been the great beneficiary of some none-too-subtle assistance by the Japanese government. Others emphasize the company's undoubted manufacturing expertise: for example, Fujitsu was the first to successfully mass-produce the SPARC microprocessor which has become the standard for RISC workstations. Having spent much of the 1980s engaged in a bitter battle to overtake IBM in the Japanese market, Fujitsu is now turning its attention more to exports in the 1990s – and unlike IBM, Fujitsu has no intention of losing market share.

The Search for Supercomputer Supremacy

Supercomputers were also invented in America, but now the lead is passing to Japan. Supercomputers are the big number-crunchers used by the military, government agencies, research institutions, and universities for tasks like missile testing, weather forecasting, materials design, and aerodynamic simulation. The performance of supercomputers in terms of speed and memory has been transformed in recent years by the use of parallel processing – that is, splitting a large problem into smaller parts and working on them simultaneously. So-called "massively parallel" machines use thousands of processors linked in parallel to achieve even better results. Supercomputers are revolutionizing computer graphics and film animation. They are also bringing about the "computerization of science," as more and more scientific experiments are simulated by, or performed with the help of, supercomputers. Because of their military and space applications, supercomputers have great strategic value: no nation can aspire to world leadership without being at least a leading player in supercomputers.

America's Control Data Corporation dominated the world supercomputer market in the 1960s. But after its guiding genius, Seymour Cray, left the company to form Cray Research in 1972, Cray Research became the one to beat. Many other US and European firms fell by the wayside while Cray consolidated its position to gain as much as 75 percent of the world supercomputer market – and along the way it sold some 220 of the 400 or so supercomputers now at work in the world.

In 1983, Control Data formed a new subsidiary, ETA Systems, charged with winning back the supercomputer initiative from Cray. Things seemed to be going well for ETA, while Cray itself was rocked by the departure of its chief designer, Steve Chen, for a new IBM subsidiary. But in 1989 Control Data suddenly folded ETA altogether, revealing that it had lost $240 million in five years. Soon after, the US supercomputer industry was plunged into further crisis when Seymour Cray announced that he was leaving Cray Research to start the ill-fated Cray Computer Corp. following a row over funding. Significantly, in the same year, Japan's NEC released the world's fastest supercomputer, the SX-3, which easily outperformed the fastest Cray and ETA machines.

Japan's quest for supercomputer supremacy began, as usual, with a MITI plan. Announced in 1980, the National Scientific Computing Project envisaged Japan catching up with the US in supercomputing by the end of the 1980s and taking the lead in the 1990s: things appear to be going according to plan. The first task for MITI was to close off the Japanese market to American suppliers: Cray Research, for instance, found that its prospective Japanese customers suddenly lost interest, claiming that they had no use for Cray's large machines. But meanwhile Japanese companies like Fujitsu and Hitachi were secretly developing just such machines with the knowledge brought back by Japanese researchers from US government laboratories such as Lawrence Livermore and NASA's Ames research facility. Cray's ex-prospective customers were among the first to buy the "too large" machines when they were eventually released![19] Japanese officials openly described supercomputers as the "Formula One cars" of computing and advocated a "buy Japan" policy to assist the Japanese "catch-up" and "take-lead" strategies.

Japan's supercomputer makers now seem to be ahead of Cray Research in terms of raw number-crunching power and speed. This is not surprising because the Japanese have a clear lead in key components such as memory chips and they are more advanced in some supercomputer architectures. But Cray probably wins in terms of software and it still has by far the largest installed user base. The Japanese also appear to be strong in computational fluid dynamics (CFD). While Cray also faces new competition in the US from Texas-based Convex, the first company in the world to introduce a commercial computer using gallium arsenide chips, the big worry for Cray is its size: while Cray's annual revenues in recent years have been about $1 billion, it is a mere tiddler in comparison with the huge, vertically integrated conglomerates like Fujitsu, Hitachi, and NEC, who have revenues of between $17 and $45 billion.

A study of the supercomputer business by the Gartner Group, financed by the US government and published in 1991, called for a $2 billion program to boost the use of supercomputers in the US and thus aid the US supercomputer industry. It pointed out, for instance, that America had 80 percent of the world's supercomputers in 1980, but only 50 percent in 1990. The Bush administration rejected the report, just as the Reagan administration had rejected a similar "shock" report from the National Science Foundation (NSF) four years earlier in 1987. The NSF report had warned that the US was in danger of losing its lead in supercomputing sometime in the 1990s.

One bright spot for the US, however, is its apparent strength in so-called massively parallel processing (MPP). The esoteric science of MPP is about designing and building computers which will compute at a teraflop, or a trillion floating point operations per second. It is early days yet for MPP, but analysts say that if it does become a significant force in supercomputing and even mainframes, US pioneers of MPP like Intel and Thinking Machines are well placed to take advantage – although the Japanese will supply much of the hardware that will go into them.

AI and the Fifth Generation: The Limits of Hype

Academics in the US and Europe have been promoting "artificial intelligence" or "AI" ever since a meeting which gave birth to the term at Dartmouth College, Massachusetts, in 1956. The term itself is attributed to John McCarthy, who developed the programming language LISP (for list processing). But in the main they have little in the way of commercial products to show for their efforts. There is as yet no machine that can remotely rival the human brain, which has 10 *trillion* circuits packed into an area of gray matter the size of a small cabbage. Early computers were actually referred to as "electronic brains," but if nearly 40 years of AI research has achieved anything, it has put to rest this naive analogy. Rather, the analogy has broadened as scientists have learned more about the complex nature of human intelligence and thought. There is still very little agreement as to whether computers will ever be able to "think."

"AI" research broadly covers two main areas: research which attempts to shed light on the nature of human intelligence by simulating it, with the eventual aim of replicating (or even surpassing) it; and attempts to build expert systems which exhibit some sort of intelligent behavior. Expert systems are not generally used as a complete replacement for human beings and human intelligence, but are used as tools for assisting humans in complex tasks such as oil exploration, medical diagnosis, chemical analysis, and fault-identification in machinery. Other activities which fall under the general rubric of AI are robotics, speech recognition or natural-language processing, image processing, and machine-learning.

Most of the early work in AI was carried out at US universities and was concerned with the construction of programs to play games such as chess. It was chess which first highlighted some of the major differences between humans and machines when faced with a demanding, intellectual task. For example, it was found that whereas computers tended to solve chess problems through the application of brute computational power, humans tended to draw upon their *experience* in the recognition of meaningful chess patterns (in order to, for example, exclude at a glance disadvantageous moves). Humans are able to do this because they have accumulated a great deal of background or "common sense" knowledge which computers do not naturally possess. Machines find it much harder to learn the vast amount of experiential information that each of us has accumulated in our brains since birth.

The lessons learned from computerized chess-playing and other experiments have repeatedly raised the questions of what exactly intelligence is and whether it can ever be replicated in the form of AI. Writers such as Jay David Bolter (*Turing's Man*, 1984) have pointed out that throughout history the brain has been thought to operate like the leading-edge technology of the era, whether it be hydraulic pistons, clockwork, or mechanical telephone exchanges. According to this view, the computer is therefore merely the latest metaphor of the mind – and there is no real evidence that the human brain works anything like a computer. Critics say that AI enthusiasts are barking up the wrong tree if they think that replicating human intelligence is simply a question of uncovering the secrets of the program that executes in the brain.

The best-supported AI research area in the West has been that of expert systems. It is estimated that thousands have been developed, but the total in commercial use is in the hundreds. There are also many different definitions of what a true expert system is – but essentially it is a computer system which encapsulates an expert's or several experts' specialist knowledge of a particular domain. From this "knowledge base," inferences can be drawn which may equal or even exceed the quality of inferences made by human experts. In the early 1980s, some apparent successes with expert systems – such as the discovery of an elusive molybdenum deposit on Mount Tolman, Washington, allegedly with the help of an expert system called "Prospector" – created a wave of interest in expert systems and there was a rush in Silicon Valley to form "AI" companies.

But progress in transferring expertise from expert to program was often very slow and the AI boom for some people became a slump. Many US start-ups went out of business altogether and most large US and European computer companies cut back on their AI research, feeling that they had been misled about the short-term prospects for commercializing AI and expert systems. Work on speech recognition also made slower than expected progress. Some speech recognition systems are available, but they tend to have vocabularies of hundreds rather than thousands of words. However, speech recognition has great potential in the long term. Voice-processing systems could make computer-based communication much more user-friendly. A system which handles instructions in English would be a boon to all computer users, while a fully developed voice-activated typewriter (VAT) or "talkwriter" would transform office work.

Many argue that AI has been dreadfully oversold in the West and that it may once again fail to deliver the goods. Most of the expert systems in use are closer to old-fashioned sequential computer programs than anything resembling real "intelligence." There is also serious concern over whether it will ever be wise to let expert systems entirely replace human judgment – especially in medical or other life-critical applications. Current technology seems best suited only to diagnosis or classification problems, whose solutions depend primarily on the possession of a large amount of specialized knowledge. If AI is to even approximate human intelligence, scientists will have to teach computers not to take things literally, to "learn" and to use "common sense" – and even then we might not be able to conclude that a computer can "think."

The search for the Holy Grail of AI has preoccupied some of the best minds in US and European universities in the postwar period and has absorbed enormous resources which could have been spent on more down-to-earth projects. As a result, the continued funding of AI research at universities like Carnegie-Mellon, Stanford, and

Edinburgh has attracted critics like Hubert and Stuart Dreyfus, who declare in their book, *Mind Over Machine* (1986): "AI has failed to live up to its promise, and there is no evidence that it ever will." Former AI researcher Terry Winograd has also mounted a grave challenge to the idea that machines will ever understand human language and has further questioned the fundamental principles underlying AI (*Understanding Computers and Cognition*, 1986).

In reply, AI boosters such as Herbert Simon, Marvin Minsky, and Edward Feigenbaum have argued that, just as the theory of evolution has changed our view of life, so artificial intelligence will change our view of the mind. As we learn more about mental processes, we will develop new perspectives on "thinking," "feeling," and "understanding" which do not see them as magical faculties. This may lead to the building of new machines and new ideas about what constitutes human intelligence. It is therefore wrong to claim that computers will *never* resemble human brains because, in truth, we do not know enough about either.

But the fact remains that the AI boosters have consistently made predictions about the imminent arrival of thinking machines which have been consistently wrong. Time and again, we have been told that computers to rival the human brain are "just around the corner" or will be available "soon." Indeed, the "Artificial Intelligentsia" have been guilty of exaggeration and hype to a degree which would not be tolerated in other fields. Theodore Roszak, author of *The Cult of Information* (1986) has even written: "AI's record of barefaced public deception is unparalleled in the annals of academic study" (*New Scientist*, April 3, 1986).

The great irony of the "AI" saga – and its relevance to our story – is that sometime in the late 1970s the Japanese began to take seriously many of the exaggerated claims being made in the West about the advances in AI and the importance of AI to the future of computing. Accordingly, MITI announced in 1981 the launch of its now-famous "Fifth Generation Computer Project," which was widely seen as Japan's attempt to overtake the West by developing the next generation of "intelligent" computers. Actually, the Fifth Generation Project was always a modest affair, employing just 90 researchers at the Institute for New Generation Computer Technology (ICOT) on loan from Japanese companies and funded to the tune of only $450 million over 10 years (compared with the $10 billion or so that NASA, for example, spends each year in the US). But it suited Japan's purposes to let the West think that it was at last going to spend more money on basic research – and it suited the purposes of the AI lobby in the West to hype up this new "threat" from Japan.

So when Stanford's Edward Feigenbaum and Pamela McCorduck declared in their somewhat evangelical best-seller, *The Fifth Generation: Artificial Intelligence and Japan's Computer Challenge to the World* (1983) that the Fifth Generation Project amounted to a "technological Pearl Harbor," the project gained instant notoriety in both the East and the West – and an importance out of all proportion to its size. The simple notion of a "fifth" generation to follow a previous "four" proved enormously powerful and could be easily understood by the public – and even by politicians. Numerous newspaper and magazine articles developed the theme that AI was to be the wave of the future in computing and that the Japanese would be the first ones to ride it unless urgent action was taken.

Few stopped to critically examine the aims, objects, and scope of the Fifth Generation Project. Had they done so, according to J. Marshall Unger, author of *The Fifth Generation Fallacy* (1987), they would have discovered that the Japanese were mainly interested in developing computers capable of handling the Japanese *kanji* writing system – which of course uses ideographic pictograms rather than a phonetic alphabet. The project did not plan to make major breakthroughs in AI or even carry out fundamental AI research, although the Japanese did little to discourage this impression. So when reports started appearing in the West in the mid-1980s to the effect that ICOT was not coming up with very much and even that the project had "failed," this was hardly surprising given the earlier misreporting of the project's aims.

In an informed discussion of the Fifth Generation Project, Sheridan Tatsuno confirms that it in fact had a modest budget and modest aims.[20] There were, he says, two main misconceptions about the project in the West. The first was that it would pursue basic research – but the intention was merely to carry out a worldwide literature search during phase I. The second misconception was that the project would come up with new products. Apart from the fact that this contradicted the alleged first aim, this was also not the case. In fact, says Tatsuno, the main goals of the project were four-fold: to erase Japan's image as a copier, to keep Japanese researchers abreast of developments in AI, to make progress with parallel processing technology (by developing a parallel inference machine), and to encourage Japanese corporations to spend more on basic research into AI and other speculative fields. On these four measures, says Tatsuno, the project must be judged a success – but the comforting myth persists in the West that it was somehow a failure.

Now Japan has launched a "sixth" generation computer project, officially called the New Information Processing Technology (NIPT) project. Again, the funding is relatively modest: $300 million over 10 years. NIPT is focusing on "intuitive" information processing modeled on the human brain, by seeking to develop neural networks – systems patterned on the neurons in the brain – and by exploiting "fuzzy logic" – systems with the capacity to make human-like judgments.

The Japanese already have a world lead in the application of fuzzy logic, although it was invented in 1965 by Lotfi A. Zadeh at the University of California, Berkeley. American scientists scoffed at Zadeh's theory that vague approximations could be represented by conventional mathematics and that computers could be taught to distinguish levels of grayness and not just black or white.[21] But in Japan, scientists and engineers soon saw the potential. They eagerly took up Zadeh's ideas and further refined them, with the result that fuzzy-logic controllers are now being used in Japan to run subway trains, elevators, air-conditioning systems, and an array of consumer goods. For example, fuzzy logic controls the auto-focus in state-of-the-art camcorders and the cycle selection in the latest washing machines. While AI research in the US appears to be stuck in a rut, American-born fuzzy logic is now giving Japanese consumer electronics companies a major competitive edge. American firms now face the prospect of having to license the technology back from the Japanese.

Computing in the Future: Japan Takes the Next-Generation Initiative

Whilst nearly 40 years of AI research has yielded much slower-than-expected progress toward replicating human intelligence, a very different route to making computers "think" like human beings has been opened up through the emergence of "neural networks." Neural networks or neural computers are based on an analogy between the switches and interconnections of a conventional computer and the neurons and synapses of the human brain. The brain is thought to contain anything from 10 billion to 100 billion neurons which are connected in parallel with each other. Whereas conventional computers simply process symbols one step at a time following a sequence of instructions, a neural computer will process instructions simultaneously across a grid or network of cells. This approach – sometimes referred to as "connectionism" – makes them particularly useful for recognizing patterns, such as sound or images.

Conventional computers are fast, accurate, and fairly well behaved. But they are also pretty stupid, in that they will only do what they have been told to do. They are poor at recognizing patterns. Neural computers are slow, they are not always accurate, and they sometimes appear to have a mind of their own. But they do not require programming for every conceivable possibility because they have the ability to learn, to exhibit associative recall, and to make decisions based on incomplete data. Conventional computers process only digital data, whereas neural computers can handle analog information. Thus conventional computers handle data in a rigid, structured way and formulate precise answers to problems. Neural computers find good, but only approximate answers to complex problems. Neural computers learn by remembering examples, not by following rules. Supporters of neural computing say that all this is more reminiscent of the sloppy, intuitive way in which humans operate.

Neural computing is therefore very different from – and amounts to a major challenge to – rule-following expert systems and traditional AI work. For decades, most AI researchers worked on the basis that human thinking involved the manipulation of symbols and that the main task for AI was to discover the symbols and rules by which the brain supposedly operates. As William F. Allman puts it: "The people who build neural nets are challenging that long-held assumption. Conventional computers, after all, are having a terrible time making the transition from number and symbol crunching to more formidable tasks such as speech and vision. In fact, computers are awful at these tasks. This failure has led to the growing suspicion that perhaps the people who brought us 'I symbol process, therefore I think' might have been putting Descartes before the horse, as it were."[22]

Neural networks have great potential, but they are still at the experimental stage. In the late 1980s, a number of US research laboratories claimed that they had built functioning neural devices and hundreds of neural network start-ups appeared. MITI in Japan began a 10-year neural network research program in 1989 and the so-called "sixth" generation or NIPT project will heavily feature research into neural networks. Meanwhile, Japanese computer companies such as NEC and Fujitsu have already announced a series of stunning advances in neural computing. The Japanese clearly see the possibilities of an entirely new generation of neurocomputers which would interpret speech, pictures, and information more like humans do – and they have the hardware and the fuzzy-logic systems with which to build them.

Another candidate for computing-technology-of-the-future is optical processing. Japan is well advanced here, too – in fact, most observers seem to agree that Japan has a clear lead in this area. Already, optical storage devices such as the CD-ROM are in regular use – indeed, the CD-ROM is one of the IT success stories of the past decade. The first CD-ROMs were introduced in 1982 by the Dutch company, Philips, and the Japanese company, Sony. A development of musical CDs, CD-ROMs come with digital information in the form of tiny pits imprinted on them by laser. A typical CD-ROM of today might contain up to 600 megabytes of information, or about 1,500 times the capacity of a floppy disk, or more than 250,000 pages of text. Publishers of dictionaries, encyclopedias, and reference books were among the first to commercialize CD-ROMs. More recent application areas for CD-ROMs have included libraries, doctors' surgeries, and financial information suppliers.

The current stage in the development of optical storage technology is the magneto-optical (MO) or erasable optical disk. An erasable optical disk can be used over and over again, with the quality of each new recording remaining high for many years. Japanese companies spotted the potential of this new technology and poured millions of dollars into MO research. Sony, Matsushita, and IBM introduced the first erasable/rewritable disks in 1988, while in the same year Steve Jobs decided to use a Canon MO disk drive in his Next computer. More than 40 Japanese companies have built, or are in the process of building, MO factories. American companies like IBM can make rewritable disks but Sony is clear market leader with 70 percent of the world market.

The next step up from optical storage is optical processing – or computing with light rather than electricity. In optical computing, photons – the basic unit of light beams – replace the electrons of conventional computing, hence this new field is also sometimes referred to as "optoelectronics" or "photonics." Optical computers work by manipulating laser-generated light beams with mirrors, lenses, and prisms incredibly fast, with optical switches substituting for electronic switches. Optical processors of various kinds have been used for many decades in such applications as radar, but it is only in the last decade or so that they have been seriously considered as the basis of a new form of computing.

The advantages of optical computers are three-fold. First, they are faster – potentially much faster – than digital electronic computers simply because light travels faster through air and optical fiber than electrons do through wires. Second, while electronic computers are sequential devices which process information one step at a time, optical devices can process information in parallel – that is, they can process information from many sources at once and can come to conclusions (for example, about an image) much quicker. Third, optical devices can switch on and off billions of times per second without overheating – there is no cooling problem with optical chips.

Many of the early breakthroughs in optical processing took place in European and American laboratories. For example, optical fiber cable was invented in England in the 1960s and developed in the 1970s by Corning Glass in upstate New York. In 1986, David Miller of AT&T's Bell Laboratories in New Jersey developed what was thought to be the first all-optical switch. But Japan had targeted optical processing in the 1970s and in 1981 MITI launched its "Optoelectronics Project." It was a great success, producing more than 300 patents and helping Japan become world leaders in semiconductor lasers, light-emitting diodes (LEDs), charged-couple devices (CCDs), compact disks and optical-storage disks – all of which are being used in Japan's world-beating VCRs, camcorders, faxes, photocopiers, printers, and point-of-sale terminals.

In 1988, the US National Research Council (NRC) published a report on optical computing, which warned that America was falling behind Japan in the development of commercial photonics products. The NRC called for a national program of R&D bringing together academics, government, and industry. A few months earlier, the Japanese company Fujitsu had stunned analysts by announcing that it had built the world's first optical switchboard with a switching speed of 512 megabits per second – or 50 times faster than a conventional electronic switchboard. The new switchboard could be used in fiber optic systems which could simultaneously carry several hundred channels of cable television. Meanwhile, Mitsubishi claimed that it had produced the world's first optical neurocomputer which could recognize the 26 letters of the English alphabet.

But in 1989 America came back into the picture when IBM – having dropped out of photonics research once before – announced that it had created the world's densest optoelectronic chip containing 8,000 transistors and four photodetectors. It was made of gallium arsenide. In 1990, long-time optical computing advocate Alan Huang of AT&T's Bell Labs demonstrated the first working, experimental optical computer. And in 1991, Texas Instruments claimed a world first with its advanced optical chip.

Some say that optical computing is still far too blue sky to warrant much attention. There are too many problems and the superfast commercial optical supercomputer is, well, light years away. It will be decades before conventional digital electronic computing faces a serious optical rival. On the other hand, optical processing has enormous potential and the linking of optical computers with fiber optic networks could have a revolutionary impact on communications.

The third candidate for computing-technology-of-the-future is molecular computing – sometimes referred to as "molecular electronics" or "bioelectronics" or "biocomputing." Although perhaps more in the realms of science fiction, the general idea is that molecular computers or "biochips" would feature switches based on molecules and would thus be much smaller and faster than even neural computers. They would be another example of nanotechnology, which is concerned with devices measured in nanometers or billionths of a meter.

Some molecular devices are already available. Biosensors "read" information from biological cells: coated with enzymes, antibodies, or antigens, they can detect substances or physical reactions such as glucose, urea, fermentation, or ion concentration. They can be used in a variety of industrial and medical applications. According to the theory (for that's what it is) of molecular computing, one stage up from this would be protein enzyme switches and biochips, which would actually function as information processors by reacting with their physiochemical environment. Molecular computing is a technology that uses physical recognition for computation and is thus an analog rather than a digital technology. Processing would be physical and dynamic rather than symbolic and passive – or at least that is one notion, for there is very little agreement as to what molecular computers or biochips could or might be.

However, the general idea of biological computing has been around for some years, with research in the US being centered on Syracuse, Wayne State, Carnegie-Mellon, and New Orleans universities. There are obvious links between work on molecular electronics and that on neural networks, as well as genetic engineering, biomaterials, and other new materials. In fact, the work of biologists probing the mysteries of slug software and the inner working of worms, squids, and leeches is very relevant to molecular computing. Cabbage leaves, magnolia petals, and toad bladders have all been studied as naturally occurring examples of biosensors.

Interest in biocomputing was stirred by a National Science Foundation conference in America in 1983 and a MITI symposium in Japan in 1985. Subsequently, more than 40 Japanese companies began work on bioelectronic devices, while in 1987 MIT announced (guess what?) a 10-year project to develop biochips and biocomputers. Among the many problems to be overcome before biochips and biocomputers become a reality are not knowing how to actually assemble them into circuits or how to make connections with input and output devices. Skeptics claim molecular computing enthusiasts are pursuing the impossible, but that has never been a very convincing argument in science. Advances of one kind or another are bound to occur in the future and when they do, we can be sure of one thing: the Japanese will be the first to commercialize them. That is the genius of the Japanese and the challenge for the rest of the world.

Notes

1 Marie Anchordoguy, *Computers Inc: Japan's Challenge to IBM* (Council on East Asian Studies/Harvard University Press, Cambridge, MA, 1989) and "How Japan built a computer industry," *Harvard Business Review*, July–August 1990, p. 65.
2 Sheridan Tatsuno, *The Technopolis Strategy: Japan, High Technology, and the Control of the 21st Century* (Brady/Prentice-Hall, New York, 1986), p. 10.
3 Sheridan Tatsuno, *Created in Japan: From Imitators to World Class Innovators* (Harper & Row, New York, 1990) and Bill Totten, "Red paper" circulated on CompuServe, Internet newsgroups and elsewhere in July 1990.
4 Charles H. Ferguson, "Computers and the coming of the US keiretsu," *Harvard Business Review*, July–August 1990, p. 55.
5 Ferguson, "Computers and the coming of the US keiretsu," p. 56.
6 Charles H. Ferguson, comment in *Harvard Business Review*, September–October 1990, p. 182.
7 Clyde V. Prestowitz, *Harvard Business Review*, September–October 1990, p. 192 and *Business Week*, October 23, 1989, p. 72.
8 Douglas K. Smith and Robert C. Alexander, *Fumbling the Future: How Xerox Invented, Then Ignored, The First Personal Computer* (Morrow, New York, 1988), p. 19.
9 Richard Florida and David Browdy, "The invention that got away," *Technology Review*, August/September 1991, pp. 43–54.
10 Florida and Browdy, "The invention that got away," p. 50.
11 David L. House quoted in *Business Week*, October 23, 1989, p. 74.
12 See, for example, *Business Week*, May 9, 1988, pp. 66–72 and *Fortune*, September 25, 1989, pp. 72–6.
13 Tom Forester and Perry Morrison, *Computer Ethics: Cautionary Tales and Ethical Dilemmas in Computing* (Basil Blackwell, Oxford, UK and MIT Press, Cambridge, MA, 1990), p. 2.
14 Forester and Morrison, *Computer Ethics*, pp. 68–76.
15 Michael A. Cusumano, *Japan's Software Factories: A Challenge to*

US Management (Oxford University Press, Oxford, UK and New York, 1991).

16 Cusumano, *Japan's Software Factories*, pp. 423 and 440–3.

17 *Business Week*, March 11, 1991, p. 67.

18 *Business Week*, April 9, 1990, p. 28.

19 Clyde V. Prestowitz, *Trading Places: How We Allowed Japan to Take the Lead* (Basic Books, New York, 1988), p. 136 and *Business Week*, December 10, 1990, p. 54.

20 Tatsuno, *Created in Japan*, pp. 167–76.

21 Arturo Sangalli, "Fuzzy logic goes to market," *New Scientist*, February 8, 1992, pp. 28–31; *Business Week*, May 21, 1991, pp. 81–2.

22 William F. Allman, "Designing computers that think the way we do," *Technology Review*, May/June 1987, pp. 59–65.

5 Manufacturing Technology: Controlling the Means of Production

The Factory of the Future Scenario – Machine Tools: The Capture of a Critical Industry – Japan's Takeover of the Robotics Industry – The US Response: A "Productivity" Panic and the "Competitiveness" Craze – FMS: Staying Ahead in the "Intelligent" Factory Stakes

At the end of World War II, American manufacturing reigned supreme. In the short space of five years, between 1940 and 1945, the US manufacturing powerhouse had churned out an amazing 5,200 ships, 50,000 tanks, 300,000 warplanes, 600,000 trucks, and 6 million guns. In fact, it was largely American industrial might that had finally won the war for the Allies in Europe and the Pacific. As "Big Bill" Knudsen, the General Motors president who headed the wartime industrial effort, so candidly put it: "We smothered the enemy in an avalanche of production."

In the immediate postwar years, and indeed right through the 1950s and into the 1960s, the whole world was queueing up to buy American-made consumer goods such as cars, trucks, televisions, typewriters, ovens, and refrigerators. Detroit in particular could sell anything it cared to build. The idea that Americans would ever want to buy anything other than cars "Made in the USA" was simply preposterous. By contrast, postwar Japanese manufacturing industry was small-scale, backward, poorly equipped, and lacking in self-confidence. Despite some wartime successes (like Mitsubishi's Zero fighter plane), budding Japanese manufacturers in the postwar era were reduced to begging for US reconstruction aid.

They also relied heavily on borrowing ideas for products and production processes from the West, where Japanese goods were considered to be shoddy knock-offs.

In this environment, it was hardly surprising that US manufacturers grew overconfident and complacent. Steady demand for their goods, cheap raw materials, plentiful labor, high profits, and an overwhelming superiority in size made them fat and lazy: they felt they could do no wrong. Just as important, it seemed there was nothing new to learn about the manufacturing process – and certainly nothing to learn from overseas. They felt that the techniques of mass production had been finally conquered: it seemed that little more could be done to improve efficiency. In his 1958 bestseller, *The Affluent Society*, leading liberal economist John Kenneth Galbraith was able to declare: "We have solved the problem of production." Partly as a result of this belief, manufacturing came to be widely seen as just plain boring. When choosing a career, the best and the brightest would opt for medicine, the law, the media, or politics – anything but engineering and manufacturing. This was not the case, however, in Japan, where working in a factory retained a strong appeal.

Then, at the turn of the 1960s and into the 1970s, the Japanese *tsunami* (series of tidal waves) hit. A flood of manufactured imports, beginning with transistor radios, motorcycles, cameras, typewriters, and black and white TVs, and then cars, trucks, color TVs, hi fis, dictation machines, mowers, and generators, began pouring into America. US manufacturers were totally unprepared for the invasion and were staggered by the lower prices and high quality offered by the Japanese. Japanese companies rapidly gained market share in sector after sector carefully targeted by Japan's MITI (Ministry of International Trade and Industry), while US producers started to struggle. Saddled with mediocre managers and a sullen, alienated workforce working on Tayloristic mass-production lines unchanged for decades, American companies were no match for the Japanese firms with their talented production engineers, dedicated workforces, and state-of-the-art manufacturing systems. The Japanese had lost the war but they were now well and truly winning the peace.

America's huge trade surplus in manufactured goods was already looking vulnerable and by 1980 had fallen to a record low of $18 billion. But worse was to follow in the 1980s, as the Japanese targeted semiconductors, computers, and telecoms and the underlying strength of Japan in consumer electronics, office equipment, and manufacturing technology became apparent. The US trade balance rapidly plunged into the red and by 1986, America had a huge, unprecedented deficit in manufactured goods of $150 billion, of which high-tech goods already accounted for $13 billion. In sector after sector, US companies were losing market share and many still didn't know why. Suddenly, "learning from Japan" became a major growth industry in itself in America and Europe, as academics rushed to discover the "secrets" of Japanese success and management consultants offered expensive seminars on such Japanese wonders as "JIT" (Just-In-Time manufacturing) and "TQM" (Total Quality Management). In America, a kind of national productivity panic resulted in a rush of government reports, studies, books, and articles on what the US was doing wrong and what the Japanese were doing right.

A central lesson of these studies was that Japanese success in consumer electronics, semiconductors, cars, office equipment, and indeed every other goods sector was underpinned by excellence in manufacturing. Sure, Japan had played the market share game to perfection, pursued protectionism and had learned early on that success in high-tech was an all-or-nothing race with victory going to those fastest along the experience curve, but the fact remained that most Japanese-made goods were more reliable than American or European-made goods. Consumers had come to recognize that "Made in Japan" now signified both better value and superior quality – and they often chose Japanese products in preference to others.

That better value and superior quality was achieved as a direct consequence of Japanese manufacturing excellence. And that excellence was achieved in three main ways: by designing a product and the process for making it in the simplest possible way and by involving concurrently both the designers and the factory-floor producers in the design process; by continually improving and refining the production process itself once it was up and running, through such techniques as JIT and "quality circles"; and by improving communication between management and the workforce, so as to maximize worker involvement in all aspects of the production process. In such ways, Japanese manufacturers have been able to achieve faster new-product cycles, lower stock levels, greater flexibility in production, better quality, and much higher productivity.

It was profoundly ironic that many of the Japanese quality control techniques that had such a devastating impact on US competitiveness were first taught to them by American quality gurus W. Edwards Deming and J. M. Juran. These two crossed the Pacific in the 1950s, having struggled to find audiences for their message in a complacent postwar America. To this day, the top Japanese manufacturing quality award is called the Deming Prize.

A second major finding of the Japan studies was that, by and large, the Japanese had achieved world-beating productivity and quality levels without spending excessively on technology. Superior management of people and of technology resources was the key to success. Unlike, for example, the hapless General Motors under chief executive officer Roger Smith in the 1980s, Japanese companies had refused to be seduced by the "high-tech fix." They realized that manufacturing success depended more on getting people and machines working together in harmony rather than throwing big bucks at a production problem. This was apparent early on when, in the late 1970s, Toyota took over a failed General Motors plant at Fremont, California and successfully turned it around simply by using improved management methods and without changing the technology (the NUMMI experiment).

Conclusive proof that superior levels of technology were not essential to Japan's success was provided by the extensive research of John Krafcik of the Massachusetts Institute of Technology (MIT), who studied 90 car assembly plants in 17 countries. Krafcik's work was incorporated into *The Machine That Changed the World* (1990, 1991), the definitive MIT study of the world auto industry by James P. Womack, Daniel T. Jones, and Daniel Roos.[1] These authors say that the "secret" of Japanese manufacturing success is the "lean production" system, which involves teamwork, continuous improvement, good communication, just-in-time (JIT) delivery, and the elimination of waste. First developed at Toyota by Taiichi Ohno, they say that lean production is universally applicable – and its adoption is essential for anyone wishing to survive long term in the auto industry.

But it would be wrong to conclude from this that the Japanese have a disdain for high technology. Far from it: Japanese factories are among the most highly automated in the world. It's just that they don't see technology as the be all and end all. Where they seem to excel is in the intelligent selection of appropriate technology and its successful integration into the production process.

Japanese companies have also been immensely successful in the postwar era in three key areas of manufacturing technology: machine tools, robotics, and flexible manufacturing systems (FMS). From a modest "Plan" in 1956, the Japanese machine tool industry rose to become No. 1 in the world by 1986, severely damaging the American machine tool industry on the way. From importing its first robots from the US in 1967, the Japanese robotics industry had almost completely destroyed the competition and had achieved world domination just 15 years later in 1982. And with a world lead in FMS and other state-of-the-art manufacturing systems, Japanese companies like Fujitsu Fanuc, Yamazaki, and Hitachi-Seiki look set to control the means of production well into the twenty-first century.

The Factory of the Future Scenario

There are basically two kinds of manufacturing industry. The *process control* industries, like chemicals, plastics, steel, and rubber, produce materials, often in liquid or extruded form, through a continuous process largely controlled by switches, pressure valves, and temperature gauges. In the 1950s and 1960s, in what has been termed the "First Age of Automation," it was the process control industries that were the first to be transformed because they were relatively simple, high-volume operations more amenable to automation.

The second type of manufacturing industry involves making physical changes to solids – most commonly metals, but also plastics, wood, and composites – with the aid of machine tools. Thus the traditional metal-bashing industries have employed millions engaged in manufacturing parts by bending, battering, cutting, shaping, and drilling pieces of metal and then welding or assembling them into finished products. The new information technologies make it possible to turn this type of manufacturing into an automated process, even when the production batches are quite small. The widespread availability of cheap, reliable, and sophisticated control systems based on microelectronics raises the possibility of the metal-bashing industries becoming totally automated.

The general idea of this wholly automated, unmanned, or "workerless" Factory of the Future is that it would be run from the order book: raw materials and information about customer preferences would go in one end, and would pass through the design, engineering, production, and packaging stages and come out the other end as finished, customized products, untouched by human hand or even committed to paper. The key components of the Factory of the Future are computer numerically controlled (CNC) machine tools, robots, computer-aided design (CAD) and engineering (CAE) systems, and flexible manufacturing systems (FMS).

Machine tools – that is, machines that make parts of products or make other tools – date back to 1897, the year that Englishman Henry Maudslay designed the first screw-cutting lathe. Milling machines soon followed, but both types of machine changed little during the course of the nineteenth century. In fact, it was not until the 1950s that the first major innovation in machine tools occurred with the introduction of *numerically controlled* (NC) systems.

NC machines were run on a program consisting of holes punched in a paper tape which contained the instructions for the movement of the drill head or cutting tool. Their logic was thus "hard-wired" and inflexible, making it difficult to change the instructions. The late 1950s saw the introduction of *machining centers*, more sophisticated machines which could change their own cutting heads and automatically carry out different tasks, such as drilling or turning.

The next big development was the arrival of computer numerically controlled (CNC) machines in the early 1960s. The addition of computer power meant that each machine could now store data and designs in its memory, making it possible to produce a range of goods on the one machine. The computer itself controls the operation of the machine tool and enables the human operator to carry out calculations and to make adjustments much more easily and quickly. In the late 1960s, the Japanese were the first to link sets of NC or CNC machines to central computers which controlled their operations. This is called *direct numerical control* (DNC), and it has the advantage of dramatically reducing manpower, because only one human operator is required to control maybe a dozen machines in the linked production "cell," to use the jargon.

Robots have been talked about and tinkered with ever since Czech writer Karel Capek's 1921 play, *Rossum's Universal Robots*, which brought the word into the English language. In Capek's play, hero engineer Rossum creates a new breed of robots to do the world's dirty work. He took the name for his human-like creatures from the Czech word *robota*, meaning forced or slave labor. After taking on all the humans' unpleasant jobs and fighting their wars, Rossum's robots eventually rise up and take over the world, like so many Frankenstein's monsters. Unfortunately, this has given "robots" a bad name and an unjustified reputation, which has been perpetuated down through the years – for example, by Isaac Asimov's science fiction writings of the 1940s and films like *2001* and *Star Wars*.

Today's industrial robots are really nothing like Capek's humanoids. For the most part, they cannot see, hear, smell, or think. They are simply machine tools, typically no more than a mechanical arm controlled by a computer which can be programmed to carry out different movements. The Robot Institute of America in fact offers the following definition of a robot: "A reprogrammable, multifunctional manipulator designed to move material, parts, tools or specialized devices, through variable programmed motions for the performance of a variety of tasks."

The arrival of the microchip in the 1970s made possible the modern science of robotics and put robots squarely into the Factory of the Future picture. Microchip controllers transformed the prospects for these "steel-collar workers," who began to be used in general manufacturing, especially in the automobile industry. Robots enjoyed something of a boom in the early 1980s in the USA and Europe, as firms flocked to join the business, but sales later slumped badly.

The "first generation" of robots in the 1970s had been "deaf, dumb, and blind" – and very inflexible. They were ideal for dirty and repetitive jobs such as spot-welding, paint-spraying, grinding, molding and casting, and loading and stacking. Of the 4,700 robots in use in the US in 1981, for instance, 1,500 were used for welding, 850 were to be found in foundries, 840 were used for loading, and 540 were used for paint-spraying. Only 100 were used for assembly tasks.

"Second generation" robots are able to "see" and to "touch." Machine vision offers the prospect of tireless and totally reliable robot eyes on the production line which can replace human quality controllers who all too often possess human fallibility. Vision systems "close the loop" on automated process control with visual feedback mechanisms: if a part is defective, it will be automatically rejected. When the sensors, computers, robots, and machine tools are all tied together – that is, when the so-called "compatibility" problem is solved by the adoption of a universally accepted protocol – we will have taken another giant step toward the Factory of the Future. A major problem at present is that the new vision systems are expensive and are slow in getting out of the lab and on to the factory floor.

"Third generation" robots will be able to "think." They will possess intelligence and massive computing power, enabling them, for example, to "infer logically" – that is, to work out for themselves how to do something. Of course, robots that exhibit real "intelligence" are years away and their prospects depend heavily on developments in AI research. But robots that not only see, feel, and hear but also "think" in certain respects are definitely on for the 1990s.

Computer-aided design (CAD) is another key component of the Factory of the Future. CAD systems enable draftsmen's drawings to be created on a VDT screen and then be manipulated, updated, and stored on a computer without even the use of a pencil. CAD leads to CAE (computer-aided engineering or "engineering without paper"), in which the three-dimensional designs can be examined, analyzed and even "tested" to simulated destruction without ever having been made! CAE, in turn, leads to CAM (computer-aided manufacturing), because the same design and prototype testing process generates a common database about the product from which a set of instructions can be derived for actually manufacturing it. The final stage, computer-integrated manufacturing (or CIM, pronounced "sim"), will see the linking up of production cells and "islands" of automation into one comprehensive, integrated manufacturing system controlled by computers.

The CAD part of CAD/CAM has its roots in the early 1960s when computerized draftsmen's aids were first displayed. For example, the SKETCHPAD system developed at MIT in 1963 used a light pen wired to a large (and very expensive) computer. The one-time industry leader, Computervision Corporation, launched its first CAD/CAM system in 1969. The arrival of the microchip in the 1970s transformed the CAD business, with the result that great strides have been made in CAD systems in the last two decades.

CAD enables a designer or draftsman to construct detailed drawings of machinery, parts, or circuits without ever touching a pencil, ruler, or compass. Instead, the designer uses a screen and keyboard, moving a special stylus over the screen or a separate graphics tablet alongside. Standard shapes and shading can be simply summoned up from the computer's memory and added to the "drawing." With CAD, designers can turn their drawings around, enlarge them, color them, or slice them in half on the screen in order to examine or modify them. If they wish to pore over their drawings, a paper copy can be provided at the touch of a button.

From the original "electronic pencils," CAD systems today have developed to a point where they offer the facilities of three-dimensional or solid modeling, engineering analysis, and testing, simulation, and interfacing with machine tools, as well as automated drafting. This enables manufacturers to design and to build life-like models, and to test, for example, projected automobiles, airplanes, and oil-drilling platforms – all on the computer screen. Once the geometric model has been completely defined, instructions for manufacturing it – even down to the tool-cutting paths – can be derived from the system's database. CAD, CAE, and CAM have therefore effectively merged into one, although most people use the term "CAD/CAM."

CAD/CAM has rapidly established itself in the automobile and aerospace industries. CAD/CAM not only allows designers to see what a car or a plane will look like when built, it can also be used to see how they will behave under certain conditions. The whole new field of computational fluid dynamics (CFD) has opened up. Finite element analysis, the mathematical method of calculating the stresses on, for example, an airplane's wing or an automobile bumper, allows realistic computer simulations to be carried out, which show exactly how the product will perform in real life. Even slow motion "movies" of the action can be made. Again, plummeting computer costs now make the necessary complex computer calculations much easier to carry out.

CAD/CAM is especially useful in routing. Airplanes and oil rigs contain many miles of pipes, and working out the best way to route them can be a designer's nightmare. Now CAD/CAM systems can locate the best possible paths in a matter of seconds. McDonnell Douglas, for example, has a system that not only plots optimum paths for the three miles of hydraulic tubing that twist and turn their way through a DC-10's airframe, but also issues instructions on how to manufacture them from standard parts. Bechtel, the giant plant construction company, is spending millions of dollars on CAD/CAM systems for plotting pipework.

Why stop at large objects? CAD/CAM is widely used in the electronics industry to design and test tiny microchips. New systems can work out the optimum layout for integrated circuits and the best route for each connection. Another CAD/CAM function is "modal testing," whereby the designer can pinpoint the moving part in a machine which is or will be responsible for a particular vibration. CAD/CAM is also being used for management systems and process planning, that is, designing and simulating the operations of an entire factory, warehouse, or supermarket before it is built. In this way, potential bottlenecks and other problems can be identified and ironed out in advance.

CAD/CAM in theory can thus greatly increase the productivity of expensive design staff, eliminate boring and repetitive tasks, cut the lead-time from design stage to final product, reduce design and manufacturing errors, increase product quality, cut the cost of updating or modifying products, and enable orders to be repeated with little or no delay. But there are obstacles to its implementation: one is the great diversity of systems available and the lack of compatible standards. Another is the very complexity of the manufacturing operations of many companies, which are not always amenable to computerization and have evolved in different ways from other firms over the years. In some companies, design and manufacturing departments are still segregated and it is often difficult to get them working together. Management indifference and union opposition have not helped.

"Flexible manufacturing systems" (FMS) are a set of machines linked up by means of handling devices in such a way that parts can be passed automatically from one to another for different manufacturing processes. Even more important, FMS – or "advanced manufacturing technologies" (AMT), as they are sometimes called – enable a company to produce small batches of components or to vary the product specifications as quickly and efficiently as if it were using a mass production line dedicated to one product. A central computer controls the whole process and keeps a check on the whereabouts of each part.

CIM was very much the buzzword concept of the early 1980s and really amounted to a bringing up to date of the early 1950s idea of what "automation" and the "automated factory" meant. It has taken 40 years of research and development – plus the invention of the microchip – to make the vision of the completely unmanned, automated Factory of the Future a distinct possibility. As the sophisticated software needed to "glue" the whole array of hardware together is further developed, that vision will take another giant step toward becoming a reality.

Machine Tools: The Capture of a Critical Industry

Machine tools are the basic building blocks of the Factory of the Future and good machine tools are the basis of all manufacturing excellence. Machine tools are the tools that make other tools: any manufactured part or product has either been made by a machine tool or by a machine made by a machine tool. The machine tool industry is therefore a fundamental one, rather like semiconductors, and maintaining a thriving machine tool industry is therefore crucial to national economic survival. When people speak of America's economic decline and the rise of Japan, they most often cite the US disasters in four key industries: cars, consumer electronics, semiconductors – and machine tools.

In 1956, Japan's MITI announced a "Plan" for its feeble machine tool industry and by 1986 it was No. 1 in the world. In 1956, the US machine tool industry had been No. 1 in the world, employing

75,000 workers and achieving annual sales of $1.3 billion. According to Clyde V. Prestowitz, the US machine tool industry was "the biggest exporter of machine tools and had the most advanced technology, the highest level of investment per worker, and by far the highest output per worker of the world's tool industries. In short, the US industry was the best."[2] By contrast, the Japanese machine tool industry was fragmented into about 1,500 small firms producing barely one quarter of the US industry's output with half as many workers. In other words, in those days it took more than two Japanese to do the work of one American. One third of Japan's machine tools were imported.

Under the 1956 plan, or more specifically the Extraordinary Measures Law for the Promotion of Specified Machinery Industries, the Japanese government offered Japanese machine tool companies financial incentives – such as cheap loans, tax credits, special depreciation, and reserves for export losses – plus a range of market-protection measures. Production targets and goals for productivity and quality were set. More intriguingly, some of the proceeds of the tax on gambling on bicycle races in Japan was to be channeled through MITI to the machine tool industry via something called the Japan Bicycle Rehabilitation Association, a body dedicated to "the promotion of industries related to machines."[3] Further plans for the machine tool industry were announced in 1967 and 1971.

Having rebuilt its machine tool industry and having consolidated its position in the Japanese domestic market in the 1960s, Japan embarked upon a massive export drive in the 1970s. By the late 1970s, Japan had swiftly overtaken both the US and France to become No. 3 in machine tools behind the USA and West Germany. The Japanese success was not without irony: decades earlier, the British firm Alfred Herbert Ltd had sent a team of engineers out to Japan to help the Japanese rebuild their machine tool industry. But by 1981 Alfred Herbert itself was bankrupt – partly because of Japanese competition. In the early 1980s, the USA was surpassed by Japan and in 1986 Japan finally overhauled West Germany to become the world's largest producer of machine tools.

In 1986, Japan produced three times as many numerically controlled machine tools as the USA. One company alone, Fujitsu Fanuc, had 60 percent of the world market for control devices.

Many US and European producers were by now wholly dependent on Japan (and Fujitsu in particular) for their controls. Japan's machine tool industry investment per worker was nearly double that of the US industry, as was productivity per worker. Japan had rationalized its industry down to 250 companies, half of whom employed over 1,000 workers, while the US still had 600 companies, only one-fifth of whom employed over 1,000 workers.[4]

By 1986, the US machine tool industry was in a parlous state. The US share of the world market had slumped from 23 percent in 1964 to 14 percent in 1979 and to just 6 percent in 1986. More startlingly, the Japanese share of the US market had rocketed from a mere 4 percent in 1964, to 23 percent in 1979 and to an incredible 49 percent in 1986 (and 70–80 percent in advanced-technology areas). America's annual trade deficit on machine tools was now in excess of $1 billion. By 1989, employment in the US machine tool industry had fallen to 47,000 from 69,000 ten years earlier: Cincinnati Milacron, for instance, had put off a third of its employees over the space of five years, despite expanding into plastics machinery. In 1989, the Japanese machine tool industry was producing an estimated $10 billion worth of equipment – approximately three times the US output by value. Because it was shipping so many machine tools to its neighbors, Japan's trade surplus with China and Southeast Asia leapt from $17 billion in 1990 to $29 billion in 1991. In the same year, America's machine tool trade deficit was still running at more than $1 billion.[5]

The Japanese thrust into machine tools caused much ill-feeling in the US and Europe. American firms could not afford to carry the inventory that Japanese firms were carrying (thanks to MITI subsidies) and thus were at a disadvantage when orders suddenly picked up in this traditionally "boom and bust" industry. It was alleged that the Japanese were conspiring together to dump machine tools at a loss in the US and European markets in order to buy market share and at the same time foreigners were effectively prevented from selling in Japan. American and European companies also found that their licenses and patents were being violated.

Matters came to a head in the US when, in May 1982, a major US machine tool manufacturer, Buffalo-based Houdaille Industries, filed a 1,000-page petition with the office of the US Trade Representative, charging that the Japanese were indulging in unfair competition. As described by former trade negotiator Clyde V. Prestowitz, the Houdaille petition detailed the various loans, subsidies, and other financial incentives given to the Japanese machine tool cartel over the years. It also described how the Japanese government, through its own laws and administrative directives, had conspired to always keep the foreign share of Japan's market below 10 percent, despite regular "trade concessions." Charging that Japan's behavior was illegal, Houdaille asked specifically that President Reagan revoke tax credits for Japanese-made machine tools.[6]

A bitter and divisive debate followed within the Reagan administration, pitting the proponents of free trade against those who questioned whether the concept of free trade could co-exist with the industry-targeting, product-dumping, and protectionist practices of the Japanese. The first group were also concerned about not disturbing America's political and military relations with Japan, while the latter group were also concerned about the national security implications of a weakened machine tool industry. Months of meetings, submissions, and counter-submissions culminated in a cabinet meeting in April 1983 at which President Reagan announced his decision to take no action on the Houdaille petition. According to Prestowitz, the President simply reiterated his faith in free trade, adding that "Nakasone (the Japanese premier) was our best friend in Japan and was trying to help the United States by expanding Japan's defense role. Therefore, said the President, he wanted to help Nakasone."[7]

In the following year, Houdaille closed down its machine tool operations, despite claiming a higher rate of productivity than the Japanese average. One of the victims was the Los Angeles-based tool maker, Burgmaster Corporation, which was owned by Houdaille. In his book, *When the Machine Stopped* (1990), author Max Holland describes how Burgmaster, founded by a Czech immigrant Fred Burg in 1944, became a thriving enterprise with annual sales of $8 million in its heyday of the mid-1960s. Short of capital to expand, Burgmaster sold out to Houdaille, who in turn were bought in 1979 by Kohlberg Kravis Roberts in a leveraged buy-out (LBO).

Holland catalogs a number of blunders made by Burgmaster/Houdaille management, which were indicative of complacency and conservatism. But much of Holland's anger is directed at the US government, with its tax laws which encouraged non-productive LBOs and speculation in strategic industries, and with its procurement policies, which were not designed to help US companies. Most important of all, Holland – like Prestowitz – charges that successive US governments in the postwar era have been too obsessed with Cold War and/or national security issues and too little concerned about the tragedies looming in fundamental industries like machine tools.[8]

Japan's Takeover of the Robotics Industry

The age of the industrial robot really began in 1946, when American inventor George Devol developed a memory device for controlling machines. The first patent for a programmable arm was filed by Devol in 1954 and in 1960 Devol teamed up with the flamboyant US engineer Joe Engelberger to form Unimation, the first company in the world to make and sell industrial robots.

By using the word "robot" to generate interest in their product, they actually succeeded in confusing everyone, because, as we have seen, these "robots" were little more than mechanical arms. But the marketing ploy worked in that Unimation's "robots" generated piles of press cuttings – if not revenue. In fact, industrial robot sales were very slow to take off: the world's first industrial robot was installed in 1961 at a General Motors factory in New Jersey, but the high costs and teething troubles delayed subsequent installations to such an extent that Unimation failed to show a profit until 1975 (Engelberger having sold out to Westinghouse as early as 1963). However, the potential of industrial robots to greatly increase productivity and to reduce manpower was steadily growing more apparent.

Nowhere was enthusiasm for robots greater than in Japan. Japan imported its first robots from the US in 1967. Within a year, Kawasaki Heavy Industries had signed a licensing agreement with Unimation to produce and sell Unimate robots in Japan. But the Japanese did more than that: to use Sheridan Tatsuno's phrase, Kawasaki "creatively refined" Unimation's robots, improving quality and reliability. For example, Kawasaki's engineers increased the mean time between failures (MTBF), which rose from 300 hours to 800 hours, and later to 1,000 hours.[9] Other big Japanese firms such as Ishikawajima-Harima Heavy Industries, Toshiba Precision Machinery, Kobe Steel, and Hitachi entered the robotics industry. By 1972, these firms had formed the Japanese Industrial Robotics Association, in order to promote the industry and to gain favors from the Japanese government.

In *The Competitive Advantage of Nations* (1990), Michael E. Porter provides an account of the growth of the Japanese robotics industry and an analysis of its underlying strength. He shows that the successful Japanese auto and domestic appliance industries created early demand for industrial robots, while the shortage of skilled labor in Japan, the 1973 oil price shock, and appreciation of the Yen provided further incentives for employers to replace people with technology. Supportive labor unions and management more open to new ways of doing things also helped. A final factor was the emergence of Japan as the center of manufacturing excellence, with world-class producers of sophisticated products like semiconductors and consumer electronics making fresh demands on the robotics industry. As a result, within five years of importing its first robot, Japan had the world's largest installed base of robotic devices. By 1980, Japan had 15,000 of the 23,000 robots at work in the world. By 1984, Japan had an even higher proportion: 67,000 out of 102,000, or two-thirds of the world total.[10]

The growing cluster of Japanese robot producers in the 1970s was joined by major players like Fanuc, Matsushita, and Yaskawa. Some had entered the robotics industry from electronics, and some from machine tools, but nearly all were major users of robots: they thus had considerable knowledge of the application of robots, which was crucial for the swift and successful development of the industry. No other country had this kind of cluster. By the mid-1980s, there were no less than 300 Japanese robot producers: competition was fierce, the pace of innovation intense, and the research effort feverish. Collaboration between robot manufacturers and the shop-floor workforce was close. So dynamic was the synergy created in the Japanese robotics industry, says Porter, that MITI and Japanese government assistance, although it existed, was hardly necessary for the success of the industry.

Exports of robots from Japan began in the mid-1970s, but did not grow rapidly until the early 1980s: by 1985, however, exports amounted to 20 percent of sales. In contrast, the US had only 70 robot makers left by the mid-1980s and imports (mainly from Japan) had grown to take about 25 percent of the US market. These imports cost the US about $161 million, while US robot exports (mainly to Europe) totaled only $34 million. In a further sign of US weakness, General Motors was forced to team up with Japan's Fanuc in order to gain access to Fanuc's superior robotics technology. Fanuc got easier entry into the huge US market. The resulting partnership, GM Fanuc, lasted ten years until Fanuc bought out GM's 50 percent stake in 1992.[11]

Robotics underwent something of a boom in the US in the early 1980s. The arrival of the microchip, of course, had created new products with cheaper, more reliable controls. The revelation that US manufacturing productivity was lagging and that foreign (mainly Japanese) competition was intensifying acted as a further spur, while continued wage inflation provided an additional incentive to employers to invest in labor-saving machinery. Robot systems already up and running appeared to demonstrate to management impressive productivity gains, while labor unions couldn't help but be impressed by the use of robots rather than humans in hazardous work environments such as furnaces, paint shops, and nuclear power plants. In fact, there was a mad scramble in the US to get into robotics, which was seen as a major growth industry of the future.

But the robot boom was followed by a robot bust in the late 1980s: analysts had confidently predicted that the US robot population would top 250,000 or more by 1990. The actual figure turned out to be 37,000 – and even some of these had already been relegated to training centers and scrap-metal dealers. American robot sales actually peaked in 1987 and went steadily downhill after, primarily because US users found the care and feeding of robots to be more costly than people. General Motors wasted millions on premature robotization and many US robot makers went bust. Critics claimed that robots had been over-hyped by boosters like Joe Engelberger, and that robot vendors had neglected to put in the hard work necessary for customers to get the maximum benefits from their robots. In fact, US manufacturers seemed remarkably wary of any kind of automated machinery. A 1988 Harvard University study found that even CNC machine tools were not as widely used as might be expected: only 11 percent of machine tools in the US metalworking industry were CNC, while 53 percent of the plants surveyed did not have even one automated machine![12]

Meanwhile, the Japanese love affair with robots showed no signs of ending. By 1989, Japan had 175,000 robots at work and by 1992 the total stood at 275,000. The Japanese were even speaking of their country as *robotto tengoku* – a robot paradise. While the robot revolution was on hold in the West, Japanese robot manufacturers were busy developing a new generation of "field" robots (also called "service" robots) which could, for example, clean up hazardous waste sites, explore the ocean floor, extinguish fires, and dispose of terrorist bombs.

Indeed, the Japanese now have a whole range of medical robots capable of performing delicate surgical tasks; a variety of agricultural robots which can, for example, milk cows and autonomously plow fields and rice paddies; and an astonishing collection of construction industry robots which can, for example, clean and/or test the exterior cladding of high-rise buildings, smooth concrete slabs, spray walls, install glass, assemble steel frames, and dig undersea tunnels. Other Japanese robots have been known to play the organ and climb stairs. There are even robot fishing rods on Japanese fishing vessels. With this growing army of steel-collar workers, it's not surprising that Japan is estimated to have a lead in robotics over other countries at between 4.3 and 7.5 years.[13]

America pioneered the robotics industry, but it is now almost completely dominated by the Japanese. Furthermore, according to Michael E. Porter, "challenges to their leadership are nowhere in sight."[14]

The US Response: A "Productivity" Panic and the "Competitiveness" Craze

As the relentless rise of Japan in machine tools and robots continued, and as Japanese successes in cars, consumer electronics, and a whole range of manufactured goods became more apparent, American manufacturers started to panic.

In 1980, newly released national productivity figures showed that growth in US manufacturing productivity had slumped from an average annual increase of 3.4 percent in the 1950s and 1960s to less than 1 percent per annum in the 1970s. US manufacturers were losing market share across the board: they could no longer compete. US companies were being "hollowed out" as more and more shifted their manufacturing operations offshore to cheap-labor countries. Many US plants were becoming mere "screwdriver" operations, assembling finished products from wholly imported parts. In Detroit, Chrysler went (temporarily) bust, just as Japanese firms grabbed 27 percent of the US automobile market.

A famous article by Harvard University's Robert Hayes and William J. Abernathy in the *Harvard Business Review* ("Managing our way to economic decline") and a landmark *Business Week* special issue, "The reindustrialization of America" (June 30, 1980) signaled that the USA was facing some kind of national productivity crisis. Prominent academics rushed to join the productivity debate, proffering their own analyses and policy prescriptions. Robert U. Ayres and Steven M. Miller of Carnegie-Mellon University confirmed the facts of the US manufacturing productivity decline and argued for more investment in the new technologies of robotics and CAD/CAM. William J. Abernathy, Kim B. Clark, and Alan M. Kantrow came out with *Industrial Renaissance: Producing a Competitive Future for America* (1983), while Robert U. Ayres followed up with *The Next Industrial Revolution: Reviving Industry Through Innovation* (1984).

Robert B. Reich of Harvard University penned numerous articles calling for the US government to adopt a European-style industrial policy. In his book, *The Next American Frontier* (1983), Reich argued for subsidies, tax breaks, generous R&D grants, and a measure of enlightened protectionism to ease the transition from "rust bowl" to "sunrise" industries. In addition, he called for social reorganization – to replace competition with cooperation through greater participation and shared ownership. A similar plea was made by MIT's Michael J. Piore and Charles F. Sabel in their book, *The Second Industrial Divide: Possibilities for Prosperity* (1985). They argued in particular for government planning of the switch to flexible factories, which they saw as the wave of the future.

One thing most of these commentators were agreed on was that the so-called "deindustrialization" process was not inevitable and that the 1970s idea that America was destined to become some kind of "post-industrial society" had to be fought. Both these notions had gained currency in public policy circles in the previous decade, but the general idea that Western nations like the US could survive in the future simply by selling services was now viewed as dangerously misleading. In the aptly titled *Manufacturing Matters: The Myth of the Post-Industrial Economy* (1987), Stephen S. Cohen and John Zysman of the University of California, Berkeley, argued forcefully that America did not have a post-industrial economy, nor was it ever likely to have one – and, what's more, it had better not try to acquire one. They pointed out – as did others – that manufacturing in the US had in fact maintained its 30 percent or so share of GNP, although its share of *employment* had shrunk to less than 20 percent. Many service-sector jobs were dependent upon manufacturing jobs, while other sectors such as agriculture, mining, construction, transportation, and utilities were inextricably linked with manufacturing. In effect, they were saying: let manufacturing go, and everything else goes with it.[15]

The "productivity panic" turned into a "competitiveness craze" when President Reagan decided to make "competitiveness" the theme of his 1987 State of the Union address. While some commentators quibbled about the precise meaning and relevance of the term, "competitiveness" became a slogan and a catch-cry of manufacturers, administrators, educators, and expensive management consultants. It soon became clear what improving competitiveness meant to most American employers: "improving competitiveness" was the reason given for slashing cut-backs in employment in the "rust belt" of American industry, just as British premier Margaret Thatcher had used the same rhetoric when engineering a savage shake-out of British industry in the early 1980s. "Restructuring" and "downsizing" became the name of the game as managers sought to make their operations "leaner and fitter" to face the foreign competition. But these terms were nearly always euphemisms for the same thing: getting rid of people.

For a while, these slash-and-burn tactics worked, producing one-off productivity gains from the extensive de-manning. But there were other, more hopeful signs that American manufacturers were getting their act together to produce longer-lasting productivity gains through reduced operating costs, the elimination of waste and improved work methods. As capacity utilization rates moved up, articles began appearing in the US business press heralding "The Rust Belt Revival" and proclaiming that "The Smokestacks Steam Again." Productivity levels began to increase, while wage claims decreased, with the result that most manufacturers were now actually making a profit. Exports shot up – although cynics pointed out that this was probably almost entirely due to the massive collapse in the value of the dollar. Even so, the Rust Belt did look to be on a roll and the US deficit in manufactured goods of $170 billion in 1987 was pegged back to exactly $100 billion in 1988.

But many experts argued that the productivity/competitiveness battle was far from won. In particular, the long-awaited report of MIT's Commission on Industrial Productivity declared: "American industry is not producing as well as it ought to produce, or as well as it used to produce, or as well as the industries of some other nations have learned to produce." Convened back in 1986, the Commission had brought together a team of MIT's top academics to examine the poor performance of US manufacturing and to appraise the many reasons advanced for it, such as high interest rates, high taxes, lack of long-term investment, takeover rules, product liability laws, bad management, lazy workers, and so on. After much discussion, debate, and analysis, the Commission identified six major areas of concern in US plants: an over-reliance on old-fashioned mass-production techniques; too much short-term thinking and a lack of long-term vision on the part of management; weaknesses in production engineering and knowledge of new technologies; the neglect of human resources, with inadequate training and worker participation; the failure of firms to collaborate in the best interests of the industry; and a lack of cooperation between government and industry, especially as regards R&D.[16]

The Commission's report concluded by listing five broad imperatives for American manufacturing: making a new commitment to the pursuit of manufacturing excellence, by, for example, measuring all aspects of a company's performance and involving top management in production details; cultivating a new sense of economic citizenship in the workforce, by increasing responsibility and by making learning a part of everyday worklife – in return for greater job security and profit-sharing; blending cooperation with individualism, both within a firm's organizational hierarchy and in its dealings with customers and suppliers; learning to live in the global economy, by learning foreign languages and customs and being ready to adopt foreign technologies and practices; and providing for the future, by improving the quality of US education, especially in basic subjects, shifting the focus of business toward the long term, creating a national "information infrastructure," and reforming economic policy so as to provide incentives for saving and investment. Practicing what it preached, MIT's Sloan School of Management promptly introduced a new master's program in manufacturing technology.

In the 1989–91 period, two themes had come to dominate the productivity debate in the US: "working smarter" and "the pursuit of quality." Neither were new ideas and in fact both were variants of the same all-embracing "competitiveness" idea. But suddenly the US business press was full of articles on "Smart factories" and "Manufacturing the smart way," which basically reiterated many of the lessons learned in the well-known studies of Japanese manufacturing techniques. The subtitle of one piece in *Business Week* proclaimed the latest panacea: "How 'concurrent engineering' can reinvigorate American industry." Then the issue became "The Push for Quality" and "The Quality Imperative" – and a further rash of articles described the latest Japanese techniques like "QFD" (quality function deployment) and detailed how US manufacturers were now adopting Japanese quality management principles (even though similar pieces had appeared in 1987). Other newspaper, magazine, and journal articles focused on the US quality "fightback" in such firms as Motorola, John Deere and General Motors (with its Saturn project), and Lehigh University's scheme for "agile manufacturing."

But by 1992 new figures showed that Japan was again surging ahead in manufacturing productivity, as its "lean production" techniques were further refined and the new generation of flexible technology came on stream. US productivity growth was slowing after notching up impressive gains in the early and mid-1980s. American industry was still saddled with the highest overhead (as a percentage of manufacturing cost) of the US, Japan, and Germany.[17] There were renewed fears that the "hollowing out" of US companies was proceeding apace and that in certain industries, like semiconductors and autos, the Japanese now appeared unstoppable. The auto industry was of particular concern, because Detroit had by now had many years in which to learn from its mistakes and to turn back the Japanese tide. But five years after its most savage shake-out, General Motors was again announcing the closure of a further 25 plants (just in time for Christmas 1991/2), while the Japanese-owned automobile plants located in the USA – the so-called "transplants" – were working at full capacity and were grabbing an ever-growing share of the US car market.

There was renewed talk in academic and government circles of the need for the US to adopt a European or Asian-style "industrial policy." But if there was one thing successive US productivity panics and competitiveness crazes had shown, it was that the "free market" theology of successive Republicans in the White House ruled out serious consideration of Washington taking a direct role in the revitalization of US manufacturing industry.

FMS: Staying Ahead in the "Intelligent" Factory Stakes

Way back in 1965, a British producer of cigarette-making equipment called Molins brought out a revolutionary machine tool called System 24. Designed by Theo Williamson, System 24 was an advanced automated machine capable of running for 24 hours a day and of making small batches as efficiently as long production runs. Unfortunately, Williamson was a few years ahead of his time: although the system was sold to Rolls Royce, IBM, and Texas Instruments, it absorbed huge sums of development money, and by 1979 Molins had plunged into the red. In 1973 the company was forced to close down its entire machine tool division.

The timing could not have been more tragic. For just as Molins was being forced to abandon System 24, cheap microelectronics from Silicon Valley was enabling US firms like Cincinnati Milacron, White Consolidated, and Kearney & Trecker to develop better, less costly controls for what came to be called "flexible manufacturing systems" (FMS). The Japanese entered the FMS business in 1977 and rapidly took the technological lead.

FMS was widely viewed as a replacement for the older "hard" automation systems of the 1950s and 1960s. "Hard" automation means that a production line is dedicated to turning out one standard product in huge volume. FMS enables a company to produce a variety of products in small volumes as cheaply and as efficiently as if it were using mass-production methods. Since a great deal of manufacturing these days is in small "batches" or variants of similar products for different markets, the advantages of this new flexibility are obvious.

FMS boosters claim that the savings and productivity gains made possible by FMS can be phenomenal, because a single, all-embracing system replaces several conventional machining lines. FMS yields savings on labor. It also saves on plant space and decreases capital requirements by dramatically reducing the amount of work-in-progress and stock inventory. It is further claimed that product quality is better, so wastage and rectification costs are reduced. Plant utilization is improved because machines can be kept running most of the time and re-programmed quickly. Reduced lead-times also enable the manufacturer to react much more swiftly to market trends. Flexible manufacturing systems are therefore said to represent not just a new technology, but an entirely new way of thinking.

Economists refer to the advantages of flexible automation as "economies of scope," as opposed to "economies of scale." Under old-fashioned "hard" automation or mass production, the greatest savings were realized only with very large-scale plants and very long production runs. FMS makes similar economies possible at a wide range of scales. Economies of scope break all the rules of traditional manufacturing. There is no long trip down the learning curve. Entrepreneurial newcomers can in theory enter the manufacturing field much more easily and may overcome less agile, older producers.

Flexible manufacturing is probably having its greatest impact in the auto industry. FMS allows manufacturers to move from design concept to prototype to production far more quickly, it revolutionizes actual production methods and it enables car makers to target a far greater variety of models to specialist niche markets. In the

1970s, most observers saw the major trend in the world automobile market as being toward a small, standardized car. FMS reversed that process, enabling producers to develop cars for specific niche markets without incurring the traditional costs of small-scale batch production. And because FMS reduces still further the labor content of a car, the expected shift to low-wage countries is not now occurring on the scale previously envisaged. In fact, many new car plants – like the Japanese-owned "transplants" in the US – are being located directly in the markets where the cars are sold.

Of the 200 or so "true" FMS installations in the world, more than half of them are located in Japan, where the major suppliers are Yamazaki, Hitachi-Seiki, and Fujitsu Fanuc. With their JIT systems, their quality control techniques and their focus on the final customer, the Japanese have taken to FMS like ducks to water. At Fujitsu Fanuc's futuristic factory near Mount Fuji, it was claimed that 30 manufacturing cells and just 100 workers in the mid-1980s were turning out as many robot parts as could be produced in a conventional plant costing ten times as much and employing ten times as many people. In Fanuc's nearby electric-motor factory, 60 cells and 101 robots were toiling night and day to produce 10,000 electric motors a month. In the early 1990s, Fujitsu opened an unmanned 24 hours a day FMS facility at its plant in Oyama which was capable of turning out a huge variety of circuit boards in batches as small as one – with parts automatically chosen from an inventory of 1,000 devices.

Yamazaki's $20 million flexible automation plant near Nagoya was said to employ just 12 workers in the day and 1 nightwatchman. Its conventional equivalent would have required 215 workers and nearly 4 times as many machines, and would have taken 3 months to turn out the machine tool parts the new plant could make in 3 days. Another "twenty-first century" Yamazaki plant 20 miles away was run by telephone from company headquarters and employed about 200 workers instead of the 2,500 in a conventional factory. It could cope with sales varying from $80 to $230 million a year without having to lay off any workers. Meanwhile, auto giant Nissan is developing an Intelligent Body Assembling System, a computer-controlled mold for holding and welding car body parts. The system is so flexible that it can be reprogrammed in three months to produce a range of new car models instead of the 12 months it takes to re-tool a conventional mold.

By contrast, American companies were slower to install FMS in the 1980s, despite the availability of advanced systems from leading US machine tool firms. Critics said that US managers, unlike their Japanese counterparts, lacked the technical expertise to understand the complex new systems and were too worried about the short-term returns to stockholders to be able to think long term. Research at Harvard Business School showed that US managers were using FMS far less flexibly than the Japanese or West Germans. And they were altogether too hooked on the idea of keeping old machine tools going. But there were honorable exceptions: Deere & Co., General Electric, and Cummins diesel engines all experimented extensively with FMS, with varying degrees of success.

Takeup of FMS in Europe was typically slow, but there were some encouraging signs. In Britain, Cincinnati Milacron (UK) and Kearney & Trecker Marwin (UK) had showpiece systems, while IBM was using FMS extensively in its computer plant at Greenock, Scotland. Construction materials company Travis & Arnold created a flexible, automated wood-cutting mill at King's Lynn, Norfolk; aerospace company Normalair-Garrett installed an FMS facility at Crewkerne, Somerset; while Rolls Royce, the aero-engine maker, managed to finance a massive investment in FMS at its Derby plant solely on savings in working capital – overall productivity was up about 30 percent. A final British example was the 600 Group's factory at Colchester, Essex, which could produce machine parts from the order book in three days rather than three months. Elsewhere in Europe, major users of FMS were Volvo in Sweden and Renault in France. In West Germany, Messerschmitt-Bolkow-Blohm's plant in Augsburg achieved impressive savings in the machining of parts for the Tornado jet fighter.

FMS does have some disadvantages, however, and these have become all too apparent in recent years. As a result, the rate of progress with FMS has slowed. FMS systems are of course very expensive, they are difficult to install, and they do not work properly unless there are reliable, linked systems for materials handling, storage, and retrieval. Manufacturers looking for a "quick fix" technological solution to their problems simply by purchasing a "turnkey" system (that is, a complete, ready-to-go system – all you have to do is turn the key) have been disappointed. Some say that FMS has been oversold. FMS installations, like anything else, have to be worked at and constantly improved by people who know what they're doing. Moreover, unless the correct management and marketing decisions are taken, no amount of new hardware can stop a sick company from losing market share. FMS must be integrated with the business as a whole, otherwise its considerable potential benefits will be dissipated.

While some in the West have become disillusioned with FMS, the Japanese are pressing ahead aggressively with innovatory manufacturing techniques such as "personalized" production. This involves using flexible systems to produce customized goods, such as shoes and bicycles, for individual customers. One such system at the National Bicycle Industrial Company, a subsidiary of Matsushita, enables customers to purchase their own, tailor-made bicycle. Orders are placed at the local bicycle store, from which the shopkeeper faxes the individual's vital statistics to the factory. An operator enters the specifications into a computer, which then instructs the manufacturing system to produce any of 11,231,862 variations of racing, road, or mountain bike in the customer's unique size.

"Desktop manufacturing" systems, which enable manufacturers to produce a part directly from a computer model on a screen, are also being developed in Japan. Some are linked to powder metallurgy processes, which enable metal objects to be made from special powders placed in molds designed and made by computer. Japan already has a lead in many areas of new materials technology. Desktop manufacturing is being explored in the US, at universities like Carnegie-Mellon and MIT, but Japanese companies are able to benefit from the expertise of other members of their *keiretsu* (family of companies), who have dominant positions in relevant technologies developed for copiers, laser printers, and high-definition television (HDTV) systems.

An indication of Japan's determination to stay ahead in the Factory of the Future race may be gleaned from the saga of the Intelligent Manufacturing System (IMS) plan, launched by MITI in early 1990. The general aim of IMS was to develop wholly integrated, flexible factories which would be totally automated and yet be very responsive to changes in consumer preferences. But the key difference with this plan was that Japan was seeking international cooperation in the project: in particular, MITI was looking for foreign partners in Germany and Switzerland, whose skills in building high-precision machinery are legendary. These, it seemed, would be welded to Japanese expertise in organizing the production process. The political purpose was to reduce trade tensions with the rest of the world, in the light of Japan's enormous trade surplus in manufactured goods.

But many observers in the US and Europe saw IMS as yet another Japanese ruse to steal Western technology and software, especially as Japan had done little to improve patent protection for Western companies. On the other hand, it was also pointed out that there was now a lot that American and European firms could learn from the Japanese, especially about JIT, quality control, and flexible manufacturing techniques. The originator of IMS, Tokyo University academic Hiroyuki Yoshikawa, was at pains to point out that he was merely seeking global cooperation in the development of a "universal theory of manufacturing" as part of Japan's new "technoglobalism." Toward the end of 1990, the three proposed partners in the project, the US, Japan, and the EC, agreed on a feasibility study with certain safeguards, such as improving the protection of intellectual property and restricting IMS to pre-competitive R&D. More than 70 Japanese companies signed up for IMS, but in the US and Europe there seemed to be a distinct lack of interest in intelligent factories.

One couldn't help but be reminded of a statement attributed to Mr Konosuke Matsushita, when talking about getting people and machines working together in manufacturing: "We are going to win and the industrial West is going to lose."[18]

Notes

1 James P. Womack, Daniel T. Jones, and Daniel Roos, *The Machine That Changed the World: The Story of Lean Production* (Rawson Associates, Boston, MA, 1990 and Harper Collins, New York, 1991).
2 Clyde V. Prestowitz, *Trading Places: How We Allowed Japan to Take the Lead* (Basic Books, New York, 1988), p. 219.
3 Prestowitz, *Trading Places*, p. 221.

4 Prestowitz, *Trading Places*, p. 222.
5 *Fortune*, September 24, 1990, p. 50 and December 30, 1991, p. 75; *Business Week*, January 13, 1992.
6 Prestowitz, *Trading Places*, pp. 223–9.
7 Prestowitz, *Trading Places*, p. 229.
8 Max Holland, *When the Machine Stopped: A Cautionary Tale from Industrial America* (Harvard Business School Press, Boston, MA, 1990).
9 Michael E. Porter, *The Competitive Advantage of Nations* (Free Press, New York, 1990), p. 227.
10 Porter, *The Competitive Advantage of Nations*, pp. 228–9.
11 Porter, *The Competitive Advantage of Nations*, pp. 230–8; *The Australian*, June 23, 1992.
12 Peter T. Kilborn, "Brave new world seen for robots appears stalled by quirks and costs," *New York Times*, July 1, 1990, p. 16. For the full story of General Motors and its robot program under CEO Roger Smith, see Albert Lee, *Call Me Roger* (Contemporary Books, New York, 1988) and Maryann Keller, *Rude Awakening: The Rise, Fall, and Struggle for Recovery of General Motors* (William Morrow, New York, 1990).
13 Estimate of Japan's lead from Robert U. Ayres (ed.), "Impacts of robotics on manufacturing," special issue of *Technological Forecasting and Social Change*, 35, nos 2–3 (1989).
14 Porter, *The Competitive Advantage of Nations*, p. 238.
15 A summary of Cohen and Zysman's argument (by themselves) may be found in Tom Forester (ed.), *Computers in the Human Context: Information Technology, Productivity and People* (Basil Blackwell, Oxford, UK and MIT Press, Cambridge, MA, 1989), pp. 97–103.
16 Michael L. Dertouzos, Richard K. Lester, Robert M. Solow, and The MIT Commission on Industrial Productivity, *Made in America: Regaining the Productive Edge* (MIT Press, Cambridge, MA, 1989). The report was also featured in *Fortune*, May 22, 1989, *Scientific American*, 260, no. 6 (1989), and a special issue of *Technology Review*, 92, no. 6 (1989).
17 *Competing Economies: America, Europe and the Pacific Rim*, Office of Technology Assessment, US Congress, Washington (USGPO, October 1991).
18 Quoted by Alec Chisholm in John Bessant and Alec Chisholm, "Human factors in computer-integrated manufacturing," in Forester (ed.), *Computers in the Human Context*, p. 309.

6
Office Equipment: Supplying the Tools of Trade

A Short History of Office Technology – The Office of the Future: California Dreamin' Meets Reality – Photocopiers: How Xerox Got Blanked by Canon & Co. – The Fax Fiasco: Japan Banks on the Not-So-"Paperless" Office

Way back in 1959, the American firm Xerox introduced its legendary 914 photocopier. Unlike its competitors, which required specially treated or heat-sensitive paper, the 914 was the first commercial copier to use ordinary paper. It was an instant success, rapidly making Xerox a household name and quickly transforming the way information was processed in the modern office. The advent of the plain paper copier was clearly an important milestone in the history of business communication and it also made a fortune for the Xerox Corporation, hitherto a small company with the name of the Haloid Company based in Rochester, upstate New York. The 914 model itself has been described as "One of the most successful, if not *the* most successful, product of all time in any industry."[1]

The 1960s were kind to Xerox. In 1965, Xerox had annual revenues of $400 million and held an estimated 86 percent of the world's plain paper copier market. By 1968, Xerox held the record for reaching sales of $1 billion faster than any other company in US history. But things went badly wrong for Xerox in the 1970s, as the booming company became immersed in litigation, grew a bloated bureaucracy, and failed to develop new products from expensive R&D. Most important of all, it totally ignored the threat from Japan. By 1979, Xerox's share of the US market had slumped to 40 percent, while little-known Japanese companies like Canon, Sharp, and Ricoh had marched in and grabbed 35 percent. In low-end machines, the Japanese were already sole suppliers. By 1984, Xerox's share of the world market for copiers was down to just 17 percent, while Japan's Canon and Sharp had held the top two spots on new copier placements in the US since 1981.[2]

A similar fate befell Xerox with that other success story of the modern office, the fax machine. Xerox had actually introduced the first commercial facsimile machine – then called a "telecopier" – back in 1964. But the company failed to capitalize on its early success and again made the mistake of ignoring the low end of the market. By 1989, 25 years later, its share of the fax market (through the Fuji Xerox joint venture) was down to a mere 7 percent, while wholly Japanese brands like Canon, Ricoh, Sharp, Fujitsu, Murata, and Panafax (plus Pitney-Bowes with its re-labeled Ricoh machines) had virtually all the rest.

Michael E. Porter, in his magisterial study, *The Competitive Advantage of Nations* (1990), says that one of *the* most significant clusters of competitive industries in modern-day Japan is the office equipment sector. The other major clusters are transport equipment, especially cars and trucks; entertainment and leisure, notably consumer electronics; steel and fabricated metal products; electronic components and computing equipment; and optical-related products, including cameras and film. Strong or emerging clusters exist in printing equipment; telecommunications equipment; ceramics products; household appliances; personal products such as pens, watches, and clocks; and business inputs such as fans, pumps, and tools.

Indeed, when Porter ranked Japan's industries in terms of their share of world markets in 1985, the office equipment sector emerged as being remarkably successful. While the motorcycle industry came out top with 82.0 percent of the entire world market and the VCR business came second on 80.7 percent, four of the next six positions were taken by categories of office equipment. Thus Japanese companies had 71.7 percent of the world market for dictating machines; 69.7 percent of the calculating machine market; 65.9 percent of the photocopier market; and 62.0 percent of the cash register and accounting machine market. Further down the list, we note that Japanese companies even had 45.0 percent of the world market for electric typewriters – all the more remarkable considering that the Japanese use an entirely different alphabet (mostly made up of *kanji* characters).[3]

A recent classification of the world's top computing companies, which included office equipment, also underlined the importance of this sector and the growing strength of the Japanese. According to these *Fortune* magazine rankings, after IBM, Fujitsu, Digital Equipment, Hewlett-Packard, and Unisys, the sixth ranked computers and office equipment company in the world in terms of revenues was Japan's Canon, best known for its copiers, and in ninth place (ahead of Apple, Bull, Wang, Compaq, and many others) was the comparatively low-profile Japanese firm, Ricoh.[4]

Thus in many respects the Japanese office equipment makers are the quiet achievers in our story. Although lacking the high media profile of the Apples and Compaqs, Japanese companies like Canon and Ricoh have quietly got on with the job of winning business in important, but somewhat humdrum areas – such as dictation equipment, calculating machines, photocopiers, faxes, and check-writing machines. Endlessly innovative and not afraid to tackle the low end of the market, the Japanese companies have succeeded where better-known American brands have failed. While US companies have persisted with outdated, expensive, and technologically glamorous products (or have made the fatal error of buying in and re-labeling products made overseas), Japanese companies have first found out what customers want – and then supplied it promptly and at the right price.

The office equipment saga also demonstrates clearly that American IT companies, unlike their Japanese counterparts, have been generally unable to diversify into other IT areas. Unlike the Fujitsus, Minoltas, Canons, and Ricohs (not to mention the Matsushitas and Mitsubishis), US companies have largely failed to become the kind of vertically integrated monoliths which seem better placed to succeed in IT in the 1990s. Thus Xerox not only squandered a world lead in copiers and fax machines: it also failed to diversify into computers and office systems. Likewise, telecoms giant AT&T, despite numerous attempts, was unable to develop a viable computer division and even IBM has enjoyed little success in its efforts to get into office copiers and telecommunications. The Japanese have made their achievements in the office equipment market look child's play.

A Short History of Office Technology

Today more people work in offices than farms, factories, shops, and services combined. For example, over 50 percent of the US labor force (or about 60 million people) are now white-collar workers. In 1900 the figure was only 5 million, or less than one fifth of the working population: at that time, two and a half times as many people worked on the land as worked in offices. Of the 60 million or so white-collars in the US today, about 34 million are clerical workers, around 19 million are professional and technical workers, and the rest are managers or administrators. For millions of people, then, white-collar work is increasingly the norm.

White-collar workers are engaged in the processes of gathering, storing, manipulating, and transmitting information in one form or another. As society grows more complex, the amount of information required to help run it increases. And as the cost of processing this information has come down – thanks to advances in microelectronics, computing, and telecommunications – the installed base of information-processing technology has increased. Together with the convergence of the computing, telecommunications, and office equipment industries, this tidal wave of new technology is bringing about a major transformation in the place where white-collar workers work: the office.

This fundamental change marks the transition from the traditional office to the electronic office, a change that hardly seemed possible 15 years ago, when the first personal computers went on sale. Yet installed computing capacity in offices doubled every two to three years during the 1980s and by 1990 there was roughly 1,000 times as much computing power in offices as there was in 1970. In less than a decade, the US population of keyboards – electronic typewriters, dedicated word processors, desktop personal computers, and computer terminals – grew to nearly 50 million. Now the total is more like 100 million.

The drive to mechanize office functions and to reduce office labor costs can be traced back to 1873, the year that American gunmakers E. Remington and Sons introduced the first typewriter. It was a huge success: by the late 1890s, scores of companies were making typewriters, and by 1900 more than 100,000 had been sold. With the typewriter came an increase in the amount of correspondence and the size of offices. The typewriter also brought women into the office for the first time. Apart from the introduction of the electric typewriter in 1935, basic typewriter technology then stayed much the same for decades. Even more recent developments like the "golfball" typewriter of 1961 and the memory typewriter in 1964 were evolutionary rather than wholly revolutionary.

Meanwhile, various attempts were being made to improve office productivity with more mechanical devices. Innovations such as ticker tape, automatic telephone switching, calculators, dictation equipment, duplicating machines, offset printing presses, and even photocopiers made regular appearances throughout the century, but their cumulative impact on productivity was not great. This long period of *mechanization* involved no fundamental change in office technology. As with typewriters, most "new" products were in fact enhancements of existing products. Key items such as that other Victorian invention, the telephone, remained essentially unchanged and the office "system" was still based on shuffling paper from typewriter carriage to filing cabinet. Offices were much the same sort of labor-intensive hives of activity that existed at the turn of the century.

The big changes started with the invention of the electronic computer and developments in what was then called data processing or "DP." The first mainframe computer for business use was installed in the USA by General Electric in 1953. In Britain, the famous LEO (for Lyons Electronic Office) data processing computer was used in the 1950s to process orders from Lyons corner teashops across London. By the 1960s, most large companies and organizations had data processing centers for dealing with routine tasks such as the payroll, issuing checks, controlling inventory, and sending out bills. The replacement of bulky, troublesome valves with solid-state circuits made mainframe computers cheaper and easier to use.

The advent of the microchip in the early 1970s got designers thinking in terms of office *automation*, which was being made possible by the growing digitization of information. Digitization meant that voice, data, and images could be reduced to a series of electronic pulses, while the notion of "automation" encouraged people to look at offices as having so many "functions" (for example, the "keying function," the "filing function," the "mailing function," etc.) of a total system. Digitization would thus be the glue that would hold together all the different elements of the modern "office information system." Strings of binary numbers would replace paper as the system's working unit.

The microelectronics revolution brought forth an avalanche of new products, such as programmable calculators, word processors, facsimile machines, remote terminals, electronic switchboards, sophisticated copiers, microcomputers, minicomputers, and superminicomputers. The migration to digital devices was spectacular and swift: the humble mechanical calculator, for instance – used for individual and often complex sums rather than the routine, repetitive calculations done by the mainframes – was displaced overnight by microelectronics-based products, which were cheaper, more reliable, and much more sophisticated. Word processors – intelligent typewriters consisting of a keyboard and a visual display terminal (VDT) linked up to a microcomputer – were an early success, while "smart" telephones, switchboards, and copiers rapidly became commonplace.

In a word processor, each keystroke operates an electronic switch rather than a mechanical linkage, which means that information coming from the keyboard can be transmitted in digital form to an electronic memory. The great advantage of a word processor is that it abolishes retyping: material can be manipulated, edited, and formatted on the screen before being printed out as hard copy or committed to memory. Once it seemed that word processors would completely oust the more humble electronic typewriter. But in fact these machines have undergone something of a renaissance in recent years, with the help of some nifty marketing by Japanese suppliers like Brother. In 1991, US producer Smith Corona again complained that Japanese suppliers Brother and Panasonic were dumping electronic typewriters at far less than fair market value.

Office automation in the late 1970s was virtually synonymous with word processing. But in the early 1980s office automation soon came to mean end-user computing. Company bosses, besieged by equipment suppliers offering a bewildering choice of wholly integrated systems, simply started taking their personal computers into the office instead. Stimulated by the launch of IBM's PC in 1981, the so-called "desktop revolution" put 8–10 million personal computers into US offices in just four years. By

1986, the installed base of IBM PCs represented roughly three times the processing power of its large 370 mainframes. US shipments of personal computers were already about two-thirds the value of mainframe computer shipments and by 1990 they were equal.

Personal computers can be used for word processing, messaging, accessing data, and spreadsheet analysis. They can be hooked up to mainframes, fax machines, printers, and databases, transforming themselves into what have been variously described as "multi-function workstations," "executive workstations," and "the electronic desk." Thanks in part to the availability of integrated software packages, the personal computer has become the basic building block of the so-called Office of the Future. The market for professional personal computers has been the scene of some of the fiercest marketing battles, the most savage shake-outs and the greatest success stories in computing.

Managers are finding that personal computers are re-making their jobs and transforming the way offices actually operate. Putting more computing power and thus information directly in the hands of executives through the use of Management Information Systems (MIS) or Executive Information Systems (EIS) and other distributed systems means that companies can dispose of some middle and lower layers of bureaucracy. The onset of professional personal computing can thus lead to major changes in the corporate structure itself and to a general flattening of the managerial pyramid. More and more companies are bringing their data processing, MIS, and telecoms units together under one roof – a kind of managerial response to technological convergence.

Spreadsheet analysis, made possible by sophisticated new software packages, has rapidly grown in popularity. Beginning with VisiCalc in 1979 and continuing through versions of Lotus's 1-2-3, spreadsheet packages have given professionals a whole new way of working. Executives are able constantly to monitor company performance: at their fingertips (in theory) are all the information and variables they need to plot future business strategy and to experiment with different scenarios. More than a million spreadsheet packages were sold in the USA alone in 1984 and their fans claim that they provide a sophisticated and flexible weapon for tackling the competition. But critics say they are not so useful: users can become addicted to playing endless "what if?" games ("spreadsheet junkies") and are at the mercy of that old truism, "garbage in, garbage out."

Digitization and technological convergence have brought computer, telecommunications and office equipment companies converging on the electronic office market. Computer companies now find they need telecommunications capabilities and they must offer the full range of office products, while telecoms companies and office equipment companies must know something about computing. US firms have struggled to diversify in response to technological convergence, while the vertically integrated Japanese conglomerates like NEC and Fujitsu appeared to have coped with the transition effortlessly and are well placed to capitalize on this trend.

The Office of the Future: California Dreamin' Meets Reality

American and European companies lost millions in the 1970s on grandiose "Office of the Future" projects. These projects had one thing in common: the belief that all existing office functions could be fairly easily automated and that the traditional paper-shuffling office was about to be replaced by the all-electronic "paperless" office.

It all began in 1971, when a team of scientists at Xerox's research center in Palo Alto, California, launched a scheme to design what they called "The Electronic Office of the Future." The notion of using digitization and convergence to create integrated office information systems was sound enough, but what was missing at the time was the hardware and especially the software to make the dream a reality (the human and organizational problems were to emerge later). But the idea was a tremendously powerful one, and soon companies, governments, and academic research establishments all over the world were rushing to develop their own Office of the Future or "paperless" office scenarios. There was a great fear that companies or countries not in the office automation market would miss out on *the* boom industry of the decade.

In 1975 – strange though it may seem with hindsight – the oil giant Exxon actually plunged into the office automation business with the purchase of start-ups Vydec (word processors), Qwip (fax machines), and Qyx (electronic typewriters). This was just the start of Exxon's bid to become a major force in the potentially huge office automation market. During the next ten years, Exxon poured an incredible $2 billion into its Exxon Office Systems (EOS) subsidiary, spending lavishly on advertising and promotion. But EOS never made money and in 1985 Exxon finally sold the remaining assets of its office automation business to Lanier Business Products for a trivial sum.

Exxon's drive to disaster in the office was mirrored elsewhere: in the UK, for example, the government-backed National Enterprise Board in the late 1970s poured millions of pounds into Nexos, a company that was to be the British entry into the Office of the Future stakes. But Nexos collapsed with huge debts in 1981 and Logica, the UK software group which was linked to Nexos, pulled out of the office automation market at the end of 1985. In continental Europe, the Dutch group Philips, France's CIT Alcatel, and even complete outsiders like Germany's Volkswagen – through its purchase of Triumph-Adler – took aim at the "paperless" office market. Volkswagen never did become a big name in word processors – nor, in fact, did Xerox.

Despite continued marketing hype, it was apparent by the mid-1980s that the Office of the Future had not yet arrived. The expensive, integrated systems had failed to sell, and many people had ended up simply taking their stand-alone personal computer into the office. Surveys in the USA and Europe showed that office automation still had a long way to go: analyst Patricia Seybold said that the promised land was still ten years away. Another authority put the state-of-the art at "about two and a half out of ten, if ten is what is being marketed." A British study found that fewer than half of the UK's 9 million office workers used any kind of electronic equipment – the nearest most employees got to office automation was the coffee machine!

To be fair, doubts about the Office of the Future scenario had crept in early on. Skeptics had pointed out during the great office automation rush in the late 1970s that this particular market was peculiar in that it was to be entirely manufacturer-driven, not consumer-driven. By the mid-1980s it was obvious that the expected sales bonanza would never materialize, although spending was rising. Articles began to appear giving reasons why the office revolution had been delayed. There was growing evidence that some executives and professionals were getting disillusioned with computers. Too many had been sold the wrong package of software, and many had suffered bad experiences with faulty and/or incompatible hardware. PBX vendors found that customers were not using the "smart" features on their devices. The buying spree had resulted in a lot of expensive gear lying around gathering dust: surveys showed that even personal computers were badly underused and in some instances had been completely discarded. Some suggested that it was time to junk the notion of the wholly integrated, all-electronic, paperless Office of the Future and to focus on more mundane matters – like producing a better copier or fax machine, which was precisely what the Japanese were doing.

The slow progress with office automation has been caused by a variety of structural, financial, technological, and human factors. One very basic – but often overlooked – reason is that there has simply been a lack of suitable buildings to receive the new technology. Existing office buildings were not designed to cope with the masses of wiring required and the amount of heat generated by the new automated equipment. Traditional skyscrapers are not flexible enough for the new working environments. In the UK, a 1983 report warned that the need to re-think office design was urgent and that the cost of remodeling old buildings to take the new technology could be almost as high as building new.

The answer seems to lie in the construction of more "smart" office buildings which are better suited to the info-tech age. These not only contain ample ducting for communications networks, but can also be made "intelligent" with the incorporation of all the latest energy control and security monitoring systems. IBM and DEC have intelligent building programs in the US. In Europe, ICL, Siemens, Olivetti, and seven other companies have teamed up to form the Intelligent Building in Europe project. But it is the Japanese who appear most advanced in smart-building techniques. NEC, Fujitsu, Hitachi, and Nippon Telegraph and Telephone (NTT) have smart-building divisions, while other computer companies have collaborative arrangements with building firms.[5] The huge Tokyo Teleport project will eventually feature a dozen or more intelligent office towers, built on land reclaimed from Tokyo Bay.

Progress with office automation has been further slowed by the lack of agreement on standards, especially the communications standards or protocols which allow machines to talk to each other. Computer vendors often try to gain advantage by selling unique, incompatible products, which are designed to "lock-in" customers to their brand. But this practice also puts off many potential customers and reduces the size of the overall market: the result is that both vendors and users suffer. The inability of machines to communicate led, in 1985, to the formation of the Corporation for Open Systems (COS), a consortium of more than 50 computer makers. The main aim of COS is to promote the "Open Systems Interconnection" or OSI protocol, a generic, seven-layer, international standard. With the backing not only of major computer vendors like IBM, Digital, and Sun, but also communication giants like AT&T and Northern Telecom and large users like General Motors and Kodak, OSI gained many adherents in the late 1980s and early 1990s.

Disappointment has been expressed with some of the heavily hyped panaceas of the electronic office, such as MIS (Management Information Systems), DTP (Desktop Publishing), and EDI (Electronic Data Interchange). MIS systems have often turned out to be expensive, hard to use, and not to contain enough of the right kind of information. DTP systems have often produced disappointing results in terms of cost-savings and the actual appearance of their products: some companies have even reverted to conventional typesetting. EDI or "paperless trading" has been slow to get off the ground and has been plagued by technical, financial, managerial, and legal problems, especially the problem of gaining international agreement on technical standards.

Management resistance has also played its part in delaying the electronic office. Too many managers prefer to carry on in the same old way and won't explore new methods of working. They feel threatened by new technology and fear loss of power to those more familiar with computers. "Wait and see" conservatism all too often triumphs. In the UK, a 1983 study on progress with the electronic office found the biggest single reason for not investing in new technology was that it had simply never been considered. Many managers lacked the knowledge or commitment to even investigate the possibility of going over to automation. Management resistance in the 230 offices surveyed had been far more effective than any resistance on the part of the office workforce. A new condition – "terminal phobia" – has also been diagnosed to explain the unwillingness of executives to use keyboards: this is caused partly by a feeling that their use is demeaning and partly by the fear that they would be shown up to be ignorant and unfamiliar with new technology in front of their staff.

The *psychology* of office automation has thus come to the fore, as it has been increasingly realized that human problems are just as important as technical problems. Managers are unwilling to change, and feel threatened and confused. Those lower down the office hierarchy see the potential disruption of traditional working methods and perhaps feel, too, that their job is on the line. Power battles have developed between different company departments; in particular, the technical experts in the DP and MIS departments have struggled to reassert control over purchasing decisions, after managers and professionals started taking their own computing equipment into the office. MIS departments have had to respond to end-user pressure for personal computers, better back-up and improved networking. Some have argued that the problem is a wider one of technological advance outstripping the ways of organizing it. Developments in office technology have raced ahead of the human ability to comprehend and manage the complexities. What was now needed was a period of learning and consolidation, so that users might learn how best to use the equipment they had already installed.

Probably the most important factor slowing progress toward the Office of the Future is the continuing fact that productivity gains are not demonstrable. While manufacturing productivity in the US grew at a healthy 4.1 percent in the 1980s, white-collar productivity rose by a negligible 0.28 percent per annum.[6] This was despite the expenditure of huge sums on office automation products. In his book, *The Business Value of Computers* (1990), former Xerox executive Paul Strassman found no link at all between IT spending and productivity in 292 companies studied. He even found a *negative* relationship between productivity and spending on MIS systems. While in *The Corporation of the 1990s: Information Technology and Organizational Transformation* (1991), Michael S. Scott Morton of MIT declares that the introduction of IT "does not indicate any improvements in productivity."[7] Likewise, research by Stephen Roach of Morgan Stanley and Martin Neil Baily of the Brookings Institution has indicated negligible improvements in white-collar productivity and little evidence of an IT payoff. This has prompted many academics and analysts to talk of an "IT productivity paradox."

Improving office productivity ought to be easy. Surveys of how office workers spend their time show clearly that long periods are spent on the phone (often playing "telephone tag," that is, trying fruitlessly to locate people), in seemingly endless meetings, simply wandering around, or apparently doing nothing. Since white-collar salaries cost the US over $1 trillion a year, even a tiny percentage gain in productivity would yield billion-dollar savings – in theory.

In theory, the potential for raising office productivity is enormous. In practice, things ain't so simple. The substitution of machines for human labor does not increase office productivity as straightforwardly as it does in a factory. Potential productivity gains can be frittered away through: the need to regularly retrain staff; the excessive re-drafting of documents; the production of additional memoranda, adding to the problem of "information overload" or "infoglut"; the excessive use of spreadsheets ("spreadsheet junkies"), faxes ("fax potatoes") and electronic mail ("e.mail addicts"); the continued existence of "busywork"; the appearance of electronic "junk" mail and "junk" faxes; and the purchase and display of under-utilized IT gear as a form of conspicuous consumption or a demonstration of up-to-dateness in order to improve the corporate image.

The inappropriate use of technology is of particular concern: after studying the use of personal computers by 1,100 accountants in the US Internal Revenue Service (IRS), Professor Brian Pentland of MIT found that only those who used their pcs *selectively* achieved the desired productivity gains. While the pc users benefited from a sense of professionalism and enhanced self-esteem, it was unlikely that the overall efficiency of the IRS had improved, despite considerable expenditure on IT. Pentland wrote: "Practitioners should be aware that policies which promote use may actually hurt productivity by encouraging users to apply technology to tasks where it is only marginally useful." Much of the perceived value of computers is "symbolic rather than substantive."[8]

With hindsight, the "paperless" office now looks to be one of the funniest predictions ever made about the social impact of IT. More and more trees are being felled to satisfy our vast appetite for paper in offices which were supposed by now to be all electronic. In the US, paper consumption has rocketed 320 percent over the past 30 years, ahead of real GDP which has gone up 280 percent. In absolute terms, this means that in 1990 American consumers gobbled up more than 4 trillion pages of paper, compared with only 2.5 trillion in 1986 – about the time that word processors and pcs were becoming really popular. The two most successful office products of recent times – the photocopier and the fax machine – are of course enormous users of paper, while technologies which do not use paper – such as electronic mail and voice mail – have been slow to catch on. The overall market for office automation equipment is not as strong as it was in the 1980s, but sales of desktop laser printers are booming – and of course they also consume vast amounts of paper. EDI might help reduce paper consumption in the future, but it will be some time before it becomes a significant force.

Despite the huge increase in telephone usage and the existence of electronic mail and videotex, old-fashioned surface mail – much of it paper-intensive "junk" mail – is still growing in volume in most industrial countries. Banks still rely on paper to a surprising degree, despite EFT (electronic funds transfer) and plastic transaction cards. A recent IBM study estimated that 95 percent of information in business enterprises is still in paper form. It has also been suggested that only 1 percent of all the information in the world is stored on computers. The US Pentagon recently declared "war" on paper: apart from the normal paper problems of all unwieldy bureaucracies, the Pentagon now has to cope with the huge amounts of documentation which go with complex high-tech weapons systems. For example, a typical US Navy cruiser puts to sea with no less than 26 tonnes of manuals for its weapons systems – enough to affect the performance of the vessel![9]

Photocopiers: How Xerox Got Blanked by Canon & Co.

Although Xerox had introduced the world's first plain paper copier in 1959 and the first commercial fax machine in 1964, all the talk in the US in the 1970s was of the "paperless" Office of the Future based on pcs displacing the old-style paperfull office. But meanwhile in Japan, corporate masterminds were quietly targeting paper-using products such as the photocopier, the fax machine, and the laser printer.

Japan had good reason to be keen on these devices: the use of some 60,000 *kanji* as well as *hiragana* and *katakana* characters in the Japanese language made typewriters and telex machines (which are best suited to roman characters) somewhat impractical. Most documents in Japan were still handwritten, so a cheap means of disseminating information in handwritten form would be a boon to business. In recognition of the importance of fax machines, the Japanese government was quick to approve the facsimile transmission of legal documents and also gave early approval for the hooking of fax machines to ordinary telephone lines.[10]

Image processing in the modern office is dominated by the plain paper copier. It is hard to imagine how we ever did without them in the days before the legendary Xerox 914 inaugurated the era of mass copying and made "to Xerox" part of our language. In their book, *Xerox, American Samurai* (1986), Gary Jacobson and John Hillkirk provide a detailed account of how Xerox first triumphed with xerography in the 1960s, then swiftly lost ground to the Japanese in the 1970s and finally fought back in the 1980s to regain some market share. Their thesis is that Xerox lost and regained the initiative in photocopiers purely on competitiveness. They say that neither Xerox nor its fierce Japanese rivals sought or benefited from government subsidies or trade barriers. In this sense, the photocopier story is a paradigm example of the competitive battle now being waged in high-tech between Japan and the USA.

Launching the world's first plain paper copier was in a way the worst thing that could have ever happened to Xerox. The company had such a huge lead and grew so quickly that it pretty soon became fat, lazy, and complacent – rather like US industry as a whole in the postwar years. The company developed a vast bureaucracy as it rapidly expanded to 100,000 employees. It poured large sums of money into expensive R&D boondoggles like the Office of the Future project at its Palo Alto, California, research center. And it soon became mired in expensive, time-consuming litigation as US competitors and the US government attempted to chip away at Xerox's powerful monopoly-supplier position. Some say that other US firms were simply jealous of Xerox's success, others argued that Xerox overcharged and generally abused its position.

But there was no doubt that the series of lawsuits launched against Xerox in the 1970s had a debilitating effect on the company – and helped divert attention from the main threat, the Japanese. Because of the US lawsuits, Xerox tended to see its main competitors as domestic firms like IBM and Kodak, who were going after the lucrative high end of the market, and not the Japanese with their funny little low-end machines. As one Xerox executive told Jacobson and Hillkirk, "It was a question of whether you concentrate on the potential elephants or the mosquitoes that were running around . . . We focussed on the elephants."[11] The company also had to endure what could only be described as harassment by the Federal Trade Commission, who at one point even tried to force Xerox to divest itself of its foreign partners, Rank Xerox in Europe and Fuji Xerox in Japan. Such action would seem unlikely today.

A potentially more serious problem was Xerox's apparent inability to develop new products. The whole emphasis of Xerox's R&D was toward huge projects, involving thousands of people, all aimed at producing the biggest, fastest, and most sophisticated of machines – a disease sometimes described as "creeping elegance." But time and again, these megaprojects simply led nowhere or the new products got pulled back for further revision close to launch. There was no solid "meat-and-potatoes" product to replace the aging 914. Instead, Xerox product planners and engineers were dreaming dreams of a more exotic kind. Most important of all, they completely failed to develop a low volume, low-end machine and by 1979 Xerox was forced to import low-end "boxes" from Japan. This proved to be fatal error because it allowed the Japanese to consolidate their technological and manufacturing supremacy in low-end machines and it gave Japanese companies a much smoother entry into the vast US market.

So Japan's strategy was, as Jacobson and Hillkirk put it, "marvelously fundamental: start at the low end of the market with a value-added product that's simpler and cheaper to build and use, and through volume production and strict attention to quality, build up the brand name and expertise to take over the industry."[12] It was here that Japanese manufacturing excellence became crucial in the battle for the photocopier market: because the Japanese were so far advanced in the 1970s in the theory and the practice of JIT, TQC, and other manufacturing techniques, US firms like Xerox were poleaxed. When Xerox management finally woke up to what was going on in about 1980, they discovered, for instance, that Japanese firms were selling copiers in the US for what it was costing Xerox to make them.

Once the Japanese had mastered the art of manufacturing highly competitive photocopiers, the only problem remaining was that of selling them in the sprawling American and European markets. Again, they tackled this problem with the customary confidence of a samurai warrior. One tactic was to supply "boxes" to US and European companies who put their own labels on them. For example, the little-known Ricoh offered to supply America's Savin and Nashua and West Germany's Kalle with state-of-the-art copiers. For a while, people like Savin's Paul Charlap did a roaring trade in this way, completely dominating the low end of the market with its 750 model – until one day Ricoh called him up and said (according to Charlap): "Ah, beginning six months from now, we decided to distribute in America. You go get yourself a different manufacturer. Bye!"[13] Ricoh refused to discuss the matter and they did the same thing to Nashua and Kalle soon after.

The other tactic was to take advantage of the greed of US dealers who didn't care whose "boxes" they sold as long as there was a good margin and perhaps something extra in it for them. Dealerships play a key role in the American distribution system and the Japanese invaders such as Sharp, Canon, and Ricoh soon won converts with their financial incentives, plentiful inventory, heavy spending on marketing, and their lavish parties at trade shows. None of this was illegal, of course, and it was quite open to US companies to tackle their marketing with such verve.

In 1980, Xerox underwent a kind of awakening. The Japanese message finally hit home. During that year, Canon overhauled

Xerox for the first time in new copier placements in the US market. Xerox was sick and dying fast. Something had to be done. The Japanese were moving ahead on productivity and quality. Canon was also moving upmarket with an aggressive marketing campaign aimed directly at Xerox's profitable niche. These developments finally precipitated a crisis at Xerox, with the result that a turnaround strategy was formulated under chairman David Kearns. After a decade of indecision, denial, and delay, Xerox was at last going to do something about the Japanese.

One by one, the problem areas were tackled. Management structures were reformed to eliminate layers of bureaucracy. "Excess" workers were laid off. New products were developed, especially the well-received 10 Series, which was launched in 1982. Xerox implemented a new system of "competitive benchmarking" – that is, tearing your competitor's products apart, to ensure that you are exhibiting *dantotsu*, or using "the best of the best." The user interface on Xerox machines was improved, while a "lean" production system was instituted at Xerox plants – as a result of the valuable lessons learned at the Fuji Xerox plants in Japan. Manufacturing costs and product defects decreased, while customer satisfaction increased.

Xerox even recaptured the lead in some segments of the medium-range copier market in the US and increased its share of the low end from 9 percent in 1984 to 15 percent in 1989. In that year, in recognition of its achievements, Xerox won one of the two Malcolm Baldrige National Quality Awards instituted by the US Congress. Even so, Xerox was still struggling in 1991 with an overall US market share of 18 percent and it was forced to fire 2,000 white-collar workers in a further bid to stay in sight of the Japanese.

The Fax Fiasco: Japan Banks on the Not-So-"Paperless" Office

Following Xerox's introduction of the first fax machine in 1964, American firms had the fax market to themselves. But Burroughs, Exxon Office Systems, and Harris/3M failed to make a go of it and they soon pulled out: Burroughs sold its fax business to Japan's Fujitsu, Harris/3M (now Lanier) stopped making faxes altogether, and Exxon sold out to Lanier. Xerox persisted – but only through its joint venture with Japan's Fuji.

While American companies were retreating from the fax market in the 1970s, Japanese companies like Sharp, Murata, Canon, and Ricoh worked on perfecting their fax technology. Although the first really commercial fax machine had only been introduced in 1971, Japanese companies, buoyed along by a thriving domestic market, boosted production of first-generation machines to about 70,000 units per annum. By 1980, the arrival of the Group 3 international standard opened up a new era for the fax machine: it meant that an A4 sheet of paper could now be transmitted to anywhere in the world in one minute. And with the introduction of second-generation, high-performance machines costing one tenth of the earlier models, demand for faxes in the early 1980s exploded: by 1985, Japanese manufacturers were producing over 1 million units per annum.

In Japan itself, by 1988, a total of 2.6 million fax machines were in use and some 59 percent of companies claimed to own one (58 percent also claimed to own a photocopier). Faxes succeeded because they were simple, speedy and they saved time. Businesses without a fax machine were threatened with extinction. By 1992, according to one estimate, there were as many as 6 million fax machines in Japanese offices. But it wasn't just commercial concerns that were using faxes: in homes, schools, and on farms faxing was becoming a way of life. "What's your fax number?" became part of daily dialog. As the office fax machine market reached saturation point, Japanese vendors like Sharp developed slender, compact models specifically for the home market. One Sharp campaign suggested that a fax could improve your social and love life. The slogan: "Say it by fax."

In Europe, sales of faxes doubled every year in the mid-1980s, while in the US fax sales leapt from just 56,000 in 1981 to 206,000 in 1986, 465,000 in 1987, and around 800,000 in 1988. In 1989, more than 1 million fax machines were sold in the US – boosting the installed base to about 3.4 million. As *Fortune* magazine enthused, faxes were now "the biggest thing since the pc."[14]

Unfortunately for America and Europe, this new boom industry is now completely dominated by Japanese companies, who supply nearly all the faxes sold worldwide. For a while in the mid-1980s, it looked as if the big battle would be between Japanese companies on the one hand and US and European companies who put their own labels on Japanese-made machines on the other. But the Japanese needn't have worried. By 1988, NEC was clear market leader in the UK, for example, while top seller in the US was Sharp (21 percent of the market), followed by Murata (15 percent), Canon (11 percent), and Ricoh (10 percent). Re-seller Pitney Bowes was in fifth place on 6 percent.

Japanese companies were outright winners in the fax business, first, because they had superior technology brought with them from the camera industry (Canon, Ricoh, Minolta, and Konica), from office machines (Matsushita, Sharp, Toshiba) and from telecommunications (NEC, Fujitsu, Oki). Second, because of the crowded conditions and limited office space in Japan, Japanese companies out of necessity worked harder at developing compact, portable, quiet, and multifunctional products.[15] Third – partly as a fortuitous consequence of this and partly as a business strategy – they again began by attacking the lower end of the market where US and European companies were most vulnerable. Once the low end, mass market had been safely captured, they were in a position to move upmarket to the more profitable high-end machines. The same game-plan had been played out in motorcycles, automobiles, semiconductors, and consumer electronics.

In the early days of the fax frenzy, Japanese manufacturers were also more than happy to supply American and European firms with key components and even complete products for re-selling under Western brand names. That way they could prevent potential competitors from developing their own production capability and there was always the possibility of restricting supplies if necessary at some time in the future.

This familiar strategem was to be adopted in the case of laser printers – but with very different results. Back in the early 1980s, the comparatively low-profile but steadily successful US company Hewlett-Packard decided that there was a huge potential market for inexpensive laser printers in the not-so-paperless office. Millions of pcs were being sold and users were demanding better quality printing than that provided by dot-matrix devices. Instead of developing its own printer "engine," the company decided to buy in a ready-made box of tricks from the Japanese company, Canon.

Ever since the debut of its LaserJet printer in 1984, Hewlett-Packard has completely dominated the US laser printer market. Even in 1991, the company still had a commanding 60 percent share, far ahead of US rivals IBM and Apple, each on 10 percent or less. The Japanese companies Panasonic, Okidata, and Epson each had a mere 2–3 percent of this $3.6 billion market. Hewlett-Packard may be congratulated on a great marketing success, but those citing laser printers as a great example of America's ability to fight back in IT should remember one thing: a Hewlett-Packard printer is basically a Canon.

Notes

1 Gary Jacobson and John Hillkirk, *Xerox, American Samurai* (Macmillan, New York, 1986), p. 56; see also David H. Brandin and Michael A. Harrison, *The Technology War: A Case for Competitiveness* (Wiley, New York, 1987), pp. 150–1.
2 Jacobson and Hillkirk, *Xerox, American Samurai.*
3 Michael E. Porter, *The Competitive Advantage of Nations* (Free Press, New York, 1990), pp. 385–6 and 394.
4 "The Global 500," *Fortune*, July 30, 1990, p. 80.
5 See, for example, David M. Gann, "Buildings for the Japanese information economy," *Futures*, June 1991.
6 Ronald Henkoff, "Make your office more productive," *Fortune*, February 25, 1991, p. 40; see also William Bowen, "The puny payoff from office computers," *Fortune*, May 26, 1986 and Catherine L. Harris, et al., "Office automation: making it pay off," *Business Week*, October 12, 1987 – both reprinted in Tom Forester (ed.), *Computers in the Human Context: Information Technology, Productivity and People* (Basil Blackwell, Oxford, UK and MIT Press, Cambridge, MA, 1989).
7 Paul A. Strassman, *The Business Value of Computers* (Information Economics Press, New Canaan, CT, 1990); Michael S. Scott Morton (ed.), *The Corporation of the 1990s: Information Technology and Organizational Transformation* (Oxford University Press, New York, 1991).
8 Brian T. Pentland, "Use and productivity in personal computing: an empirical test," in *Proceedings of the Tenth International Conference on Information Systems*, Boston, MA, 1989 (ACM, Baltimore, MD), pp. 211–22.
9 *Business Week*, February 6, 1989 and June 3, 1991.
10 Porter, *The Competitive Advantage of Nations*, pp. 403 and 415.

11 Jacobson and Hillkirk, *Xerox, American Samurai*, p. 71.
12 Jacobson and Hillkirk, *Xerox, American Samurai*, p. 105.
13 Quoted in Jacobson and Hillkirk, *Xerox, American Samurai*, p. 136.
14 Frederick H. Katayama, "Who's fueling the fax frenzy?" *Fortune*, October 23, 1989, pp. 95–7.
15 Porter, *The Competitive Advantage of Nations*, pp. 403 and 407.

7
Telecommunications: Switching to a High-Fiber Diet

Deregulation American and Japanese-Style – ISDN: Japan's Dash Down the Digital Superhighway – Optical Fiber: How Japan Denied the US the Fruits of Innovation – The Battle for the Global Telecoms Equipment Market – Targeting Future Phone Technologies

When the American regional telephone company US West recently wanted to offer a new service to people who call and get a busy signal, it had to ask Japan's NEC Corp. to supply the basic software. Not bad for a nation that supposedly can't write software and is widely thought to lag behind the US and Europe in telecommunications technology.[1]

Not many people realize that Japan is *already* No. 1 in production of telecoms equipment, having overhauled the US in the late 1980s. While America's share of total world production slumped from 48 percent to 34 percent between 1980 and 1989, Japan's share leapt from 28 percent to 41 percent. Japan now has three out of the top eight telecoms equipment suppliers in the world (NEC, Hitachi, and Fujitsu), while France (Alcatel), the USA (AT&T), Germany (Siemens), Canada (Northern Telecom), and Sweden (Ericsson) have just one each. Japan exports about seven times as much telecoms equipment to the US as it imports, giving it a trade surplus with the US of some $2 billion.[2] Japan's dominant phone company, Nippon Telegraph and Telephone (NTT) is the most valuable company in the world, with a stock market valuation twice that of General Motors, IBM, and AT&T combined. Japan is also well advanced with plans to fully digitize its phone network, it has a world lead in fiber optics technology and is well placed to capitalize on the boom in mobile phones, satellite communications, and value-added network services (VANs).

With the second largest telecoms market in the world, Japan in the 1990s will be able to take full advantage of the fundamental economic and technology trends affecting the global telecoms industry. Japanese corporations have access to patient capital and they have deep pockets. With one very large consumer and several large suppliers of telecoms equipment, Japan will be better able to withstand the twin pressures of rising R&D costs caused by rapid technological advance and falling prices caused by increased international competition. With their manufacturing expertise and a world lead in chips, certain types of switches, and in fiber optics, Japanese companies are poised to conquer as private branch exchanges (PBXs) and other telecoms hardware become commodity items – and future "smart" phones come to resemble computers, complete with LCD screens, keyboards, and other features borrowed from the world of consumer electronics.

In contrast, America's AT&T will struggle to find overseas markets and the US telecoms manufacturing industry will become progressively hollowed out: the share of the US telecoms market actually produced in American factories fell from 95 percent to 81 percent between 1979 and 1989 and seems set to fall further. While the post-deregulation US telephone service is beset by wrangles over who has done what to whom in the long-distance market and what AT&T, the regional "Baby Bells", and the cable TV companies are and are not allowed to do, deregulation Japan-style appears to be working more harmoniously. And while American academics and politicians argue over whether the US should build a fiber optic "National Information Highway" and if so who should pay for it, the Japanese have already decided to get every household, school, hospital, office, and factory wired up with broadband optical fiber at a cost of about $200 billion by the year 2015. By then, the Japanese government estimates that fully 30 percent of Japan's GDP will come from services made possible by the new telecoms infrastructure.

Although millions of words have been written in recent years about computers and the computer revolution, the traditional phone network is undergoing a less well-publicized but equally far-reaching technological transformation which will have a huge impact on society. The largely unseen and unknown fiber optic cable is every bit as important as the mighty microchip. With the arrival of ISDN (the Integrated Services Digital Network), the old analog phone network which was built to carry the human voice is being rapidly replaced by a high-speed, high-capacity system which can carry all manner of digital data – including text, facsimile, and video pictures. The new telecoms infrastructure now being built has been likened to the construction of the railroads or the highway network.[3] The intelligent use of telecoms will create new businesses and new competitive advantage for existing businesses. Sometime in the next century, we will have in place a worldwide digital superhighway which will truly herald the Information Age and make Marshall McLuhan's "global village" a reality.

Deregulation American and Japanese-Style

The key event in the recent history of telecommunications – and arguably the biggest thing to happen in the telecoms industry since the invention of the telephone in 1876 – was the divestiture of American Telephone and Telegraph's long-standing monopoly over the US telephone network, announced on January 8, 1982, and implemented on January 1, 1984. The breaking-up of AT&T – or "Ma Bell," as it was called – into one smaller company and seven regional operating companies was by far the most important example of "deregulation" in the USA and it sparked a wave of "liberalization" and "privatization" throughout the Western world, including Europe, Japan, Canada, Australia, and New Zealand.

Deregulation led to increased competition, and this in turn has led to the internationalization of the telecoms industry, now worth over $100 billion a year and expected to be worth $200 billion by the end of the decade. New and surprising alliances between companies and countries have been formed. Telecoms companies have had to get into computers and computing companies have had to develop telecoms capabilities. The old publicly owned PTT (post, telegraph, and telephone) monopolies have mostly been bust apart. This major upheaval in an industry whose frontiers had been fixed for decades has stimulated rapid growth, dramatic technological advances and a whole variety of new services. But it has also brought with it headaches for governments as they struggle to develop appropriate telecommunications policies for the 1990s and the twenty-first century.

History records that it was Alexander Graham Bell who first demonstrated his "harmonic telegraph" on March 10, 1876. But it was Theodore N. Vail who built up AT&T's Bell System between 1878 and 1887 in the crucial years before Bell's last patent ran out in 1894. For very nearly the next 20 years, AT&T fought hard in the marketplace as competitors tried to get in on the act. But AT&T, bolstered by Vail's return to the helm after two decades in 1907, not only won out against the independents, but defeated nationalization proposals as well. State-owned postal PTTs were being formed all over the world. There was a widespread consensus that, because of the economies of scale involved in planning and operating a public network, considerations of efficiency made the telecommunications industry a "natural" monopoly to be entrusted to a single, publicly owned carrier. This enabled the PTTs to introduce pricing structures and cross-subsidization practices based on social criteria rather than strictly commercial ones.

On December 19, 1913, the US government settled the American argument when AT&T agreed to submit itself to tight government regulation in return for a *private* monopoly over the US telephone network. That monopoly remained wholly intact until 1968 and mostly intact until January 1, 1984. In the interim years, AT&T grew into a corporate colossus: in 1929, for example, it became the first US company to generate revenues of $1 billion. By 1983, it had revenues of $65 billion. It also had 84 million customers, 3.2 million shareholders, and nearly 1 million employees. Thus for around seven decades, the US telephone system was quietly run as a public service by a private company – a company that was regulated, but was basically untroubled by competition. Overseas the set-up was similar, although these state-owned PTTs usually inhabited an even more sleepy and cozy world in which monopoly suppliers of telecoms equipment grew fat and lazy on regular orders and guaranteed profit margins.

Yet underneath this apparently serene surface, technology-driven forces were shaping a major realignment of the telecoms business. Changing technology, in the form of microelectronics, fiber optics, cellular radio, and microwave communications, was creating new products and new services as computers and telecommunications converged. Aware of the growing demand for data transmission, AT&T itself needed to get into computing, while computer firms like IBM were demanding the right to participate in the telecoms revolution. It was increasingly apparent to everyone that the old PTT-style monopolies were no longer appropriate to the modern world.

By the late 1960s, the liberalization of US telecoms was underway. In a pioneering decision, the Federal Communications Commission (FCC) in 1968 allowed a Texas company to sell its Carterfone, a non-AT&T device which connected mobile radios to AT&T's own lines. More significant still, in 1969 the MCI Communications Corporation won the right to connect its own long-distance network to AT&T's local phone network. Even so, by the end of the 1960s AT&T still controlled over 90 percent of the US telephone service. Finally, on November 20, 1974, the US Justice Department filed an antitrust suit against AT&T, with the immediate purpose of breaking off Western Electric, the company's manufacturing division, from the rest of AT&T.

The suit dragged on and on. The first judge on the case died, there were lengthy pre-trial hearings, and it wasn't until January 1981 that the actual trial began. Even as the trial got underway, there was a growing feeling among AT&T and government officials that the time had come to settle the case. Accordingly, on January 8, 1982, the world was stunned by the announcement that AT&T had agreed to be split up. Thus, on January 1, 1984, the "new" AT&T came into being, together with seven newly independent regional operating companies or "Baby Bells." The new AT&T was far smaller than the old AT&T and was made up of five parts: a long-distance phone-service division; Western Electric, a telephone equipment manufacturer; Bell Labs, the famous research and development facility; an equipment and services marketing division; and AT&T International, which would sell AT&T goods and services overseas.

Divestiture day did not settle things for good. There was soon a plethora of lawsuits as the "Baby Bells" tried to expand outside their territory and AT&T tried to become a local operating company again. The Baby Bells were already branching out into everything from computer retailing and cellular radio to directory publishing and even real-estate development – but they were *not* free to sell information services or long-distance services or to manufacture telecoms equipment, according to the terms of the divestiture judgment. In 1985, the FCC gave AT&T permission to market office automation and computer services, while in 1986 Judge Greene gave Pacific Telesis permission to operate outside its area – by allowing it to purchase a Dallas-based provider of paging and mobile phone services. But he stopped Bell Atlantic from undertaking a similar expansion on the grounds that they hadn't asked permission first!

AT&T's monopoly of the long-distance market had been under minor attack for 15 years prior to deregulation by the independent networks. Their origins went back to the immediate postwar period, when some companies had experimented with their own microwave radio networks. But it was not until the late 1960s that the FCC gave them permission to operate public systems. MCI, led by Bill McGowan, was the pioneer of alternative long-distance networks, while GTE Sprint began with cables run along the Southern Pacific Railroad. The new networks achieved rapid growth after the re-sale of circuits became legal in 1978. Allnet, United Telecom, Western Union, RCA, and ITT among others began offering long-distance and international satellite services.

From divestiture day on, an all-out battle for long-distance traffic developed between the alternative carriers and AT&T. In the divestiture agreement, Judge Greene ruled that local phone companies had to provide "equal access" for customers to the alternative networks by September 1, 1986. Individual subscribers would be able freely to elect a long-distance carrier as the new system was phased in. After September 1, subscribers wishing to change their carrier would have to go through a complicated procedure and pay a fee. But it was also agreed that the 55 percent discount on local connections enjoyed by the alternative carriers would also be phased out: they would eventually have to pay the same as AT&T. In order to meet the new competition, AT&T made progressive cuts in its long-distance rates so that by mid-1986 they were 19 percent lower than they had been on divestiture day.

AT&T went into the great long-distance telephone election with nearly 90 percent of the market and came out with less than 80 percent. MCI achieved a large enough market share to remain viable, but GTE Sprint and United Telecom were forced to merge in order to survive (forming US Sprint). MCI and US Sprint both sustained huge losses in 1987 as they struggled with rising costs and technical problems. But by the end of the decade things were looking up for them: AT&T's share of the long-distance market slipped even further to 68 percent, with MCI taking 12 percent and US Sprint 8 percent. The very rapid growth in long-distance traffic – spurred by further price cuts of about 10 percent a year – transformed the bottom line for MCI and US Sprint, who were now suddenly flush with cash. When MCI swallowed up the fourth-placed Telecom USA in 1990, industry observers concluded that the long-distance market looked more than ever like a three-horse race.

So has US deregulation worked? The answer depends upon who you ask. By and large, business customers are happy with cheaper long-distance calls (down in total by about 50 percent) and the new services on offer, while residential customers are unhappy with increased charges (up about 40 percent) and a lower level of service. Drawbacks for all include the loss of one-stop telephone service, higher charges for equipment installation and confusion over telephone bills and the various new "options" available. On the plus side, it is claimed that competition has led to the faster introduction of new technologies and services and lower equipment costs for the phone companies. This, it is claimed, will enable US companies to be more competitive in overseas markets.

Whilst AT&T held the No. 2 position in the world market for telecoms equipment in 1990 with a 13 percent share, the American giant's performance has been criticized in recent years. Rather like IBM, AT&T is said to be bureaucratic and slow at turning the fruits of its Bell Labs research into commercial products. The company that invented the transistor has a poor record in computers: successive acquisitions and joint ventures have so far failed to improve AT&T's showing. Earlier joint ventures with Philips and Olivetti led nowhere, while it remains to be seen whether the recent takeovers of Paradyne, Istel, and NCR will make a difference. In view of its size and the strength of its domestic market, AT&T has also made slow progress in its efforts to go global, in comparison with firms like Ericsson and Northern Telecom. Overseas income is still less than 20 percent of AT&T's total revenues.[4]

Should there be more deregulation? Debate about the exact role to be played by the Baby Bells has continued in the 1990s. Usually, either Judge Greene or the FCC have been called upon to adjudicate on such matters as: whether the Baby Bells should be allowed to buy computer stores (it was OK); whether the Baby Bells would have to set up separate subsidiaries to offer computer services (no); whether the Baby Bells should be allowed to manufacture and sell telephone equipment (yes overseas, but not in the USA); whether the Baby Bells could offer cellular telephone and paging services (the Federal Appeals Court, over-ruling Judge Greene, said yes); and whether the Baby Bells would be allowed to compete in the long-distance market (not yet).

The Baby Bells launched a concerted "Free-the-Bells" campaign in 1990 – mainly using the international competitiveness argument – and started lobbying in Washington for oversight of their activities to be removed from the redoubtable Judge Greene and placed entirely in the hands of Congress and the FCC. The campaign achieved a major success in 1991 when the US Supreme Court ruled that the Baby Bells could offer cable TV services (confirmed by the FCC in 1992) and Judge Greene himself gave them permission to provide information services over their phone networks. But the prospect of deregulated Baby Bells enjoying a monopolistic position in their own region has alarmed many industry observers and the Free-the-Bells campaign ran into considerable opposition from consumer groups, cable TV companies, newspaper publishers, and the long-distance carriers.

For their part, the Baby Bells claim they are losing revenue because many companies are now "bypassing" their local phone network by installing their own satellite-based systems. Since a very high proportion of their business comes from just a few big customers, metropolitan Bells are extremely worried about the growth of "bypassing". The Port Authority of New York and Merrill Lynch, for example, have built a giant $84 million Teleport on Staten Island. Its dishes and cables can carry 38.8 billion bits of data per second – or 300,000 simultaneous phone calls – into Manhattan and right up Wall Street. More than 20 other teleports are planned for US cities. The Baby Bells also say they face further threats from the fiber optic networks planned by the cable TV companies and the mooted wireless phone networks or PCNs – like that announced by MCI in November 1992 – which will allow people to make calls without using the conventional phone network.[5]

Deregulation in the USA has been accompanied by deregulation overseas. In 1982, the British government gave permission to Mercury Communications to set up an alternative network to British Telecom (BT) using fiber optic cables run along British Rail lines. It also announced the proposed sale of BT to private investors – the sale was accomplished in November 1984. During 1985–6, steps had to be taken by the government watchdog Oftel to safeguard competition by bolstering Mercury's position and reducing BT's dominance. On May 15, 1986, Mercury started its alternative phone service – in the first instance, for business customers only. But by early 1987 there was already concern that the performance of BT had not been transformed by the change of ownership. Customer surveys by Oftel indicated similar levels of dissatisfaction with BT as existed prior to privatization. Amid a barrage of criticism, the chairman of BT, Sir George Jefferson, resigned.

In the period 1988–9, Oftel took a number of steps to increase competition and to introduce new services. The mobile phone market, for instance, was thrown open to four new players offering "Telepoint" services, which allowed people to make calls by standing within 150 yards of a base station. Six satellite operators in addition to Mercury and BT were licensed to offer satellite services. And, in a very significant move, the Post Office was allowed to resell surplus capacity on BT lines running between its offices dotted all over the country. BR Telecommunications, which manages British Rail's extensive private network running alongside its railway tracks, was also pushing for the right to sell space on its lines. By November 1990, when the first major review of British telecommunications since the licensing of Mercury in 1982 began, there was a growing feeling that a third or even a fourth major player might be needed to shake up what some were already seeing as a cozy duopoly of BT and Mercury.

Meanwhile in Japan, Nippon Telegraph and Telephone (NTT) – modeled on AT&T when it was founded in 1952 – has been privatized and a measure of competition in the telecoms market has been introduced. The initial plan, conceived by NTT chairman Mr Hisashi Shinto in 1982, was for NTT to be split up into one central company and five regional companies along the lines of the AT&T divestiture. However, after studying the plans for British Telecom, Shinto and the Japanese government decided simply to privatize NTT and allow competition to spread inwards from the boundaries. But unlike Britain, more than one competitor would be licensed.

NTT became a private company on April 1, 1985 and in 1986 the Japanese government began to sell 50 percent of its shares in stages. With over 50 million customer lines, NTT is the most valuable company in the world. It has so much buying power in Japan that it can dictate the development of the Japanese microchip and fiber optics industries.[6] NTT also has considerable political influence: chairman Hisashi Shinto, for instance, had very close links with Japan's ruling Liberal Democratic Party. Unfortunately for him, when the Recruit Cosmos stock and influence-peddling scandal broke he was forced to resign. The scandal ultimately brought down premier Takeshita. In 1990, Shinto was jailed for two years and fined about $150,000.

During the late 1980s, a lively battle had developed between the newly formed independent carriers. For example, Japan Telecom, backed by Japan National Railways, was proposing to lay fiber optic cables alongside its tracks. Teleway Japan planned to lay cables alongside major highways, while Daini-Denden was to use microwave radio links. But the newcomers were only making very slow progress against NTT. In fact, together they had gained less than 0.5 percent of the long-distance market by the end of 1988. All were making financial losses, although Daini-Denden was nearly breaking even. The vast size of NTT ensured that it remained overwhelmingly dominant, assisted by its chain of shops, a huge advertising budget, and close links with leading Japanese companies. Moreover, customers wishing to use the service of a new carrier had to dial extra digits in order to get connected: there was no "equal access."

To some, all this suggested that deregulation Japanese-style had not worked because it had failed to produce the kind of cut-throat competition evident in the US and elsewhere. There were growing calls for NTT to be broken up along the lines of AT&T and further calls for drastic measures to be taken in order to ensure a more open telecoms market in Japan. In fact, two newcomers, IDC and ITJ, were licensed to provide international calls in competition with monopoly supplier and close NTT associate, KDD. But others, including MITI officials, argued that it would be foolish to undertake a 1980s-style break-up of NTT: the public policy pendulum in the 1990s was now swinging back toward big being beautiful again. A strong, highly profitable NTT would be better placed to push ahead with ISDN and to undertake the mammoth task of wiring the whole of Japan with fiber optic cable by 2015. It would also be in a stronger position to pick off the foreign competition at a time of its choosing.

ISDN: Japan's Dash Down the Digital Superhighway

The "convergence" of computers and telecommunications is occurring because telecoms systems are going digital. This means that all data transmission equipment will soon be talking the same language – the language of the *binary code*. In the binary code, a low-voltage pulse equals "1" while its absence equals "0". Each number is a "bit" of information and a stream of such numbers – a "bit stream" – can be transmitted over conventional copper wires or over modern fiber optic cables.

Existing phone systems – which some refer to as the POTS (Plain Old Telephone Service) – were built to carry the human voice and are therefore based on analog devices in which the message signal rises or falls in line with the original signal. But analog systems are slow, they have a low capacity and translation is required before data can be transmitted on the network. In fact, a vast array of devices and services has been developed in recent decades to make machine noises palatable to the network. For example, *modems* provide MOdulation and DEModulation of digital signals into analog signals suitable for the phone network; *multiplexers* of various kinds collect signals from more than one slow-speed device and send them over a cheaper high-speed line; *network processors* switch signals or concentrate them once they are in the network; and *packet-switching services* process digital signals into large chunks and send them quickly over rented telephone lines.

Digital exchanges have no need for such elaborate decoding equipment. Digital technology is fast, flexible, reliable – and is getting cheaper by the minute. Thus, digital exchanges are fast replacing electromechanical exchanges, just as word processors have largely replaced typewriters, fax machines are replacing surface mail, and electronic storage systems are replacing filing cabinets. High-speed, high-capacity fiber optic cable is replacing conventional copper co-axial cable. It is remarkable just how much data can be carried on the conventional analog network, which has seen great technological changes in the last two decades. But ultimately the real explosion in telecommunications will occur with the full realization of the Integrated Services Digital Network (ISDN).

The ISDN will be able to handle all kinds of services that can be transmitted in digital form – voice, text, data, facsimile, even moving pictures. In effect, the telephone will become a computer terminal communicating with a huge range of sophisticated devices and services. ISDN is fast: typically ISDN will send data at 6,400 characters per second, compared with 1,000 characters per second on the POTS. ISDN will make possible interactive banking and retail services, give access to a variety of general and specialist databases, and deliver information to your desktop terminal using new forms of electronic mail and electronic newspapers. ISDN will operate on a worldwide basis, and remote access will mean that it won't matter where your terminal is located – it could be in the car or on the beach. In theory, a US salesman in Australia, for example, could call up his boss in California and discuss a graph of Asian sales displayed on his portable terminal, which is based on data provided directly from the company's European headquarters in Brussels.

ISDN will not happen overnight. In most nations, it will evolve over the next decade or so as more and more exchanges and phone lines are converted to digital technology. A huge investment in new lines, new message switches, and translation devices will be required. But by 1992, France, Hong Kong, and Singapore were already claiming that 100 percent of their phone lines had ISDN capability and Japan was claiming 87 percent (compared with just 50 percent in the USA).[7] The Japanese plan to have the basics of their more ambitious and more sophisticated ISDN, called Information Network System (INS), in place by 1995 – although wiring up the entire nation with fiber optic cable will not be accomplished until 2015.

The idea of INS was first announced by Dr Yasusada Kitahara, executive vice-president of NTT, at an international telecommunications forum held in Geneva in 1979. Kitahara described INS as the "marriage" of computers and telecommunications, and said that the Japanese expected it to be *the* key infrastructure of what they called the "advanced information society" of the twenty-first century. In Japan, INS would link major cities and regional cities with the chain of "technopolises" envisaged under the Technopolis Plan. INS would enable Japanese society to save on time, space, and transport and energy costs. There were also strong political pressures for NTT to undertake the construction of an entirely new system, partly because it was felt that NTT had become bureaucratic and bloated (after doing sterling work rebuilding Japan's telephone system in the postwar years) and partly because MITI saw in INS an opportunity for Japan to dominate the world market for telecoms equipment.[8]

Accordingly, Mitaka, a Tokyo suburb, was chosen for an experiment with "telecommuting" or working from home in "satellite offices" on the prototype INS. Households were provided with special digital phones, video telephones, fax machines, videotex terminals, and other equipment like so-called "sketchphones," hooked up via digital exchanges and high-capacity optical fiber cables. The experiment cost about $80 million. Unfortunately things did not go as planned and the Mitaka experiment was not a great success: after an initial surge of enthusiasm, residents showed little interest in using on a regular basis most of the gadgetry provided.[9] This meant, among other things, that NTT could not rely on a surge in demand for new residential services to help pay for the huge investment in INS. The assumption that the new services would automatically become part of daily Japanese life proved to be incorrect. Even so, NTT pressed ahead with an ambitious research program to develop advanced INS computers and automatic translation telephones.

The Europeans, on the whole, have not announced such grand strategies as the Japanese, but France has been quick to undertake a much-needed modernization of its phone network and Britain, Belgium, Holland, Italy, Germany, Norway, Sweden, and Switzerland are steadily installing electronic digital systems. But there are still major incompatibilities between the systems adopted by the many European nations, despite a 1986 request from the EC Council of Ministers that they develop a common ISDN standard.

One development that was originally seen as aiding the achievement of ISDN was the rapid proliferation of *local area networks* (LANs). LANs are basically high-speed wires that link the mainframe to terminals in a building for the purpose of swapping information. People on the network often share add-ons such as storage disks and printers. The remarkable and somewhat unexpected rise of the personal computer gave "networking" a big boost and now it is one of the hottest areas in computing. There are over 50 different brands of net on the market. Most local networks are one of two kinds: "star" networks have a central control unit, usually a mainframe computer, with devices coming off it in a star-shaped configuration; "ring" or "bus" networks lack a central core, with the devices joined together in a circular or ring configuration.

Ironically, because so many sophisticated local and wide area private networks have come into existence in the past few years, some are now suggesting that ISDN may no longer be necessary. It is said that large corporate customers have already satisfied their communication needs and low-level users such as residential subscribers (as the Mitaka experiment showed) do not really need any of the new ISDN services. In this view, ISDN has thus come to stand for "Innovation Subscribers Don't Need" (or even: "I Smell Dollars Now"!). Many applications, such as electronic mail, small file transfer, and even graphics transmission will be no better served by ISDN and are quite adequately catered for on the existing POTS. Critics like the Cambridge, Massachusetts-based Electronic Frontier Foundation also claim that too much has been spent on ISDN marketing hype by major international suppliers, who are simply interested in selling more telecoms gear and services to the military, academia, and big business. It remains to be seen whether the critics are proved correct.

Optical Fiber: How Japan Denied the US the Fruits of Innovation

One of the new technologies transforming telecommunications – indeed by far the most important one – is a remarkable innovation, fiber optics. Although various Europeans and Americans including Alexander Graham Bell experimented with using light to transmit speech over a century ago, modern optical fiber technology dates from 1966, when two British engineers at Standard Telecommunications Laboratories in England, Charles Kao and George Hockham, first demonstrated its potential. However, it was the Corning Glass Works of Corning, upstate New York, that produced the first commercial version in 1970, and latterly it has been Japanese companies like Sumitomo that have exploited the invention most dramatically on world markets.

Optical fibers are tiny strands of pure glass no wider than a human hair that can carry thousands of telephone conversations or other digitized data in the form of extremely fast streams of light pulses. Many such strands can be bundled together into a cable, which is typically about one fifth of the size of a conventional copper cable. Light travels down the strands and is converted back into sound or whatever at the other end. There are basically three kinds of optical fibers: the simplest is "step-index" fiber, in which light zigzags down the central core, bouncing off the sides which are covered with reflective cladding; in "graded index" fiber, the glass in the core varies in density toward the edges, so the light travels in a smooth, curving path; and finally, in single or "monomode" fiber the core is very small in relation to the wavelength of transmitted light, which therefore travels very efficiently in almost a straight line.

Optical fibers have a number of advantages over conventional copper cable, which is costly, slow, and has a low capacity. Optical fibers have a much higher capacity – a single strand can carry literally thousands of simultaneous telephone conversations – and they are much faster. They are also becoming cheaper to produce because copper is more expensive than sand, the main ingredient of glass: in 1977 a meter of fiber cost $3.50; by 1985 it was down to 25 cents. Thus, optical fiber is quickly becoming the preferred medium for transmitting voice, data, and video, especially over long distances. Telecoms applications account for more than 60 percent of the optical fiber market. US sales of optical fiber leapt from $55 million in 1981 to $550 million in 1986, to $1 billion in 1989 and to nearly $3 billion in 1992.

Optical fibers are easier to handle because they are thinner and lighter and thus fit more easily into crowded underground ducts. They are also easier to use because fewer "repeaters" are required on the line to boost the signal, and the few that are needed can be installed in warm and dry telephone exchanges rather than damp holes in the ground. Optical fibers are free from the kind of electrical and environmental interference that plagues satellite communications and they offer greater security because they cannot easily be "tapped." They are particularly suitable for applications in defense, airplanes, and automobiles and for use in hazardous places, although recent British research has raised some doubts about their durability. But clearly, they have a lot going for them.[10]

The glass used in fiber optics has to be extremely pure. Two things can cause light to be lost and thus transmission impeded: "absorption" of light, which is caused by impurities in the glass as few as even one or two parts per million, and "scattering," which occurs when the light wave is deflected by even quite small changes in the density of the glass medium. The breakthrough at Corning in 1970 came with the demonstration that it was possible to produce very pure glass of uniform quality suitable for transmitting light over long distances. In the production process invented at Corning – known as "vapor deposition" – high-purity vapors of silicon and germanium are reacted by applying heat to produce layers of glass. The composition of the glass can be altered by changing the proportions of the ingredients to produce the different densities required for graded-index fibers. It is said that, if the oceans were as transparent as the glass in state-of-the-art optical fibers, it would be possible to see the bottom of the Mariana Trench from the surface of the Pacific – 32,177 ft down! Scientists believe that they will eventually be able to send a typical light pulse as far as 9,000 km. without it having to be recharged.

The process of transmission used in optical fibers is called pulse code modulation and is rather like a fancy version of Morse code. The light pulses are originated by laser diodes which are capable of millions of blinks per second. Repeaters boost the signal if necessary, and a photo-detector receives the signals and converts them back into their original form at the other end. Today, the fastest commercial lasers in use can pulse at around 2.5 billion times a second, enough to transmit 30,000 phone calls along a single optical fiber. In 1991, US researchers at Bell Labs demonstrated an experimental ultra-high-speed laser that could blink 350 billion times a second. That roughly means that it could transmit the entire contents of 350 *Encyclopedia Britannicas* every second! Sending the same amount of information over a conventional telephone line would take weeks.

Japan's thrust into fiber optics began in 1970, as soon as the breakthroughs at Corning Glass became known. As Clyde V. Prestowitz explains, while Corning swiftly obtained patents on its new process in the USA, patents in Japan were not issued for more than 10 years. In the 1970s, Corning had a huge competitive advantage in optical-fiber production, but when it tried to sell its cable in Japan to monopoly buyer NTT, Corning was told simply that the Japanese were developing their own version. Indeed, NTT had already formed a joint venture with the Japanese companies Furukawa, Sumitomo, and Fujikura, intending to share R&D costs and future profits. Corning then entered into endless negotiations with possible Japanese venture partners, supplying them with useful data and information, but ultimately this proved fruitless because NTT said flatly that it would not buy from consortiums involving foreigners.[11]

Under international pressure, especially from Washington, NTT finally signed an agreement in 1979 to open its procurement process to foreign bidders. Encouraged by this, Corning formed a joint venture with Germany's Siemens called Siecor with a view to selling in Japan. Siecor claimed to have a superior product available at a third of the price NTT was paying its own suppliers. But according to Prestowitz, NTT would not accept bids from suppliers whose products did not conform to precise Japanese specifications: when asked to provide a copy of the specifications, they stalled. It was only after months of inter-governmental haggling that the specifications were finally made available. Even this was not enough, because NTT then insisted in effect that Siecor build a new factory in order to produce the Japanese design – but offered no guarantee of market share if they did. At times it seemed that Siecor was not trying hard enough, but there was little doubt that NTT was determined to deny Siecor any Japanese business – and thus deny Corning the full fruits of its innovation.

By the mid-1980s, the battle was effectively over. Japanese companies had come up with an improved version of Corning's vapor deposition process and had developed a new technique which made possible the mass production of optical fiber: tens of kilometers of thin filament could now be drawn from one hot glass rod, compared with 5 km. using first-generation technology. Even more disturbing, Sumitomo, Furukawa, and Fujikura had built enough capacity to supply the Japanese market three times over: pretty soon, they were dumping optical fiber in the US and Canadian markets at well below market price. Corning filed suit against Sumitomo for patent infringement and began the laborious march through the American courts: Corning eventually won a modest victory in December 1989, when Sumitomo were forced to pay Corning $25 million in compensation.

But by then it was too late for Corning to reap the rewards of its earlier risk-taking. Japanese industrial policy had systematically denied Corning access to the large Japanese market, it had reduced the risk for local entrants into the optical fiber industry and it had generated domestic over-capacity leading to very aggressive overseas pricing. Meanwhile, as Prestowitz puts it, "the US government ignored its [optical fiber] industry. It assumed that the free play of the market would allow the best man to win. Although the Japanese market remained effectively closed while the US market was open, the US government took no action . . . The result was that Japan became a powerful competitor, and various US observers congratulated it for its diligence and foresight . . . Virtually every industry has had the same experience . . . Japanese policy since 1952 has been systematically to deny foreigners the profits of innovation."[12]

Worldwide progress with the installation of fiber optic cables is now very swift. In the USA, the three major long-distance carriers, AT&T, MCI, and US Sprint have their backbone networks linking major cities mostly in place. Production of cable and transmitters is rocketing, but even so it will be many years before all US households are supplied with optical fiber cable by the phone companies. The state of New Jersey in conjunction with Bell Atlantic recently decided to rewire the entire state by 2010, but the new challenge from cable TV companies may dissuade the regional phone companies from pressing ahead in many areas.

Meanwhile, work is proceeding on what will soon become a worldwide network of submarine fiber optic cables. Already transatlantic and transpacific links have been completed, while new branches of a much more extensive Pacific Rim network linking Australia, New Zealand, Guam, the Philippines, Taiwan, Hong Kong, China, Japan, Hawaii, Alaska, British Columbia, and California are planned or are being built. Submarine fiber optic technology is advancing so fast that each new section seems to have a much higher capacity and requires dramatically less amplifiers or repeaters than earlier sections.

While most EC countries are recording steady progress with the changeover to fiber optics, Japan appears to be racing ahead with its ambitious $200 billion plan to run fiber optic cable into every home by 2015. By 1990, more than 200 Japanese cities had been connected – admittedly with narrowband rather than broadband cable, which only has 50 times the capacity of conventional phone lines! However, it is often difficult to distinguish between the hype and the reality of such Japanese megaprojects and it is also clear that Japanese "wired city" experiments like Hi-Ovis and Mitaka have not been a great success.

The Battle for the Global Telecoms Equipment Market

The worldwide wave of deregulation of the old PTT monopolies over telephone services and the opening-up of telecoms equipment markets to competition in most countries has turned the formerly staid telecommunications business into a bloody, global battlefield. Once upon a time, each nation had its own favored suppliers of telecoms equipment. They enjoyed a cozy relationship with the old PTTs, from which they received a steady stream of orders. Now deregulation, technological revolution, and rapidly rising costs have forced traditional domestic suppliers to merge, to join cross-national partnerships, and to launch global marketing ventures. The world market for telecoms equipment passed the $100 billion mark in 1991 and is expected to reach $200 billion by 2000. A dozen or so "national champions," plus three Japanese conglomerates and scores of smaller suppliers, are currently battling it out for market share. But by the end of the decade, most analysts agree, there will be room for only about five or six global telecoms equipment suppliers.

Deregulation has given telecom consumers more choice, but for vendors of telecoms equipment the new competition has been a nightmare. Being forced to compete for the first time is one thing, but deregulation has also occurred just as the world's telephone systems are switching over from analog to digital technology. The upfront investment required by telecoms equipment manufacturers has been enormous: typically, the cost of putting a state-of-the-art digital telephone exchange into production is about five times what it cost to develop an analog exchange. The next generation of optical exchanges could cost twice as much again. Developing the software for the new digital switching systems has also proved to be very expensive. With no guaranteed customers anymore, the only way for suppliers to survive has been to share costs with their domestic or international counterparts.

Thus the last decade or so has seen a whole series of mergers and acquisitions in the telecoms supply business. For instance, France's Alcatel emerged out of a merger in France with CGE, who had earlier picked up what was left of ITT's European telecoms business. Alcatel also acquired both the telecoms division of the US firm Rockwell and the Italian company Telettra. Germany's Siemens picked up Rolm after IBM's period of ownership had proved to be a disaster. Siemens also formed a partnership with Britain's GEC to take over Britain's Plessey, which had earlier taken over America's Stromberg-Carlson. AT&T bought out the telecoms interests of the Dutch firm Philips, GTE's switch business, and Paradyne Corp., while Canada's Northern Telecom took over Britain's STC. Scores of other deals have been done with, for example, suppliers of cellular phone services and makers of cellular phone equipment. Some companies, including GTE, the once-powerful ITT and the once-fancied IBM are now out of telecoms equipment business altogether.

The US itself is the largest telecoms equipment market in the world. It has in recent years proved to be a happy hunting ground for foreign suppliers such as Canada's Northern Telecom, France's Alcatel, Germany's Siemens, Sweden's Ericsson, and Japan's NEC, Hitachi, and Fujitsu. Although US companies led by AT&T have been pushing into overseas markets as diverse as Mexico, the Netherlands, Italy, Indonesia, and South Korea, US exports have not been enough to offset US imports: as a result, America was running a telecoms equipment trade deficit of $2.5 billion a year at the end of the 1980s. Intense competition in the US market has reduced prices for customers such as the Baby Bells, but it has also put pressure on the profits of suppliers. It is most unlikely that all the suppliers currently in the US market will be around at the end of the decade.

Despite deregulation, the fast-growing European market has been a tough nut to crack for North American and Japanese telecoms equipment suppliers. Basically, of the large markets, Britain is tied up by Siemens-GEC-Plessey and Ericsson, Germany by Siemens and Alcatel, and France by Alcatel and Ericsson. But AT&T sells to the Netherlands and in the late 1980s AT&T won a hard-fought battle to supply Italy's Italtel with new equipment. Northern Telecom has picked up useful sales in Britain and elsewhere. Scandinavia is dominated by Ericsson and Nokia. Siemens and Alcatel look well placed to win the business of rewiring Eastern Europe and the states that comprise the former Soviet Union – although creative financing arrangements will be required. Japanese suppliers seem to be looking more at Asia.

Despite the occasional gestures to placate international opinion, the huge Japanese market remains largely closed to foreign competitors. Back in the late 1970s, the head of NTT confidently forecast that the only things foreign companies could sell his company would be "mops and telephone poles." But under intense international pressure – mainly from the US government – the Japanese government in 1985 moved to liberalize the sale of telecoms equipment. For a while, it looked like sales by American and European suppliers would surge. But the big Japanese manufacturers continued to pressure NTT to buy Japanese and Japan's powerful Ministry of Posts and Telecommunications began to quietly close the door on foreign companies. By 1990, only 6 percent of NTT's capital budget was spent on foreign equipment: most of it was sophisticated American and Canadian switching gear and switching software not yet developed in Japan.

But America's Motorola persisted with its plans to provide one of two proposed cellular phone networks which the Japanese government said it would license to compete with NTT's own nationwide cellular network. The only problem was that NTT's two competitors would only get half the country each – and Motorola was awarded the half that did not include Tokyo. Thus a Motorola customer visiting Tokyo would not be able to make or receive calls. Motorola then asked to use a spare sliver of the Tokyo radio spectrum and was told by NTT – who just happened to control spectrum allocation in Tokyo – that none was free. Motorola knew that there was plenty of space and began a long campaign for fair treatment. It was only after the US government's trade representative Carla Hills intervened to threaten an all-out trade war that the Japanese finally relented.[13]

Targeting Future Phone Technologies

Japan has been quick to adopt and adapt the telecommunications technologies of the future. Take cellular or mobile phones, for example: whilst in America, AT&T first proposed a cellular system as early as 1971, the license to run a trial in Chicago was not granted by the FCC until 1977. The trial was an instant success, but because of legal and regulatory wrangles, AT&T's Chicago system was not able to go commercial until October 1983. Other major US cities obtained cellular networks in rapid succession in 1984, but meantime NTT in Japan had put in place an extensive cellular network, with 300 systems serving all of Japan's major cities. Likewise, the Scandinavians had pioneered cellular phones in Europe when Ericsson's NMT system went commercial in 1982. But Britain's two competing systems did not get started until January 1985 and most of the rest of Europe followed along behind.

Even so, mobile phones have proved to be one of the great boom industries of the late 1980s and early 1990s. Some 4.4 million units were sold worldwide in 1991. In the US, the total number of subscribers leapt from 1 million in 1987, to over 3 million in 1989, to 5 million in 1990, and to 7.4 million in 1991. Lucky winners of the FCC lotteries held to award local cellular franchises became millionaires overnight and sales of mobile phones, assisted by plunging prices, leapt month upon month. In the late 1980s, the huge, lucrative US market was largely shared by three companies: America's Motorola – and Japan's NEC and Mitsubishi. Meanwhile in Europe, sales of mobile phones also took off, with the two UK networks alone signing up 1 million subscribers by 1990.

However, a cheaper alternative to the regular cellular network, known as CT2 or Telepoint, flopped badly. The British government licensed no less than four competing Telepoint systems, which enabled users to make but not to receive calls within range of a local station. All four services folded in 1991. But another new type of service, called PCN (for Personal Communications Network) or "Rabbit" might prove more successful.

In the global cellular phone market, Motorola is battling it out with its Japanese rivals and Sweden's Ericsson. Ericsson has teamed up with other European companies like Siemens, Alcatel, and Philips to first develop a European-wide cellular network and then go global with its GSM or Global System for Mobile communications by the year 2000. This will enable anyone, anywhere to make and receive mobile calls anywhere in the world. Australia has already indicated that it will adopt the GSM standard. Obviously, success for GSM will strengthen the hands of European manufacturers like Ericsson. But meanwhile America's Motorola has announced ambitious plans to create its own worldwide mobile phone network linked to 77 satellites called Iridium. Motorola says that Iridium (like GSM) will be all digital and will be in place by the mid-1990s.

Satellite communications has been another boom industry in recent years. By the late 1980s, no less than 3,300 satellites had been launched into orbit, with related revenues amounting to more than $10 billion a year.[14] In recognition of this, the Japanese government has sought to give Japan a capability in rocket launching and to develop a new generation of Japanese communication satellites which do not depend on US technology. Accordingly, Japan hopes to have its H-2 launch vehicle perfected soon: this will offer stiff competition for America's Titan rockets and Europe's Ariane system. As for direct broadcasting by satellite (or DBS), the Japanese launched their first DBS satellite in early 1984, just as US and European services were getting underway. DBS has experienced somewhat mixed fortunes in Europe and the US, but Japan, with so many outlying islands and mountainous regions, has a special interest in developing DBS services.

The Japanese have also taken to videoconferencing, voice-mail, and VANS (Value-Added Network Services) in a big way. Videoconferencing (or teleconferencing as it was earlier called) has been slow to take off in the US and Europe, where businessmen seem to prefer their business travel. But in Japanese companies, where daily conferences are a way of life, videoconferencing has been eagerly taken up by overworked executives. NEC, Fujitsu, Mitsubishi, and NTT are all marketing advanced videoconferencing systems. Despite some opposition, voice-mail or voice-messaging systems have proved popular in the West since their introduction in 1980. But their installation has been patchy and usually has been the result of individual company initiative. In Japan, voice-messaging is offered over the public phone network. As early as late 1986, for example, NTT in Tokyo overnight gave every phone a voice-mail capability. About the same time, Japan started going crazy over VANS, particularly those developed to link manufacturers and suppliers in JIT (Just-In-Time) delivery systems. Market leaders NEC and Fujitsu saw VANS as a way of beating IBM in the pc market.

Perhaps Japan's greatest competitive challenge is likely to come in the supply of the next generation of "smart" phones which will resemble computer terminals and borrow many features from the world of consumer electronics – which, of course, Japan already dominates. With their miniaturized manufacturing expertise and control of key technologies like LCD screens, Japanese office-equipment companies like Sharp and consumer electronics companies like Toshiba will be the first to market phones which double as answering machines, personal organizers, computer terminals, and TVs. With the coming of broadband fiber optic networks, smart telephones of the future will be able to receive, transmit, and manipulate all manner of digital data. Whilst stand-alone video telephones have not proved very popular with consumers in either America, Europe, or Asia, the experience gained by Mitsubishi, Matsushita, and Sony in the production and marketing of video telephones will be invaluable as "multimedia" devices become standard.

Notes

1 *Business Week*, October 7, 1991.
2 *Fortune*, March 9, 1992.
3 See, for example, Frederick Williams, *The New Telecommunications: Infrastructure for the Information Age* (Free Press, New York, 1991); John Pierce and A. Michael Noll, *Signals: The Science of Telecommunications* (Scientific American Library, New York, 1990).
4 *Fortune*, June 19, 1989; *Time*, December 17, 1990; *Business Week*, January 20, 1992.
5 Reports in *Business Week*, March 12, 1990, March 25, 1991, April 29, 1991, and July 15, 1991.
6 *Fortune*, October, 10, 1988.
7 *Fortune*, March 9, 1992; UPI report on a University of Southern California study in *The Australian*, January 11, 1993.
8 Ian Mackintosh, *Sunrise Europe: The Dynamics of Information Technology* (Basil Blackwell, Oxford, UK, 1986), pp. 57–9; Sheridan Tatsuno, *The Technopolis Strategy: Japan, High Technology and the Control of the 21st Century* (Brady/Prentice-Hall Press, New York, 1986), pp. 52–7; Sheridan Tatsuno, *Created in Japan: From Imitators to World Class Innovators* (Harper & Row, New York, 1990), pp. 178–81.
9 Robert Chapman Wood, "NTT squanders a lead," *High Technology Business*, May 1988, p. 15.
10 Jeff Hecht, *Understanding Fiber Optics* (Sams & Co., Indianapolis, 1987); C. David Chaffee, *The Rewiring of America* (Academic Press, San Diego, CA, 1988).
11 Clyde V. Prestowitz, *Trading Places: How We Allowed Japan to Take the Lead* (Basic Books, New York, 1988), pp. 131–4.
12 Prestowitz, *Trading Places*, p. 134.
13 *Fortune*, November 4, 1991, p. 74.
14 Heather E. Hudson, *Communication Satellites: Their Development and Impact* (Free Press, New York, 1990).

8
Japan, the US, and Europe: The Winner and the Losers

How Japan Won the IT Industry – Why the US Lost – What's Wrong with Europe? – Winning the 1990s: What Will Japan Do Next?

We have seen how Japan has effectively become No. 1 in consumer electronics, semiconductors, manufacturing technology, office equipment, and telecommunications. Only in computers and software per se are the Japanese not yet dominant – but this may only be a matter of time, given Japan's growing stranglehold over key computer components and the merging of computers with consumer electronics, telecommunications, and office equipment.

In each sector of the IT industry, the Japanese have followed the same general pattern of conquest, with minor variations. In each sector, Japan's "catch-up" and "take-lead" strategies have gone more or less according to plan. Success has sometimes come fairly slowly and sometimes quite fast: for example, it took Japanese companies about two decades to patiently build a leading position in TV production, whilst the battle for the market leadership in microchips was all over in barely five years. Sometimes a particular Japanese onslaught was anticipated, but more often than not the West was completely taken by surprise by the sudden arrival, for example, of superior Japanese robots or new ranges of highly competitive Japanese faxes and photocopiers. Despite the warnings of some commentators, it has been more usual for American and European industrialists and politicians to seriously underestimate rather than exaggerate the competitive threat posed by Japanese companies.

In this concluding chapter, we review the reasons why the

Japanese have won the battle for the global IT industry, why the US and Europe lost ground so spectacularly, and what the future might hold for all concerned: who will win the 1990s and in particular, what will Japan do next?

How Japan Won the IT Industry

Japan is now No. 1 in information technology because it has adopted more appropriate industrial, trade, and technology policies; because of its industrial and financial structure; because of its emphasis on manufacturing excellence; and because of the nature and values of Japanese society.

Japan's policy toward the IT industry has been characterized by close government–industry collaboration and the targeting of markets and technologies by MITI. MITI has successfully nurtured "infant" IT industries, providing subsidies and protection until they were strong enough to stand on their own two feet. As Chalmers Johnson explained in his famous study, *MITI and the Japanese Miracle* (1982), typically MITI officials would target a particular market or technology. They would then analyze the opportunities in detail; develop business strategies based on consensus-building among the major players (who were often chosen by MITI); provide funds for research; and offer "administrative guidance" to companies about what products to produce, what overseas markets to enter, and even what size to grow to. In other words, MITI was both the pilot and the engineer of Japanese economic growth.[1]

Subsequent authors claimed that Johnson had over-estimated the role of MITI in Japan's postwar success story. They argued that laissez-faire economic policies and a highly competitive domestic market rather than central planning had been more significant factors. For example, Sheridan Tatsuno attacked the "myth" of Japan Inc., showing that MITI had gone through five very different phases since its formation in 1949. Tatsuno argued that Western perceptions were still stuck in the 1960s, when MITI was much more important, and that this had led to "exaggerations" of MITI's power.[2] Michael E. Porter also chose to highlight the declining role of MITI planning in recent years and to emphasize the role of

MITI in encouraging domestic competition. Rather than MITI planning, it was fierce domestic rivalry and a saturated domestic market which led to the massive Japanese export pushes, said Porter. Competition, dynamism, and continuous innovation were the real keys to Japanese success.[3]

Nevertheless, government indicative planning via MITI still appears to play a much greater role in Japan than it does in either America or Europe. In his recent study of MITI, Daniel Okimoto shows that while MITI has not been a great spender of money, it has played an absolutely crucial role as an adviser, an information provider, a consensus-builder, a target-setter, and a lobbyist on behalf of Japanese firms.[4] Fred Warshofsky, in his book on the battle for the microchip market, also describes how MITI orchestrated the highly successful VLSI (Very Large Scale Integration) "catch-up" program in great detail – even to the extent of deciding which Japanese companies would be allowed to participate in the burgeoning semiconductor industry. Here, the term "administrative guidance" seemed to have a very broad meaning.[5]

Moreover, Tatsuno himself provides an account of how, in the early 1980s, MITI targeted 14 high-tech industries for rapid development, providing direct loans, subsidies, and trade protection – not bad for a "lion without teeth" (Tatsuno's earlier description of MITI). In addition, MITI has in recent years announced 10-year plans to develop next-generation computing technologies such as neural networks, optical processing, and molecular computing. MITI is also encouraging Japanese companies to investigate more speculative areas like nanotechnology. As usual, MITI is offering generous loans and subsidies to companies wishing to participate in relevant research projects and is providing the entire gamut of MITI "guidance." Nothing on this scale occurs in either the US or Europe.

Japan's trade policies have been based on protectionism at home – that is, keeping foreigners out of its large domestic market – and supporting free trade abroad – that is, taking full advantage of more open markets like the US and Europe. As Clyde V. Prestowitz explains it, the basic strategy in IT has really been quite simple: in an industry where the first firm down the learning curve is more likely to dominate a new technology, a closed domestic market can provide a critical competitive advantage. The big markets for IT goods are America, Japan, and Europe – in that order. If US firms can sell and achieve volume in the American and European markets – but not in Japan – while Japanese firms can achieve volume in all three markets, then the eventual triumph of Japanese companies is highly likely. On a wider scale, says Prestowitz, if America sticks with laissez-faire and Japan continues with the same set of trade, industry, and technology policies in place, the economic dominance of Japan is a foregone conclusion.[6]

Despite years of talks, successive trade agreements, and renewed pressure – mainly from Washington – the Japanese IT market remains a very difficult one for Americans and Europeans to crack. Foreigners still only had 14.6 percent of the Japanese chip market in early 1992, despite the 1986 US–Japan chip accord which was designed to give foreign firms a 20 percent market share. In recent years US manufacturers have found it almost impossible to sell supercomputers in Japan and the Japanese have refused to buy American optical fiber and telecoms equipment, even when offered a superior product. In most cases, the Japanese have stalled on buying foreign IT goods altogether or have purchased only minimal quantities, whilst waiting for the Japanese technology to "catch-up" and for Japanese production to come on stream. In reply to critics, the Japanese are fond of claiming that foreigners "do not try hard enough" to sell in Japan. This may well be true in many instances, but there is now enough evidence from the IT sector to show that a complex web of formal and informal rules have worked to keep foreign IT companies out of Japan – or at least to severely limit their market share.[7]

Japan's unique approach to technology transfer and to R&D has enabled Japanese companies to systematically "catch-up" and then "take-lead" in most areas of IT. Once known as "copycats" and "imitators," the Japanese emerged in the 1980s to become world-class innovators, to borrow Tatsuno's phrase.[8] Among the "catch-up" or technology transfer techniques used by the Japanese have been the licensing of Western technology, the offering of "partnerships" or "joint ventures" to cash-starved Western companies possessing useful technology, the direct acquisition of Western companies (especially promising start-ups), the systematic scouring of Western universities, research institutions, and academic journals for technology secrets, and the less savory transfer of intellectual property back to Japan using more underhand industrial espionage techniques. Even the MITI-inspired "projects" have been as much about keeping the Japanese abreast of developments in the West as about doing original research in Japan.

The Japanese have a very different view of the R&D process, intellectual property, and the notion of creativity itself. The Japanese approach to R&D may be characterized as practical, pragmatic, and clearly focused on rapid commercialization. The Western approach to R&D emphasizes basic scientific breakthroughs above all else. The Japanese say they believe that ideas belong to everyone and are not concerned about their origins – they will take them from anywhere and everywhere. The Western approach emphasizes the protection of intellectual property, in the form of copyright and patents. The Japanese see creativity as a collective, organized process in which ideas are gathered, assimilated, and applied in a new product. The Western approach emphasizes the innate creativity of a small number of brilliant individuals. In short, the West is more into Science (especially "Big Science") while Japan is more interested in Technology.

While one half of all R&D money in the US comes from the government and over one half is spent on military research, in Japan less than 20 percent of R&D money comes from the government, more than 80 percent of all R&D money is provided by corporations, and hardly anything is spent on military research. Unlike the US and Europe, the significant Japanese R&D efforts are mainly located in commercial organizations rather than universities. Indeed, the Japanese tend to be suspicious of academic whiz kids and PhDs, preferring practical people who can handle down-to-earth tasks. The net result is that while the US is big on "R" rather than "D," the Japanese are bigger on "D" rather than "R." Despite the well-publicized MITI projects to boost investment by Japanese companies in basic research, recent surveys have indicated that corporate spending on development is still growing at the expense of research.[9] Akio Morita, the highly successful boss of Sony, even said recently that too much basic research prevents companies from being competitive. Pointing to the success of the Walkman, a device that contained no new technology, Morita said the "most important task" for company researchers was to come up with products that would sell.[10]

The Japanese focus on technology rather than science is borne out by data which show that whereas America has produced the greatest number of Nobel prize winners (40 percent of the total), Japan ranks only twelfth overall.[11] The number of Japanese scientific publications has grown only slowly, by about 0.5 percent a year. And yet Japan has been so successful at technological innovation that as early as 1984 the Japanese had obtained more US patents than inventors in the UK, France, and West Germany combined.[12] Even so, Japan still relies on imported technology to a high degree: in recent years, Japan has been paying out 3.3 times as much (about $3 billion versus about $900 million) for licenses, patents, and royalties as it earns from selling Japanese know-how abroad.[13] Recent court cases have probably boosted the level of Japanese payments. Most of this technology is being imported into Japan for further "creative refinement" by Japanese engineers who will turn it into highly competitive products. The Japanese always have their eye on the main game.

Japan's industrial and financial structure has greatly facilitated the Japanese conquest of IT. Much of Japanese industry is organized into *keiretsu*, or families of companies with close ties. Many different types of *keiretsu* have been identified, but broadly speaking there are two main kinds: "industry" or "vertical" *keiretsu* based on a single industry, like the auto company Toyota, and "financial" or "horizontal" *keiretsu* like Mitsubishi, which straddle a variety of industries and are primarily based on banks. The *keiretsu* have their origins in the rise of Japan's great banking families in the nineteenth century. By the 1930s, they had developed into huge conglomerates, known as *zaibatsu*, which played a key role in Japanese militarism. The *zaibatsu* were dismantled by the American occupation forces after World War II, but some of them regrouped to form today's *keiretsu*.

The six largest *keiretsu* in Japan – Mitsubishi, Mitsui, Sumitomo, Fuyo, DKB, and Sanwa – now control 12,000 companies which account for about one quarter of Japan's entire GNP. *Keiretsu* companies trade together, work together, plan together, offer guidance and provide information to each other, restrict imports together, and hold shares in each other – no less than 70–80 percent of shares on the Tokyo stock exchange comprise interlocking shareholdings of *keiretsu* members. This means that company directors can plan for the long term without having to bother too much about short-term returns to shareholders. Because they are all linked to banks, *keiretsu* companies can also depend on the support of patient capital. The *keiretsu* system is a deep-rooted social tradition in Japan, which draws its strength from old-boy networks, close physical proximity and cultural homogeneity. As a result, *keiretsu* companies generally enjoy a high degree of corporate loyalty and smooth management–labor relations.[14] All these factors have been critically important to Japan's remarkable success in IT.

Much of Japan's success in IT can also be explained by manufacturing excellence. Paying greater attention to manufacturing has given Japan the competitive edge in most high-tech products. As Richard J. Schonberger explained some time ago, Japanese companies have been able to achieve higher productivity and superior quality by borrowing ideas from overseas (like total quality management) and continuously improving upon them. In Japan, manufacturing has a higher social status and engineers rather than generalists tend to be at the helm of Japanese manufacturing companies. Japanese manufacturers of IT products have worked harder at reducing the number of parts, at standardizing parts, at creating a steady stream of new products, and at reducing costs by producing to a target price rather than creating a product and then pricing it. Above all, the Japanese have placed extreme emphasis on quality control in order to achieve "zero-defect" products – this has been made much easier by more cooperative shop-floor relations.[15]

Finally, the nature and values of Japanese society have contributed greatly to Japan's success in IT. Japan has unique national characteristics and these have provided a powerful combination, especially when it comes to mobilizing national efforts to catch up and take the lead in areas of high technology.

Japan has tremendous human resources. It has a disciplined, hard-working, well-educated, highly motivated workforce of "corporate soldiers" who are dedicated to the success of their company and their country. Japanese workers or "salarymen" work on average 2,150 hours per year and rarely take more than about 10 days' holiday per year. The Japanese work on average some 225 hours (or nearly six weeks) more per year than their American counterparts and a staggering 545 hours (or nearly 14 weeks) more per year than the French and the Germans![16] There is a downside to this, of course, with frequent reports coming out of Japan of the high incidence of *karoshi*, or "death by overwork" and studies which show that stress levels are extremely high in the Japanese workplace.[17] Government attempts to reduce the working week in Japan have for the most part failed because of opposition from employers and peer group pressure from fellow employees.

Japan also benefits from a largely homogeneous workforce – migrant workers and non-Japanese speakers make up less than 1 percent of Japanese employees. In a patriotic nation where "nails which stick up are hammered down" and "protruding bits of hedge snipped off," employers have the advantage of a largely docile, disciplined, and above all unified workforce. With a greater respect for education and a strong emphasis on re-training, Japan's human resources are being continuously upgraded. And with a greater emphasis on cooperation rather than conflict in the workplace, this makes for more harmonious working relationships. All these factors make it easier for Japanese companies to achieve greater things.

Another feature of Japanese society which has helped finance Japan's push into high technology is the frugality of most Japanese. The Japanese save more and spend much less than Americans and Europeans, with the result that the Japanese economy benefits from a higher savings ratio. Moreover, Japanese values strongly emphasize the supremacy of production over consumption – hence the Japanese strength in manufacturing, the striving to get the production process right, and the desire to boost exports before even considering imports. Japanese society further teaches people to be more concerned about the collective good rather than individual aggrandizement, and so it is much easier to mobilize support for economic, social, and technological goals.

Every so often, reports appear in the Western media to the effect that Japan is changing, that the successful Japanese formula is failing, and that Japan's competitive advantage will soon disappear. These reports usually question the "price of Japanese success" by highlighting the incidence of alcoholism, suicide, and divorce in modern Japan, as well as poor housing conditions and environmental degradation. They also reflect the official US government view (recently under attack from the "revisionists") that

Japan will inevitably change in time and will become "more like us" – and as a result, hopefully suffer the same competitiveness problems!

Two particular favorites of mine, which date back some years, are "Cracks in the Japanese work ethic" (*Fortune*, May 14, 1984) and "Japan's troubled future" (*Fortune*, March 30, 1987). Unfortunately for the authors of these and other pieces, there is still very little sign of serious cracks appearing in the Japanese work ethic or of Japan plunging into serious social "trouble". Instead, in the intervening years Japan has gone from strength to strength. The absurd idea that Japan is about to collapse under the weight of its own internal contradictions is simply a comforting myth for those in the West who are unable to confront reality.

Why the US Lost

America has lost out in the global IT battle because of misguided industry, trade, and technology policies; because of its inappropriate industrial and financial structure; because of its neglect of manufacturing; and because of the nature and values of US society.

America's failure to capitalize on its inventions is legendary. In 1948, the transistor was invented at Bell Labs in New Jersey, but it was the Japanese who first commercialized this breakthrough device by finding a mass market in transistor radios. The US company Raytheon had introduced the first microwave oven as early as 1947, but today over three-quarters of the microwaves sold in the US are made in Asia. Then there was the color TV, the VCR, video games, the microprocessor chip, the memory chip, LCD screens, the industrial robot, the photocopier, the fax machine, optical fiber, and all the other American IT disasters detailed above.

In attempting to explain how the US was able to squander such a huge lead in consumer electronics in the 1950s, Ian Mackintosh puts the blame on "management complacency" – and specifically the inability of the managers of major US electronics companies to spot technologies and markets.[18] Sheridan Tatsuno, focusing on the semiconductor industry, also finds US management to have been lazy, ignorant, arrogant, and totally unprepared for the new wave of international competition. For example, he shows how

American chip makers were badly caught napping by the arrival of Japanese memory chips – pointing out, among other things, that US companies at the time were not bothering to monitor developments in Japan, or even to read major Japanese electronics magazines and journals – in fact, they had no one who *could* read them![19]

But incompetent management alone doesn't wholly explain America's long list of lost opportunities in IT. The US decline has been going on for so long now that there must be something fundamentally wrong with the American system – and in particular the way that US industry, technology, and trade policies interact with industrial, financial, and social structures to create a recipe for repeated failure.

In the postwar era, the American government's industrial policy was to have no industrial policy. Despite the evident success of MITI targeting and of the close government–industry collaboration prevalent in Japan and other booming Asian nations, successive US governments have refused to intervene in the economy or even to participate in milder forms of indicative planning in industrial sectors like IT. So distant are government–industry links that Ian M. Ross, upon ending a 12-year tenure as president of the powerful Bell Labs, revealed that in all those years, "No one in the Administration ever called me up."[20]

Throughout the 1980s, as America's economic decline became more obvious, certain academics, politicians, and policy analysts urged Washington to adopt various forms of industrial policy, but to no avail. Major US business magazines like *Business Week* also joined the chorus of calls for the US government to help fund research into targeted technologies, to encourage greater use of new technologies, to provide more information on market and technology trends, to directly assist exporters, and to boost education and training in science, mathematics, and engineering.[21] But apart from setting aside some extra money for research into generic, "pre-competitive" technologies such as high-performance computing and funding a small Critical Technologies Institute, the Bush administration did little more for the IT industry than was done by the Reagan administration – which was virtually nothing.

However, opponents of industrial policy point out that pre-competitive research consortiums do not have a very good record in America. Neither the Microelectronics & Computer Technology

Corp. (MCC), nor the Sematech consortium – launched respectively in 1983 and 1987 to help revive the fortunes of the US semiconductor industry – have been conspicuous successes, while the Pentagon's VHSIC (Very High-Speed Integrated Circuit) project of the late 1970s is said to have led to very few applications in operational equipment.[22] The proposed memory chip consortium, US Memories, collapsed in 1990 through lack of support before it could even get started. Some critics, like Harvard's Michael E. Porter, say that pre-competitive or generic research is never likely to feed through to commercial products, whilst others have suggested that cooperation is simply not the American way. It remains to be seen whether the election of President Clinton and the appointment of Laura D'Andrea Tyson to head the Council of Economic Advisors will turn the tide in favor of industrial policy.

There is little doubt that America spends too much on "R" and not enough on "D." The problem is not one of overall spending on R&D: despite the regular protestations to the contrary by members of the US scientific community, America is spending more than ever on R&D – and more, in fact, than Japan and Western Europe combined.[23] The problem is that over a half goes on military R&D, which has few commercial spin-offs, and too much of the rest goes on "big science" projects like atom smashers and space stations. As for the remainder, it is still by no means clear whether basic science generates much technology, let alone useful commercial products. Sony chairman Akio Morita has been quoted as saying that America spends too much on basic science and does not put enough effort into developing technologies. He also says that the US seems to have forgotten how to innovate: that is, to turn technologies into products.[24]

One helpful suggestion made by Morita is that America should borrow more technologies from abroad – just as Japan does. Indeed, there are all sorts of ways in which the US could turn the tables on the Japanese and at the same time overcome its "not invented here" syndrome, which has made it blind to developments overseas. For example, there are 7–10 times as many Japanese researchers at work in the US as there are American researchers in Japan – among graduate students, the Japanese lead by 30 to 1. More US companies should set up R&D facilities in Japan, where they will find an abundance of publicly available information – much of which has never been translated into English. Instead of trying to develop every technology itself, America could take a leaf out of Japan's book by buying in more technology from abroad: in recent years, Japan has outspent America 3–5 times in this area, saving itself billions of dollars on development costs. US companies could also do a lot more to guard their intellectual property from foreigners and to take much greater care when entering into joint ventures, especially with the Japanese.[25]

The American IT industry has clearly suffered from Washington's rigid adherence to free-trade ideology and its touching belief in level playing fields. Free trade yields great mutual benefits if it is reciprocated by nations that hold the same principles. But it is useless if major trading partners – like Japan – simply do not play the game. Throughout the postwar era, Japan has cynically manipulated its trade relations to ensure that the benefits flow in one direction only. Whilst it is perfectly true that many American IT companies have not tried hard enough to penetrate the Japanese market, those that have tried have run into all sorts of subtle and not-so-subtle barriers erected by the Japanese, especially the *keiretsu*. American products which sell well in Europe and elsewhere often have trouble finding a market in Japan. If America did take action to reduce its enormous high-tech trade deficit with Japan by temporarily managing its trade, it might provide a breathing space in which the US could rebuild its IT industry.

But in the process the US would also have to thoroughly reform its industrial and financial structure. Whilst the economic and technology trends in the IT industry have played to Japan's industrial and financial strengths, they have also clearly exposed America's weaknesses. These weaknesses include chronic entrepreneurialism in an industry where big has become beautiful again; the prevalence of short-term thinking among managers, stockholders, and bankers; and the tyranny of stockholders over management, which also inhibits long-term planning. As a result, the American IT industry is too fragmented, too undercapitalized and too shortsighted to remain viable as a major competitive force, as Charles H. Ferguson has argued.[26] Moreover, the underlying IT trends suggest that Japan's dominance is set to increase rather than decrease in the future.

Yet there is much that the American IT industry could learn from the Japanese – such as the need to replace short-term speculation with long-term strategic planning. Some analysts like Charles H. Ferguson and Lester Thurow are even advocating that American industry consider developing a US version of Japan's *keiretsu*. A start could be made by encouraging greater cooperation between manufacturers, suppliers, and financiers over such matters as research, design, production, and marketing. This would avoid duplication of effort (too many companies "reinventing the wheel"), decrease the incompatibility of products, improve product quality, and reduce the pressure from impatient investors. There should also be a much greater emphasis on manufacturing rather than financial manipulation. Lester Thurow even suggests that groups of US companies should own shares in one another, Japanese-style, that short-term share-trading be discouraged and that stockholders' voting rights be amended to favor long-term investors.[27] A number of US commentators have also observed that if the Japanese were running General Motors, the *keiretsu* partners would have stepped in long ago to fix the problems.

Finally, the nature and values of American society have not been conducive to long-term success in IT, despite the fact that most major IT inventions are American in origin.

Despite being one of the richest nations on earth for many years, America lacks quality human resources. The US workforce is less disciplined, less hard-working, less well-educated, less motivated, and much more heterogeneous than other workforces, especially the Japanese. Manufacturers complain that a workforce made up of people from different ethnic backgrounds with a poor command of English can lead to racial tension and severe problems with shop-floor communication. In high-tech plants where absolute cleanliness is essential, some US managers say that it is impossible to persuade their employees not to smoke for an hour before entering the clean room or not to wear make-up, beards, or mustaches. This is not a problem in Japan.[28] Drugs are also used by employees in many US plants and their prevalence has even resulted in the installation of spy cameras in the toilets. This is unheard of in Japan. One recent survey found that American workers admitted to spending more than 7 hours a week on average goofing off work – malingering, doing drugs, drinking, or calling in sick when they weren't.[29]

About 23 million Americans are judged to be functionally illiterate and another 47 million or so are borderline illiterates. Recent surveys such as the International Assessment of Educational Progress have shown US schoolchildren to be near the bottom of the class on standard science and math tests. Another study found that Japanese children spend 52–60 percent more time in the classroom than American children and spend an astonishing 4–5 times more hours doing homework: overall, 12 years of Japanese schooling was equivalent to an incredible 22.3 years of American education![30] More than half of US high-school graduates have not even done one year of science and many commentators have suggested that US science, math, and engineering education is in decline, if not in serious crisis.[31]

Individualism has been one of America's great strengths and, in the past, Americans have shown themselves to be great pioneers. But the flipside is a lack of cohesion in companies, industries, and society as a whole. The American IT industry has probably relied too much on individualistic entrepreneurship, whilst the more successful Japanese IT manufacturers have been more collectivist in orientation. The Japanese focus more on collective cooperation rather than individualistic competition, and collective production rather than individual consumption. For example, American CEOs (chief executive officers) often show no long-term loyalty to any particular firm, but instead hop around from company to company seeking to get the best financial deal for themselves. Japanese CEOs usually stay with their firm for life. One result is the astonishing disparity in CEO pay between the US – where the average compensation package for a CEO in one of the top 30 companies was $3,200,000 in 1992 – and Japan – where the same executive would have got just $525,000.[32]

Because the US has had it so good for so long, Americans have often appeared to be arrogant, ignorant of foreign ways, and suffering from self-delusion. Now the chickens are coming home to roost, as Americans finally realize that American products and indeed everything American is not necessarily the best in the world. American companies abroad have been accused of not paying enough attention to detail, of offering poor customer service, and refusing to listen to other people's opinions. Two recent books have painted a frightening picture of the average American as shallow, materialistic, cynical, greedy, and amoral, as someone who couldn't care less about the local community and would sell their family for $2 million.[33] Some, like pc pioneer Steve Jobs, say the problem is that America lacks national goals – Americans really have no idea what America is about these days and where it should be heading. Optimists like Jobs believe that the US can still be turned around, given the right political leadership, whilst pessimists like Brandin and Harrison believe that the problems of American society are so deep-rooted that the prospects for change are not good. In fact, for America, they say that it is basically all over: "The American system is presently geared to self-destruct."[34]

What's Wrong with Europe?

Europe has failed in IT for broadly the same reasons as the US, but with some interesting differences. The history of European IT is a long history of lost technological opportunities, of complacent management, of fragmented markets, of featherbedded "national champions," of poor entrepreneurship, and of defeatist attitudes.

European companies once held the lead or were up with the best in consumer electronics, semiconductors, mainframe computers, telecoms technology, robotics, NC machine tools, and CAD systems. From 1945 right through to the end of the 1970s, Europe ran a positive trade balance on IT goods. But in 1979 Europe plunged into deficit on IT for the first time and has stayed there ever since. Despite efforts to turn the tide in the form of government assistance, trade tariffs, and EC-funded research consortia, the European IT deficit grew steadily worse to reach a staggering $40 billion in 1991. Although Europe now has the second largest domestic IT market in the world, European companies have only about 20 percent of the world IT market – and about 10 percent of the world semiconductor market. You cannot now buy a European-sourced laptop computer or supercomputer.

What went wrong? Throughout the postwar period, the large European market was fragmented into a number of smaller national markets. Each market had its own "national champions," who were often directly subsidized or otherwise featherbedded by their respective governments – this had the twin effect of stifling domestic competition and of keeping out foreign products. National rules and regulations created very effective trade barriers and pan-European cooperation was exceedingly difficult. But market fragmentation also meant that European companies could not achieve the economies of scale necessary to compete effectively in world markets – even if they wanted to. This made Europe very vulnerable to imports of high-tech goods from nations with large domestic markets, such as the US and Japan. It was not until 1993 that the EC finally became a genuine "common market" – but by this time, most of the damage to the European IT industry had been done.

In the run-up to 1993, there was much talk of Europe finally getting its act together and of Europe being about to enter a period of unprecedented growth and prosperity – in fact, the mood in European capitals was so buoyant in 1988–9 that the whole continent was said to be caught up in "Europhoria." Press reports also suggested that Europe would soon provide serious competition in high-tech and that the European IT industry in particular was about to "catch up" with Japan and the US – thanks partly to innovative EC research projects like JESSI and ESPRIT.[35] But the period of "Europhoria" was short-lived and as European economic growth slowed, as interest rates increased, and as exports, capital investment, and stock markets slumped, "Euro-pessimism" again became the order of the day in 1990.

There was a sudden realization that the European IT industry, far from getting its act together, was actually facing its greatest crisis ever. Holland's Philips and France's Bull were heading for record losses, Germany's Siemens had been forced to take over its ailing compatriot, Nixdorf, Italy's Olivetti was in deep financial trouble, and Britain's ICL and Apricot Computer were both snapped up by the Japanese. This was not what was meant to be happening: in the run-up to 1993, the European IT industry was supposed to be consolidating in order to *take on* the Japanese, not sell out to them. In early 1991, the true extent of the European IT disaster became apparent: for example, Bull, despite having received a total of $1.3 billion in direct aid from the French government in the previous seven years, announced a record annual loss of $1.2 billion in 1990; Philips beat that with a massive $2.5 billion loss in 1990 and actually called it quits in semiconductors; Olivetti was forced to lay off another 7,000 employees; Siemens laid off 3,500 at Nixdorf; and both Thomson and SGS-Thomson announced record losses. The EC had poured $11 billion into IT research since 1984, but the European IT industry was fast becoming a sickly, hollowed out shell of its former self.

It's no wonder that the IT crisis not only prompted a European IT "summit" meeting chaired by EC president, Jacques Delors, but also started a major policy debate in Brussels between "liberals," who questioned the effectiveness of state and EC aid for the IT industry, and *dirigistes*, who argued that continued financial support was necessary if any kind of European IT industry was to survive. In particular, certain politicians and bureaucrats began to focus on the billions spent on pre-competitive research projects like EUREKA, JESSI, and RACE, and to ask what they were getting for their money. For example, critics claimed that the largest project, ESPRIT (European Strategic Program for Research & Development in Information Technology) had failed to speed the pace of innovation in IT and had done little to strengthen Europe's ability to maintain an independent IT industry capable of resisting Japan. Instead, critics alleged that ESPRIT had become a cozy "club" of established IT manufacturers who had made no real attempt to become internationally competitive. A new proposal, the ENS (or European Nervous System) project, was seen as merely another attempt to milk the European taxpayer.

A second response to the European IT crisis was a flurry of mergers – partly out of necessity and partly as a last-ditch attempt to create groups large enough to compete with the Japanese. Some of these mergers also involved tie-ups with America's IBM. Europe's four surviving suppliers of complete IT systems are Siemens, Bull, Philips, and Olivetti – but even the largest, Siemens, is only about the eighth largest IT company in the world and together they have less than 10 percent of the world IT market. Moreover, the "big" four Europeans are already buying in many components and even complete products from the Japanese and Japan's NEC has actually purchased a direct stake in Bull. Given the poor track records of these companies in IT in the past two decades, the question may really be one of how much longer can an independent European IT industry survive. More than six years ago, I wrote that time was running out for European IT and that it looked like being the big loser in the global IT battle.[36] Nothing has changed in the interim to alter that view.

There are many puzzling aspects to the European IT flop. While an industrial policy of government–industry collaboration seems to have worked in Japan, in Europe it has not. While Europe – unlike the US – has used tariffs in an effort to keep out foreigners, this has not stopped the Japanese from doing an end run by setting up plants in Europe, nor has it stopped the practice of European firms buying in critical components from Japan. While the Japanese have seemingly made a success of their pre-competitive research projects on targeted technologies, the Europeans apparently have not. While big has been beautiful for the Japanese in IT, in Europe it has spelt bureaucracy, featherbedding, little innovation, and poor overseas marketing efforts. In the US, the chill winds of international competition have forced manufacturers to boost productivity, in Europe they have not been so effective. In Japan, picky consumers have pressurized manufacturers into greatly improving quality, but in Europe they appear to have not.

All this suggests that there is something about the nature and values of European society which makes Europe fundamentally incapable of competing with the Japanese in IT. That something could be attitudes. Thus UK consultant Ian Mackintosh, in his analysis of the European IT industry's "components of collapse," stresses the fact that European managers in the 1970s simply failed to understand the significance of the microchip and of developments in "far-off Silicon Valley."[37] (This did not seem to be a problem for the Japanese.) European captains of industry, academics, government officials, and even research directors, he writes, tended to dismiss the speculations of West Coast "whiz kids" as being not worthy of consideration – and yet they were inventing the future. European managers also completely failed to understand the economics of high-tech production and the necessity of developing local high-tech skill "clusters."[38]

In short, the Europeans were complacent and conservative, and lacking in dynamism and entrepreneurship. It was almost as if they did not want to succeed. Fred Warshofsky quoted Sheldon Weining, European CEO of chip manufacturing equipment maker MRC, as saying: "The Europeans literally chose to be third in a peculiar way . . . They chose literally to not compete because of an inability to commit monies and ideas . . . In other words to make a commitment. Siemens, Philips and so on should have sat down and said we want to be on the frontier. But in typical European fashion, we don't see any entrepreneurship; we don't see any new companies. There are no Intels coming up . . . But what the Europeans are doing is studying the shit out of every problem. They must make a decision: do we go from 4K to 16K? They'll have to think about it; they have to set up a study commission. They didn't have the balls to make a commitment. Let's do it, pow! Which at least the Japanese do. When we come out with a new piece of equipment, the first one is sold to Japan. And everyone has found this to be true. The ninth one, or the ninety-third one, is sold to Europe."[39]

Winning the 1990s: What Will Japan Do Next?

Four times in the past 20 years, American and European commentators have proclaimed the Japanese miracle to be over. First there was Oil Shock of 1973, which was supposed to put paid to Japan's industrial competitiveness. Then there was the Second Oil Shock of 1979 and the Yen Shock of 1986, which were also supposed to deliver death blows to Japan's economic aspirations. On each occasion, there was relief in the West that the game was finally up for the Japanese: now they were really finished! Yet each time the Japanese economy actually emerged from the crisis stronger, leaner, fitter, and more internationally competitive than ever before.

Much the same thing happened in 1990–2, with the bursting of the so-called "bubble economy" in Japan. Once again, some Western observers of the "Japan is finished" school simply looked at the Nikkei index and declared that the end was nigh for Japan, not realizing that the early 1990s recession – although deeper than expected – could still be seen as a period of readjustment, which would help purge the Japanese economy of dangerous excesses. Besides, the Japanese recession was always a pretty odd one by Western standards: not many recessions in the West are accompanied by 2 percent unemployment, record balance of payments surpluses, higher savings rates, and increased spending on R&D. In their "readjustment," the Japanese authorities took the opportunity to cap inflation and to take the heat out of the stock market and property markets. Japanese manufacturers took the opportunity to upgrade their facilities, to trim product lines, to lengthen product cycles, to move upmarket, and to move offshore – but there were no lay-offs on the scale seen in the US and Europe.[40] Not bad for a recession.

But profits for many Japanese corporations – especially in the IT sector – did fall substantially and this prompted some to rethink their traditional policy of relentlessly pursuing market share at the expense of profits. Akio Morita, the high-profile chairman of Sony, was one of those urging Japanese companies to boost their "razor-thin" profit margins and to return higher dividends to shareholders – as happens in the West. In fact, Morita argued forcefully that Japanese companies should become more like Western companies by reducing working hours, granting longer holidays, treating employees more humanely, and paying more attention to environmental and community concerns.[41] Other observers have noted that "job hopping" from company to company is starting to become common in Japan, especially among younger workers. The tradition of lifetime employment is also being slowly eroded, as are other time-honored practices such as rigid seniority systems. And in one remarkable break with tradition, the giant Mitsubishi Corp. actually appointed a British-born American resident, Minoru "Ben" Makihara, to be president and CEO in 1992. Until recently, Japanese executives who had spent even a few years overseas were usually said by their colleagues to "stink of butter."

None of these modest changes to the way Japan's companies do business is likely to make much difference in the short term. In the foreseeable future, nothing seems likely to derail the Japanese industrial juggernaut. As Richard I. Kirkland Jr recently put it, "What can you say about an economy that was less than 10 percent of the size of America's in 1960 and is now just over 60 percent; whose trade surplus had doubled in seven years despite a 50 percent increase in the value of its currency; that habitually spends 70 to 100 percent more of its gross domestic product on capital investment than the US, and 33 percent more on nonmilitary R&D; whose household savings rate is more than three times higher than America's; and that, compared with the US, employs

70,000 more scientists and engineers on R&D in its labs and ten times the number of robots on its assembly lines?"[42] What indeed.

In IT, the Japanese juggernaut is developing a stranglehold over key computer components such as flat-panel displays/LCD screens, memory chips, and floppy disk drives. Next on the hit list are such items as microprocessor chips, high-definition TV screens, gallium arsenide chips, laser diodes, and tiny nickel-hydride batteries. Press reports in 1992 indicated that American chip manufacturers, led by Intel, were fighting back strongly in EEPROM (electronically erasable programmable read-only memory) chips – better known as "flash memory" chips and cards – but it later emerged that Intel had licensed its EEPROM technology to Japan's Sharp and NMB Semiconductor, among others, with inevitable results. Likewise, US manufacturers appeared to be well placed in DSP (digital signal processing) chips, especially programmable DSPs, which have a wide range of applications (converting analog signals into digital and vice versa) in consumer electronics and telecommunications. But a temporary strength in one technology hardly guarantees a US comeback in consumer electronics, which is totally dominated by the Japanese, or a major US advance in telecoms, where the Japanese have shown themselves to be adept at working around such problems.

The Japanese are in the process of introducing a whole new generation of high-tech whiz-bangs such as "smart" cards (originally a French concept), for storing all kinds of transactional data, electronic dictionaries, personal organizers, shirtpocket computers, wristwatch pagers, "intelligent" vacuum cleaners, "smart" ovens, wall-hung TV screens, filmless cameras, tapeless answering machines, automatic translation telephones, and so on. Most of these will be stylish, user-friendly, consumer appliances which will fit easily into the modern home or office. They will have in common multimedia capabilities and some form of "intelligence," such as fuzzy logic. In fact, just as we saw happen with cars, the Japanese are now setting standards for leading-edge design in IT products which the rest of the world is being forced to follow.

We have seen how the Japanese have targeted just about every conceivable future information technology for further investigation. Thus the projects to develop neural, optical, and molecular computers. The Japanese are also looking at micromachines or "microbots" as part of an expected push into nanotechnology and they have massive R&D programs in biotechnology, new materials technology, and aerospace, all of which have links with IT. In his study of how the Japanese have made the transition from imitators to innovators, Sheridan Tatsuno declares: "By the mid 1990s, Japan's technological prowess could overwhelm the West, and the political shock waves of losing one next-generation industry after another to Japan will be severe. By the late 1990s, Japanese companies will have mastered the entire 'mandala of creativity.' They will excel not only at refining and recycling ideas but also at exploring and generating new ideas . . . By the year 2000 we may be left behind unless we wake up and reconsider our notions of creativity."[43] The year 2000 is just six years away.

Will the Japanese share their new-found expertise with others? Will Japan continue to pursue unbridled nationalism, or is it about to embark on a new internationalist era of what some Japanese are calling "techno-globalism," in which a spirit of harmony and cooperation will reign in a so-called "borderless" world? The two key litmus tests of Japan's seriousness about techno-globalism are (1) whether Japan will truly open up its domestic market, not only to America and Europe, but to emerging Asian nations which Japan has said it wants to "help;" and (2) whether Japan will share its technology secrets by changing its technology-transfer policies in order to return the many favors it owes the West and to help Asia.

The problem with Japanese credibility on the technology-transfer issue is that technology transfer to the Japanese has always been a one-way street. Ideas go back to Japan, but very few come out. As G. Dan Hutcheson, president of the US company VLSI Research, recently put it, "There's not a single instance in the past 20 years where a US company that licensed its technology to Japan was able to avoid losing that technology and the edge it provided over the next decade." Michael Borrus, of the Berkeley (California) Roundtable, states: "The data are pretty clear. The Japanese don't transfer high technology, period." While T. J. Rodgers, president of Silicon Valley company, Cypress Semiconductor, when explaining why his company won't enter joint ventures with the Japanese, was quoted as saying: "We concluded that every company we negotiated with was after our technology, would blow us out of the [Japanese] market, and would come after our US market."[44]

If it was serious about techno-globalism, the Japanese government would change its patent system to stop awarding patents to companies who are the first to file (rather than the first to invent) or who "flood" the patent office with similar patents on devices first seen overseas. It would open up Japanese research laboratories, especially corporate research laboratories, to foreign researchers. And it would consent to Korean, Taiwanese, and Singaporean requests that it help out emerging Asian nations who have huge trade deficits with Japan by transferring more technology to them. For years, Japan has done little to discourage the belief that it wanted to "help Asia," but the truth is that the Japanese see the Asian "Tigers" – especially the Koreans – as potential rivals who may one day out-Japan Japan. Asians find it just as hard as Westerners to penetrate the Japanese domestic market and they are even more dependent on Japan for high-tech components. This raises the possibility that the Japanese could at some time in the future dramatically raise prices or even cut off supplies. The Japanese have also switched production of things like TV sets to very low wage countries like Thailand and Malaysia in order to undermine the competitiveness of Korea, Taiwan, Singapore, and Hong Kong.

In recent years, we have witnessed a literally massive transfer of wealth and economic power from America and Europe to Japan. This is because Japan has structured its industry, trade, and technology policies and tailored its domestic arrangements to ensure that it emerges as the dominant player in industry after industry it has targeted. Much of that wealth has been transferred via the IT industry, which makes the second largest hole in Western trade balances after the auto industry. In the 1990s, the size and importance of the IT industry is likely to grow and the dominance of Japan will be complete. Unless drastic action is taken to ensure that America and Europe do a better job of competing in the 1990s than they did in the 1970s and 1980s, then Americans and Europeans will continue to get poorer and the Japanese will get richer. You have been warned.

Notes

1 Chalmers Johnson, *MITI and the Japanese Miracle* (Stanford University Press, Stanford, CA, 1982).
2 Sheridan Tatsuno, *The Technopolis Strategy: Japan, High Technology, and the Control of the 21st Century* (Brady/Prentice-Hall Press, New York, 1986), pp. 23–31.
3 Michael E. Porter, *The Competitive Advantage of Nations* (Free Press, New York, 1990), pp. 414–21.
4 Daniel I. Okimoto, *Between MITI and the Market: Japanese Industrial Policy for High Technology* (Stanford University Press, Stanford, CA, 1989).
5 Fred Warshofsky, *The Chip War: The Battle for the World of Tomorrow* (Charles Scribner's & Sons, New York, 1989), pp. 121–8.
6 Clyde V. Prestowitz in *The Economist*, reprinted in *The Australian*, December 5, 1991.
7 Warshofsky, *The Chip War*, pp. 177–81; *Fortune*, September 7, 1992.
8 Sheridan Tatsuno, *Created in Japan: From Imitators to World-Class Innovators* (Harper & Row, New York, 1990).
9 *New Scientist*, January 5, 1991.
10 *New Scientist*, February 15, 1992.
11 Reuters report in *The Australian*, October 1, 1991.
12 Francis Narin and J. Davidson Frame, "The growth of Japanese science and technology," *Science*, 245 (1989), pp. 600–5.
13 Report in *The Economist*, reprinted in *The Australian*, April 18, 1989.
14 Carla Rapoport, "Why Japan keeps on winning," *Fortune*, July 15, 1991; see also *Business Week*, February 17, 1992.
15 Richard J. Schonberger, *Japanese Manufacturing Techniques* (Free Press, New York, 1982); Porter, *The Competitive Advantage of Nations*, pp. 409–10; see also *Fortune*, August 12, 1991.
16 Juliet B. Schor, *The Overworked American: The Unexpected Decline of Leisure* (Basic Books, New York, 1992), pp. 152–4.
17 See, for example, Mike Parker and Jane Slaughter, "Management by Stress," *Technology Review*, 91, no. 7 (1988).
18 Ian Mackintosh, *Sunrise Europe: The Dynamics of Information Technology* (Basil Blackwell, Oxford, UK, 1986), pp. 23–4; see also Ian M. Ross, "Sun sets over Silicon Valley," *New Scientist*, September 19, 1992, reprinted from *The Bridge*.
19 Tatsuno, *The Technopolis Strategy*, pp. xii–xiii, 18–19 and 34.
20 *Business Week*, April 20, 1992.
21 *Business Week*, April 6, 1992.
22 Jay Goldberg, "Integrating the Pentagon's circuits," *Technology Review*, 93, no. 3 (1990), pp. 19–20.

23 Daniel Greenberg, "The phoney crisis in American science," *New Scientist*, February 2, 1991.
24 Morita quoted in *Fortune*, September 25, 1989 and February 15, 1992.
25 *Fortune*, January 1, 1990 and March 25, 1991.
26 Charles H. Ferguson, "Computers and the coming of the US keiretsu," *Harvard Business Review*, July–August 1990, pp. 55–70.
27 Lester Thurow, *Head to Head: The Coming Economic Battle Among Japan, Europe and America* (Morrow, New York, 1992).
28 Warshofsky, *The Chip War*, p. 145.
29 James Patterson and Peter Kim, *The Day America Told the Truth: What People Really Believe About Everything That Really Matters* (Prentice-Hall, Englewood Cliffs, NJ, 1991).
30 Reports in *Newsweek* and elsewhere, March 1992 and *Business Week*, July 22, 1991.
31 Simon Ramo, *The Business of Science: Winning and Losing in the High-Tech Age* (Hill and Wang, New York, 1988), pp. 193–5; David H. Brandin and Michael A. Harrison, *The Technology War: A Case for Competitiveness* (Wiley, New York, 1987).
32 *Business Week*, January 27, 1992.
33 Patterson and Kim, *The Day America Told the Truth*; Donald L. Kanter and Philip H. Mirvis, *The Cynical Americans: Living and Working in an Age of Discontent and Disillusion* (Jossey-Bass, San Francisco, 1989).
34 Steve Jobs in *Fortune*, December 30, 1991, p. 42; Brandin and Harrison, *The Technology War*, p. 202.
35 For example, *Business Week*, June 25, 1990, pp. 60–78; "How not to catch up," *The Economist*, January 9, 1993.
36 Tom Forester, *High-Tech Society: The Story of the Information Technology Revolution* (Basil Blackwell, Oxford, UK and MIT Press, Cambridge, MA, 1987), pp. 283–9.
37 Mackintosh, *Sunrise Europe*, p. 71.
38 Mackintosh, *Sunrise Europe*, pp. 70–87; *Business Week*, December 14, 1992.
39 Warshofsky, *The Chip War*, p. 233.
40 *Business Week*, March 2, 1992; *Fortune*, May 18, 1992.
41 *Business Week*, January 27, 1992; *Fortune*, March 9, 1992.
42 *Fortune*, May 18, 1992, p. 30.
43 Tatsuno, *The Technopolis Strategy*, pp. 267–8.
44 *Fortune*, January 1, 1990, p. 58 and May 18, 1992, p. 32.

Selected Bibliography

Abegglen, James C. and Stalk Jr, George, *Kaisha: The Japanese Corporation* (Basic Books, New York, 1986).

Abernathy, William J., Clark, Kim B., and Kantrow, Alan, M., *Industrial Renaissance: Producing a Competitive Future for America* (Basic Books, New York, 1983).

Anchordoguy, Marie, *Computers Inc: Japan's Challenge to IBM* (Council on East Asian Studies/Harvard University Press, Cambridge, MA, 1989).

Anchordoguy, Marie, "How Japan built a computer industry," *Harvard Business Review*, July–August 1990.

Ayres, Robert U., *The Next Industrial Revolution: Reviving Industry Through Innovation* (Ballinger, Cambridge, MA, 1984).

Ayres, Robert U., "Technology: The wealth of nations," *Technological Forecasting and Social Change*, 33, pp. 189–201 (1988).

Bolter, Jay David, *Turing's Man* (University of North Carolina Press, 1984 and Penguin Books, Harmondsworth, UK, 1986).

Brandin, David H. and Harrison, Michael A., *The Technology War: A Case for Competitiveness* (Wiley, New York, 1987).

Braun, Ernest and Macdonald, Stuart, *Revolution in Miniature: The History and Impact of Semiconductor Electronics*, 2nd edition (Cambridge University Press, Cambridge, UK and New York, 1982).

Burstein, Daniel, *YEN: Japan's New Financial Empire and Its Threat to America* (Random House, New York, 1988).

Burstein, Daniel, *Euroquake: Europe's Explosive Economic Challenge Will Change the World* (Simon & Schuster, New York, 1991).

Chaffee, C. David, *The Rewiring of America* (Academic Press, San Diego, CA, 1988).

Choate, Pat, *Agents of Influence: How Japan's Lobbyists in the United States Manipulate America's Political and Economic System* (Knopf, New York, 1990).

Cohen, Stephen S. and Zysman, John, *Manufacturing Matters: The Myth of the Post-Industrial Economy* (Basic Books, New York, 1987).

Crichton, Michael, *Rising Sun* (Knopf, New York, 1992).

Cusumano, Michael A., *Japan's Software Factories: A Challenge to US Management* (Oxford University Press, Oxford, UK and New York, 1991).

Davidow, William H., *Marketing High Technology* (Free Press, New York, 1986).

Dertouzos, Michael L., Lester, Richard K., Solow, Robert M., and The MIT Commission on Industrial Productivity, *Made in America: Regaining the Productive Edge* (MIT Press, Cambridge, MA, 1989).

Dietrich, William S., *In the Shadow of the Rising Sun: The Political Roots of America's Economic Decline* (Penn State Press, University Park, PA, 1991).

Dreyfus, Hubert and Dreyfus, Stuart, *Mind Over Machine* (Free Press, New York, 1986).

Dutton, William H., Blumler, Jay G., and Kraemer, Kenneth L., *Wired Cities: Shaping the Future of Communications* (G. K. Hall & Co., Boston, MA, 1987).

Fallows, James, *More Like Us* (Houghton Mifflin, New York, 1990).

Feigenbaum, Edward A. and McCorduck, Pamela, *The Fifth Generation: Artificial Intelligence and Japan's Computer Challenge to the World* (Addison-Wesley, Reading, MA, 1983).

Ferguson, Charles H., "From the people who brought you voodoo economics," *Harvard Business Review*, May–June 1988.

Ferguson, Charles H., "Computers and the coming of the US keiretsu," *Harvard Business Review*, July–August 1990.

Florida, Richard and Browdy, David, "The invention that got away," *Technology Review*, August/September 1991.

Forester, Tom, *High-Tech Society: The Story of the Information Technology Revolution* (Basil Blackwell, Oxford, UK and MIT Press, Cambridge, MA, 1987).

Forester, Tom and Morrison, Perry, *Computer Ethics: Cautionary Tales and Ethical Dilemmas in Computing* (Basil Blackwell, Oxford, UK and MIT Press, Cambridge, MA, 1990).

Fransman, Martin, *The Market and Beyond: Cooperation and Competition in Information Technology in the Japanese System* (Cambridge University Press, Cambridge, UK and New York, 1990).

Freiberger, Paul and Swaine, Michael, *Fire in the Valley: The Making of the Personal Computer* (Osborne/McGraw-Hill, Berkeley, CA, 1984).

Friedman, George and Le-Bard, Meredith, *The Coming War With Japan* (St Martin's Press, New York, 1991).

Gilder, George, *Microcosm: The Quantum Revolution in Economics and Technology* (Simon & Schuster, New York, 1989).

Ginzberg, Eli and Vojta, George, *Beyond Human Scale: The Large Corporation at Risk* (Basic Books, New York, 1985).

Graham, Margaret, *RCA and the Videodisc: The Business of Research* (Cambridge University Press, Cambridge, UK and New York, 1986).

Gregory, Gene, *Japanese Electronics Technology: Enterprise and Innovation* (Japan Times Ltd, Tokyo, 1986).

Halberstam, David, *The Reckoning* (Morrow, New York, 1986).

Halberstam, David, *The Next Century* (Morrow, New York, 1991).

Hecht, Jeff, *Understanding Fiber Optics* (Sams & Co., Indianapolis, 1987).

Holland, Max, *When the Machine Stopped: A Cautionary Tale From Industrial America* (Harvard Business School Press, Cambridge, MA, 1990).

Holstein, William J., *The Japanese Power Game: What It Means for America* (Charles Scribner's & Sons, New York, 1990).

Hudson, Heather E., *Communication Satellites: Their Development and Impact* (Free Press, New York, 1990).

Ishihara, Shinto, *The Japan That Can Say No: Why Japan Will Be First Among Equals*, translated by Frank Baldwin (Simon & Schuster, New York, 1991).

Jacobson, Gary and Hillkirk, John, *Xerox, American Samurai* (Macmillan, New York, 1986).

Johnson, Chalmers, *MITI and the Japanese Miracle* (Stanford University Press, Stanford, CA, 1982).

Kahn, Herman and Pepper, Thomas, *The Japanese Challenge* (Harper & Row, New York, 1979).

Kearns, David T. and Nadler, David A., *Prophets in the Dark: How Xerox Reinvented Itself and Beat Back the Japanese* (Harper Business, New York, 1992).

Kearns, Robert L., *Zaibatsu America: How Japanese Firms Are Colonizing Vital US Industries* (Free Press, New York, 1992).

Kobayashi, Koji, *Computers and Communications: A Vision of C&C* (MIT Press, Cambridge, MA, 1986).

Levy, Mark R. (ed.), *The VCR Age: Home Video and Mass Communication* (Sage, Newbury Park, CA, 1989).

Mackintosh, Ian, *Sunrise Europe: The Dynamics of Information Technology* (Basil Blackwell, Oxford, UK, 1986).

Malone, Michael S., *The Big Score: The Billion Dollar Story of Silicon Valley* (Doubleday, New York, 1985).

Morita, Akio with Reingold, Edwin M. and Shimomura, Mitsuko, *Made in Japan: Akio Morita and Sony* (Dutton, New York, 1986).

Moritz, Michael, *The Little Kingdom: The Private Story of Apple Computer* (Morrow, New York, 1984).

Morris-Suzuki, Tessa, *Beyond Computopia: Information, Automation and Democracy in Japan* (Kegan Paul, London, 1988).

Morton, Michael S. Scott (ed.), *The Corporation of the 1990s: Informa-*

tion Technology and Organizational Transformation (Oxford University Press, New York, 1991).

Narin, Francis and Frame, J. Davidson, "The growth of Japanese science and technology," *Science*, 245 (1989).

Noll, A. Michael, *Introduction to Telephones and Telephone Systems* (Artech House, Norwood, MA, 1991).

Ohmae, Kenichi, *The Borderless World* (Harper, New York, 1990).

Okimoto, Daniel I., *Between MITI and the Market: Japanese Industrial Policy for High Technology* (Stanford University Press, Stanford, CA, 1989).

Ouchi, William, *Theory Z: How American Business Can Meet the Japanese Challenge* (Addison-Wesley, Reading, MA, 1981).

Parker, Mike and Slaughter, Jane, "Management by stress," *Technology Review*, 91, no. 7 (1988).

Pascale, Richard Tanner and Athos, Anthony G., *The Art of Japanese Management* (Simon & Schuster, New York, 1981).

Patterson, James and Kim, Peter, *The Day America Told the Truth: What People Really Believe About Everything That Really Matters* (Prentice-Hall, Englewood Cliffs, NJ, 1991).

Pierce, John R., and Noll, A. Michael, *Signals: The Science of Telecommunications* (Scientific American Library, New York, 1990).

Piore, Michael J. and Sabel, Charles F., *The Second Industrial Divide: Possibilities for Prosperity* (Basic Books, New York, 1984).

Porter, Michael E., *The Competitive Advantage of Nations* (Free Press, New York, 1990).

Prestowitz, Clyde V., *Trading Places: How We Allowed Japan to Take the Lead* (Basic Books, New York, 1988).

Ramo, Simon, *The Business of Science: Winning and Losing in the High-Tech Age* (Hill and Wang, New York, 1988).

Rapoport, Carla, "Why Japan keeps on winning," *Fortune*, July 15, 1991.

Reich, Robert B., *The Next American Frontier* (Times Books, New York, 1983).

Reich, Robert B., *The Work of Nations: Preparing Ourselves for 21st-Century Capitalism* (Knopf, New York, 1991).

Reid, T. R., *The Chip: How Two Americans Invented the Microchip and Launched a Revolution* (S&S Publishing, North Carolina, 1985).

Report of the Defense Science Board Task Force on Defense Semiconductor Dependency, Office of the Under-Secretary of Defense for Acquisition, Washington, DC, 1987.

Rogers, Everett M. and Larsen, Judith K., *Silicon Valley Fever: Growth of High-Technology Culture* (Basic Books, New York, 1984).

Roszak, Theodore, *The Cult of Information* (Pantheon Books, New York, 1986).

Schonberger, Richard J., *Japanese Manufacturing Techniques* (Free Press, New York, 1982).

Schonberger, Richard J., *World Class Manufacturing* (Free Press, New York, 1986).

Schor, Juliet B., *The Overworked American: The Unexpected Decline of Leisure* (Basic Books, New York, 1992).

Sharp, Margaret (ed.), *Europe and the New Technologies* (Pinter, London, 1985).

Shooshan III, Harry M. (ed.), *Disconnecting Bell: The Impact of the AT&T Divestiture* (Pergamon, Elmsford, NJ, 1984).

Smith, Douglas K. and Alexander, Robert C., *Fumbling the Future: How Xerox Invented, Then Ignored, The First Personal Computer* (Morrow, New York, 1988).

Strassman, Paul A., *Information Payoff: The Transformation of Work in the Electronic Age* (Free Press, New York, 1985).

Strassman, Paul A., *The Business Value of Computers* (Information Economics Press, New Canaan, CT, 1990).

Tatsuno, Sheridan, *The Technopolis Strategy: Japan, High Technology, and the Control of the 21st Century* (Brady/Prentice-Hall Press, New York, 1986).

Tatsuno, Sheridan, *Created in Japan: From Imitators to World Class Innovators* (Harper & Row, New York, 1990).

Taylor, Jared, *Shadows of the Rising Sun* (Morrow, New York, 1983).

Thurow, Lester, *The Management Challenge: Japanese Views* (MIT Press, Cambridge, MA, 1985).

Thurow, Lester, *Head to Head: The Coming Economic Battle Among Japan, Europe and America* (Morrow, New York, 1992).

Tolchin, Susan J. and Tolchin, Martin, *Dismantling America: The Rush to Deregulate* (Houghton Mifflin, New York, 1984).

Tolchin, Martin and Tolchin, Susan J., *Selling our Security: The Erosion of America's Assets* (Knopf, New York, 1992).

Tuck, Jay, *High-Tech Espionage: How the KGB Smuggles NATO's Strategic Secrets to Moscow* (Sidgwick & Jackson, London, 1986).

Tunstall, Jeremy, *Communications Deregulation: The Unleashing of America's Communications Industry* (Basil Blackwell, Oxford, UK and New York, 1986).

Tunstall, W. Brooke, *Disconnecting Parties: Managing the Bell System Break-Up – An Inside View* (McGraw-Hill, New York, 1985).

Unger, J. Marshall, *The Fifth Generation Fallacy* (Oxford University Press, Oxford, UK and New York, 1987).

Vogel, Ezra F., *Japan as Number One* (Harper & Row, New York, 1980).

Warshofsky, Fred, *The Chip War: The Battle for the World of Tomorrow* (Charles Scribner's & Sons, New York, 1989).

Williams, Frederick, *The New Telecommunications: Infrastructure for the Information Age* (Free Press, New York, 1991).

Winograd, Terry, *Understanding Computers and Cognition* (Ablex, Norwood, NJ, 1986).

Wolferen, Karel van, *The Enigma of Japanese Power* (Knopf, New York, 1989).

Womack, James P., Jones, Daniel T., and Roos, Daniel, *The Machine That Changed the World: The Story of Lean Production* (Rawson Associates, Boston, MA, 1990 and Harper Collins, New York, 1991).

Index